Evangelical Apologetics

Edited by
Michael Bauman
David W. Hall
Robert C. Newman

CHRISTIAN PUBLICATIONS, INC.
CAMP HILL, PENNSYLVANIA

Christian Publications
3825 Hartzdale Drive, Camp Hill, PA 17011

Faithful, biblical publishing since 1883

ISBN: 0-87509-685-9

96 97 98 99 00   5 4 3 2 1

Table of Contents

Preface

At its forty-seventh annual meeting held in Philadelphia November 16-18, 1995, the Evangelical Theological Society featured the topic "Defending the Faith: Christian Apologetics in a Non-Christian World." Some 1,100 people attended these sessions, and over 80 of the nearly 200 papers presented were on this topic. This book is a selection from those papers.

We have organized these papers under four headings: Defending the Faith Philosophically, Defending the Faith Historically, Defending the Faith Scientifically and Defending the Faith Theologically—the subjects assigned to our four plenary speakers. Their papers appear first in each section, followed by others in that category. Some good papers were left out of this collection because they were very specialized or did not fit under one of these categories. Others were passed over due to lack of space. A catalog of all the papers given and audio tapes of each presentation can be obtained from ACTS, 1-800-642-2287.

We send out these papers with the prayer that God may use them to strengthen His people and to turn the hearts of others to find rescue and rest in Jesus Christ, His only Son.

Robert C. Newman
President, ETS
September 19, 1996

Part I

Defending the Faith Philosophically

Philosophical Apologetics,
the Church and
Contemporary Culture

J.P. Moreland

*I*n 1756, John Wesley delivered an address to a gathering of clergy on how to carry out the pastoral ministry with joy and skill. In it, Wesley cataloged a number of things familiar to most contemporary believers—the cultivation of a disposition to glorify God and save souls, a knowledge of Scripture and similar notions. However, at the top of his list Wesley focused on something seldom highly valued by most pastoral search committees: "Ought not a Minister to have, First, a good understanding, a clear apprehension, a sound judgment, and a capacity of reasoning with some closeness?"[1] Time and again throughout the address, Wesley unpacked this remark by admonishing ministers to know what would sound truly odd and almost pagan to the average congregant of today: logic, metaphysics (including the first principles of being), natural theology, geometry and the ideas of important figures in the history of philosophy.

Wesley's remarks were not unusual in his time. A century earlier, the great Reformed pastor Richard Baxter was faced with lukewarmness in the church and unbelief outside the church. In 1667, he wrote a book to meet this need and in it he used philosophy to argue for the existence of the soul and the life to come. The fact that Baxter turned to

3

philosophy instead of small groups or praise hymns is worth pondering. Over a millennium earlier, Augustine summarized the view of many early church fathers when he said: "We must show our Scriptures not to be in conflict with whatever [our critics] can demonstrate about the nature of things from reliable sources."[2] Philosophy was the main tool Augustine used in this task.

Today things are different. Most evangelical seminaries with which I am familiar do not have professional philosophers on their faculties nor do they train ministerial candidates to do philosophy or motivate them to see philosophical acumen as part of their calling. In my experience of speaking in literally hundreds of churches, the first thing that comes to many Christian minds when they hear the word "philosophy" is that Colossians 2:8 (in their view) warns them to stay away from it. It is no accident that these facts run concurrently with an increasingly marginalized evangelical community which, as a result, is struggling with a crisis of self-image as the culture turns neo-pagan.

I do not pretend to have a thorough answer to these latter two difficulties, but I do believe there is a causal connection between them and the diminished role of philosophy in our collective evangelical worship and witness. Social historian John Gager has pointed out that even though the early church was a minority movement that faced intellectual and cultural ridicule and marginalization, the early church maintained internal cohesion and a courageous witness thanks in no small measure to the powerful role in the broader Christian community of the philosophically trained apologists in the first centuries of the Christian faith.[3] The same point applies with real force to our current condition. In my view, if the evangelical community would give greater attention to philosophy, especially philosophical apologetics in formal educational settings, publishing and local church life, this could help a great deal in our efforts to penetrate our culture effectively and proclaim Christ and a Christian worldview to outsiders and to our own brothers and sisters. However, if we continue to eschew philosophy, we will continue to speak largely to ourselves and our dialect will, I fear, be fideistic.

Space does not permit me to attempt to prove this claim directly. Instead, I shall do three things: (1) clarify the nature and tasks of philosophical apologetics, (2) describe the current scene in order to indentify areas where we need to focus our attention as a community and (3) offer some brief remarks about a strategy for the future. I hope that my discussion of these three desiderata will show, even if only implicitly, just why we need to be more intentional and intense about promoting philosophical apologetics within our ranks. Let us begin with fullness of heart then and look first at the different purposes of philosophical apologetics.

Different Types of Philosophical Apologetics

If philosophy is hard to define, philosophical apologetics is harder still. Nevertheless, as a working definition, let us characterize philosophical apologetics as a philosophical activity which has as its goal (or perhaps its result) the increasing or maintaining of the epistemic justification of a Christian worldview in whole or in part.[4] Let us accept this gloss as adequate.

Note two things about the definition. First, philosophical apologetics involves the direct use of philosophy. Thus, historical evidences *per se* are not part of philosophical apologetics. Second, philosophy, as well as its employment by Christians, goes beyond philosophical apologetics. All cases of philosophical apologetics are cases of philosophy but the converse does not hold. As I see it, there are at least four different types of philosophical apologetics. My aim in delineating these is not simply informational. My hope is that when these are clarified, they can help all of us be more intentional in trying to relate our academic work to philosophical apologetics, whatever other purposes we may have.

1. Direct Defense

In direct defense, one uses philosophy with the primary intent of enhancing or maintaining directly the epistemic justification of Christian theism or some proposition taken to be explicit to or entailed by it (hereafter I will simply refer to Christian theism). There are two basic forms of direct defense, one negative and one positive.[5] The less controversial of the two is a negative direct defense where one attempts to remove defeaters to Christian theism. If you have a justified belief regarding some proposition P, a defeater is something that weakens or removes that justification. Defeaters come in two types.[6] A *rebutting* defeater gives justification for believing *not P*, in this case, that Christian theism is false. For example, attempts to show that the biblical concept of the family is dysfunctional and false or that homosexuality is causally necessitated by genes or brain states and that, therefore, it is not a proper object for moral appraisal are cases of rebutting defeaters. An *undercutting* defeater does not give justification for believing *not P*, but rather seeks to remove justification for believing P in the first place. Critiques of the arguments for God's existence are examples of undercutting defeaters. When defeaters are raised against Christian theism, a negative defense seeks either to rebut or refute those defeaters.

By contrast, a positive direct defense is an attempt to build a positive case for Christian theism. Arguments for the existence of God, objective morality, the existence of the soul, the value and nature of virtue ethics and the possibility and "knowability" of miracles are examples. This type of philosophical apologetics is not accepted by all Christian intellectuals, e.g., various species of what may be loosely called Reformed epistemology run the gamut from seeing a modest role for a positive direct defense to an outright rejection of this type of activity.

2. Philosophical Polemics

In philosophical polemics, one seeks to criticize views that rival Christian theism in one way or another. Critiques of scientific naturalism, physicalism, pantheism and normative ethical relativism are all cases of philosophical polemics.

3. Theistic Explanation

Suppose we have a set of items x_i through x_n that stand in need of explanation and we offer some *explanans* E as an adequate or even best explanation of the *explananda*. In such a case, E explains x_i through x_n and this fact provides some degree of confirmation for E. For example, if a certain intrinsic generic statement explains the various data of a biblical text, then this fact offers some confirmation for that statement. Christian theists ought to be about the business of exploring the world in light of their worldview and, more specifically, of using their theistic beliefs as explanations of various desiderata in the intellectual life. Put differently, we should seek to solve intellectual problems and shed light on areas of puzzlement by utilizing the explanatory power of our worldview. For example, for those who accept the existence of natural moral law, the irreducibly mental nature of consciousness, natural human rights or the fact that human flourishing follows from certain biblically mandated ethical and religious practices, the truth of Christian theism provides a good explanation of these phenomena. And this fact can provide some degree of confirmation for Christian theism. I will mention shortly how the discipline of philosophy enters into this type of intellectual practice because it overlaps with the way philosophy is relevant to the next type of philosophical apologetics.[7]

4. Integration

a. *The Nature of Integration.* The word *integration* means to form or blend into a whole, to unite. The human intellect naturally seeks to find the unity that is behind diversity, and, in fact, coherence is an important mark of rationality. In conceptual integration, one's theological beliefs are blended and unified with propositions from other sources judged to be justifiably believed as true into a coherent, intellectually satisfying worldview. One of the goals or results of integration is to maintain or increase both the conceptual relevance of and epistemological justification for Christian theism. To be engaged in the task of integration is to embark on a journey that is at once exciting and difficult. Integration is no easy task, and it is a life-long project that should occur within an individual believer's life and among the various members of the Christian community working together. Part of the difficulty of this journey is due not only to the massive amount of information and vast array of studies that need to be consulted, but also to the fact that there are many different aspects of and attitudes toward integration itself. It is beyond my present scope to attempt to give anything even approximating a topology of these aspects and attitudes.[8] However, it may be helpful to list some examples where the need for integration arises, as well as some of the different ways that Christian theology interacts with other disciplines in the process of developing an integrated Christian worldview.

b. *The Need for Integration.* Here are some cases that illustrate the need for integration:

(1) A biblical exegete becomes aware of how much his own cultural background shapes what he can see in the biblical text, and he begins to wonder whether meanings might not reside in the interpretation of a text and not in the text itself. He also wonders if certain hermeneutical methodologies may be inappropriate given the nature of the Bible as revelation.

(2) A psychologist reads literature regarding identical twins who are reared in separate environments. She notes that they usually exhibit similar adult be-

havior. She then wonders what free will amounts to, if there is really any such thing, and if not, she ponders what to make of moral responsibility and punishment.

(3) A political science professor reads John Rawls's *Theory of Justice* and grapples with the idea that society's primary goods could be distributed in such a way that those on the bottom get the maximum benefit even if people on the top have to be constrained. He wonders how this compares with a meritocracy wherein individual merit is rewarded regardless of social distribution. Several questions run through his mind: What is the state? How should a Christian view the state and the church? What is justice, and what principles of social ordering ought we to adopt? Should one seek a Christian state or merely a just state?

(4) A neurophysiologist establishes specific correlations between certain brain functions and certain feelings of pain and puzzles over the question of whether or not there is a soul or mind distinct from the brain.

(5) An anthropologist notes that cultures frequently differ over basic moral principles and wonders whether or not this proves that there are no objectively true moral values that transcend culture.

(6) A businesswoman notices that the government is not adequately caring for the poor. She discusses with a friend the issue of whether or not businesses have corporate moral responsibilities or whether only individuals have moral responsibility.

(7) A mathematician teaches Euclidean geometry and some of its alternatives and goes on to ask the class if mathematics is a field that really conveys true knowledge about a subject matter or if it merely offers internally consistent formal languages expressible in symbols. If the former, then what is it that

mathematics describes? If mathematical entities exist and are timeless, in what sense did God create them?

(8) An education major is asked to state her philosophy of education. In order to do this, she must state her views of human nature, truth, how people learn, the role of values in education and so on. She wonders how her Christian convictions inform these issues.

c. *Different Ways Integration Is Done.* In each of the cases listed above, there is a need for the person in question, if he or she is a Christian, to think hard about the issue in light of the need for developing a Christian worldview. When one addresses problems like these, there will emerge a number of different ways that theology can interact with an issue in a discipline outside theology. Here are some of the different ways that such interaction can take place.

The Two Realms View. Propositions, theories or methodologies in theology and another discipline may involve two distinct, non-overlapping areas of investigation. For example, debates about angels or the extent of the atonement have little to do with organic chemistry. Similarly, it is of little interest to theology whether a methane molecule has three or four hydrogen atoms in it.

The Complementarity View. Propositions, theories or methodologies in theology and another discipline may involve two different, complementary, non-interacting approaches to the same reality.[9] Sociological aspects of church growth and/or certain psychological aspects of conversion may be sociological or psychological descriptions of certain phenomena that are complementary to a theological description of church growth or conversion.

The Direct Interaction View. Propositions, theories or methodologies in theology and another discipline may directly interact in such a way that either one area of study offers rational support for the other or one area of study raises rational difficulties for the other. For example, certain theological teachings about the existence of the soul raise rational problems for philosophical or scientific claims that deny the existence of the soul. The general theory of evolution raises various difficulties for certain ways of understanding the book of Genesis. Some have argued that the Big Bang theory tends to support the theological proposition that the universe had a beginning.

The Presuppositional View. Theology tends to support the presuppositions of another discipline and vice versa. Some have argued that many of the presuppositions of science (e.g. the existence of truth, the rational and orderly nature of reality, the adequacy of our sensory and cognitive faculties as tools suited for knowing the external world) make sense and are easy to justify given Christian theism, but are odd and without ultimate justification in a naturalistic worldview. Similarly, some have argued that philosophical critiques of epistemological skepticism and defenses of the existence of a real, theory-independent world and a correspondending theory of truth offer justification for some of the presuppositions of theology.

The Practical Application View. Theology fills out and adds details to general principles in another discipline and vice versa, and theology helps one practically apply principles in another discipline and vice versa. For example, theology teaches that fathers should not provoke their children to anger, and psychology can add important details about what this means by offering information about family systems, the nature and causes of anger, etc. Psychology can devise various tests for assessing whether one is or is not a mature person, and theology can offer a normative definition to psychology as to what a mature person is.

These are some of the ways that integration takes place. From the examples and models listed above, it should be clear that philosophy is central to the task of integration. Nevertheless, the task of forming an integrated worldview is a very difficult one, and there is no set of easy steps that exhaustively describes how that task is to be conducted or what role philosophy should play in the quest for integration. With this in mind, the following is a list of principles that can aid someone unfamiliar with philosophy to think more clearly about its role in integration.

d. *The Role of Philosophy in Integration.*

1. *Philosophy can point out that an issue thought to be a part of another discipline is really a philosophical issue.* It often happens that scholars, untrained in philosophy, will discuss some issue in their field and, without knowing it, cross over into philosophy. When this happens, the discussion may still be about the original discipline, but it is a discussion of philosophy.

For example, attempts to put limits on a given discipline and attempts to draw a line of demarcation between one field of study and another, say between science and theology, are largely philosophical matters. This is because such attempts assume a vantage point outside and above the discipline in question where one asks second-order questions about that discipline. Philosophy focuses on these kinds of second-order questions.

Consider the following six propositions that allow science to limit theology and vice versa:

(S1) Theological beliefs are reasonable only if science renders them so.

(S2) Theological beliefs are unreasonable if science renders them so.

(S3) Theological beliefs are reasonable only if arrived at by something closely akin to scientific methodology.

12

(Tl) Scientific beliefs are reasonable only if theology renders them so.

(T2) Scientific beliefs are unreasonable if theology renders them so.

(T3) Scientific beliefs are reasonable only if arrived at by theologically appropriate methods.

Contrary to initial appearances, these propositions are not examples of science or theology directly placing limits on the other, for none is a statement *of* science or theology. Rather, all are philosophical statements *about* science and theology. Principles *about* science and theology are not the same as principles *of* science and theology. These six principles are philosophical attempts to limit science and theology and show their relationship.

Here is a second example where a discussion crosses over into philosophy almost unnoticed.

Evolutionist: "The origin of life from inanimate matter is a well-established scientific fact."

Creationist: "But if life arose in the oceans as you claim, then dilution factors would have kept the concentration of large, macromolecules to levels so small as to have been negligible."

Evolutionist: "Well, so what? I do not think abiogenesis took place in the ocean anyway. Rather, it took place in some isolated pool that had some concentrating mechanism in place."

Creationist: "But there is no geological evidence for such pools. Further, the probabilities for such a process are incredibly small, and in any case, evidence appears to be coming in that the early earth's atmosphere was not a reducing atmosphere, in which case the relevant reactions could not occur."

Evolutionist: "Give us more time, and we will solve these problems. The only alternative, creationism, is too fantastic to believe. It involves religious concepts and is not science at all."

Creationist: "Well, evolution is not science. Science requires firsthand observation, and since no one was there to observe the origin of first life, any theory about that origin is not science, strictly speaking."

The discussion starts out as a scientific interaction about chemical reactions, probabilities, geological evidence and so on. But it slides over into a second-order philosophical discussion (one that represents a misunderstanding of the nature both of creationism and science) about what science is and how one should define it. These issues are surely relevant to the debate, but there is no guarantee that two disputants trained in some first-order scientific discipline have any expertise at all about the second-order questions of what science is and how it should be practiced. If scientists are going to interact on these issues, then philosophy will be an essential part of that interaction.

2. *Philosophy undergirds other disciplines at a foundational level by clarifying, defending or criticizing the essential presuppositions of that discipline.* Since philosophy operates as a second-order discipline that investigates other disciplines, and since philosophy examines broad, foundational, axiological, epistemological, logical and metaphysical issues in those other disciplines, then philosophy is properly suited to investigate the presuppositions of other fields. Thus, philosophy plays a regulative role for Christian intellectual activity, including apologetics, and is critical to our community if we are to articulate and defend our theology to thinking people, especially to those outside the church. Philosophy can provide structure and sharpness to our discourse in the public square.

For example, in linguistic studies, issues are discussed regarding the existence, nature and "knowability" of meaning. These issues, as well as questions about whether and how language accomplishes reference to things in the world, are the main focus of the philosophy of language and epistemology. Again, science assumes there is an external world that is orderly and knowable, that inductive inferences are legitimate, that the senses and mind are reliable, that truth exists and can be known and so on. Orthodox theology assumes that religious language is cognitive, that knowledge is possible, that an intelligible sense can be given to the claim that something exists that is not located in space and time, that the correspondence theory of truth is the essential part of an overall theory of truth and that linguistic meaning is objective and knowable. These presuppositions, and a host of others besides, have all been challenged. The task of clarifying, defending or criticizing them is essentially a philosophical task.

If evangelicals wish to speak out on issues and move beyond a surface analysis of them, we need philosophy. Training in logic, metaphysics, epistemology and ethics are crucial parts of local church discipleship in this regard.

3. *Philosophy can aid a discipline by helping to clarify concepts, argument forms and other cognitive issues internal to a field.* Sometimes the concepts in a discipline appear to be contradictory, vague, unclear or circular. Philosophers who study a particular discipline can aid that discipline by bringing conceptual clarity to it. An example would be the wave/particle nature of electromagnetic radiation and matter. These concepts appear to be self-contradictory or vague, and attempts have been made to clarify them or to show different ways of understanding them.

Another example concerns certain conceptions of the mechanisms involved in evolutionary theory. Some scientists have held that evolution promotes the survival of the fittest. But when asked what the "fittest" were, the answer was that the "fittest" were those that survived. This was a problem of circularity within evolutionary theory, and attempts have been made to redefine the notion of fitness and the goal of evolution (e.g., the selection of those organisms that are reproductively favorable) to avoid circularity. Whether or not these responses have been successful is not the point. The point is, rather, that philosophers have raised problems for a scientific theory regarding issues of conceptual clarity. In these and other examples like them, philosophy can help to clarify issues within a discipline. When philosophy is brought to bear on questions of this sort, the result may be that the theory in question is problematic because it involves an internal contradiction or is somehow self-refuting.

For example, the sociological claim that there is no difference between *intellectual history* (roughly, the attempt to trace the development of ideas through history by focusing on the rational factors involved in the ideas themselves, including their own inner logic and relationships to ideas coming after them) and the *sociology of knowledge* (the attempt to trace the development of ideas as a result of non-rational factors in a given culture, e.g., social status, economic conditions and so on) is sometimes justified by an appeal to conceptual relativism. The claim is made that different cultures have different language games, different views of the world and so forth, and that all of one's views are determined by non-rational factors and thus are not to be trusted. Such a claim is self-refuting, for presumably this theory itself would be untrustworthy on its own terms.

By way of application, Christians need to be involved in political, social and ethical issues. However, the evangelical voice in this regard often sounds tinny and sloganistic because our proclamations do not express a well-developed political, social or ethical theory. We do not have the latter because we often fail to articulate the philosophical issues necessary to developing these theories.

4. *Philosophy provides a common language or conceptual grid wherein two disciplines can be directly related to one another and integrated.* Sometimes two different disciplines will use a term in a slightly different but not completely unrelated way. When this occurs, philosophy can help to clarify the relationship between the inter-disciplinary uses of the term in question.

For example, sometimes an operational definition of some notion can be related to an ordinary language definition of that notion or a definition from another field. An operational definition is, roughly, a definition of some concept totally in terms of certain laboratory or experimental operations or test scores. Thus, one could operationally define a number of sociological concepts (minority group, traditional family roles, group leadership) or psychological terms (depression, intelligence) completely in terms of some operation or test score. A person could be said to be depressed if and only if that person scored between a predetermined range on some standard psychological test.

Now these operational definitions may be related to our ordinary language notions of the relevant concepts in question; but they may not be clearly related, and in any case, they are certainly not identical to them. So philosophical clarity needs to be given before we can specify the relationship between *depression* as it is understood in ordinary language and *depression* as it is operationally defined in some test.

This type of philosophical elucidation is especially important when the term in question appears to be normative in nature. Thus, if one tries to give an operational, psychological definition of a "mature" or "healthy" adult, then all one can give is a descriptive definition, not a prescriptive one, for psychology as it is currently practiced is a descriptive field. Philosophy focuses on moral prescriptions and "oughts"; psychology focuses on factual descriptions. So philosophy becomes relevant in clarifying the relationship between a "mature" adult, psychologically defined, and a "mature" adult taken as a normative notion (i.e., as something we ought to try to be like).

Philosophy also helps to clarify and relate the different disciplinary descriptions of the same phenomenon. For example, biologists describe a human being as a member of the classification *Homo sapiens*. Philosophy, theology, law and political science (to name a few) treat a human being as a living entity called a *human person*. It is a philosophical question as to whether the two notions are identical and, if they are not, how they relate to one another.

5. *Philosophy provides **external conceptual problems** for other disciplines to consider as part of the rational appraisal of theories in those disciplines* (and vice versa). A philosophical external conceptual problem arises for some theory T, in a discipline outside of philosophy, when T conflicts with a doctrine of some philosophical theory P, when P and its doctrines are rationally well-founded. For example, suppose there were a good philosophical argument against the view that history has crossed an infinite number of events throughout the past to reach the present moment. If this argument is a reasonable one, then it tends to count against some scientific theory (e.g., an oscillating universe) which postulates that the past was without beginning and actually infinite. If there were a good philosophical argument for the claim that space and time are absolute, then this argument would tend to count against scientific theories to the contrary.

Again, if there are good philosophical arguments for the existence of libertarian freedom and agency or arguments for the existence of real moral responsibility and the necessity of libertarian freedom as a presupposition of moral responsibility, then these would tend to count against sociological, economic or psychological theories which entail the sufficiency of event causality. In cases like these, a rationally defensible position is present within philosophy, and it runs contrary to a theory surfaced in another field. The philosophical external conceptual problem may not be sufficient to require abandonment or suspension of judgment of the theory in the other discipline; it may merely tend to count against it. Even so, these kinds of conceptual problems show that philosophical considerations are relevant to the rationality of theory assessment in other disciplines.

Areas of Focus for Philosophical Apologetics

Happily, the state of Christian philosophy in general, and philosophical apologetics in particular, is stronger today than at any other time in the last half-century.[10] As Mark Noll correctly points out, "Christian philosophers have made their presence felt in the world of scholarship more substantially than intellectuals in any other discipline."[11] The incredible growth, vitality and influence of the Society of Christian Philosophers alone is nothing short of a miracle given the intellectual climate since its inception in April of 1978. It is now one of the most influential groups among professional philosophers in the West and its journal *Faith and Philosophy* is widely recognized as one of the top journals in the discipline.

In spite of these gains, however, it would be misleading to speak as if all were well on the battle front. There is much work to be done and it would be wise for us to think carefully about where our efforts are most needed. But how is one to think about this since there are dozens of branches and sub-branches in philosophy that could be fruitful realms of philosophical apologetical activity? Any taxonomy here would likely express the interests and biases of the taxonomist and I am no exception to this rule. Still, I think the following reflections are not too wide of the mark and I have used three criteria in formulating them. First, philosophical apologetics should be focused on those areas of study that seem to be intrinsically more central or foundational to the Christian theistic enterprise. For example, work in religious and moral epistemology would get high marks on this criterion. Second, philosophical apologetics should be focused on areas that are currently under heavy attack. Philosophy of mind comes readily to mind in this regard. A third and perhaps less important criterion is this: philosophical apologetics should be focused on those areas of study in which such activity is under-represented relatively speaking. Political and social philosophy would get my vote here.

With this in mind, here are some areas where I think more concentrated efforts would bear fruit for the kingdom of God.

1. Two Important Intellectual Trends

There are two broad approaches to the intellectual life that are, in my view, dangerous rivals to Christian theism even if we grant that some modest positive value is to be found in each. First, there is *philosophical naturalism*, roughly, the view that the spatiotemporal physical universe studied by natural science—especially physics—is all there is.[12] Many (or even most) philosophical naturalists would take this view to entail the following: 1) scientism as an approach to epistemology along with a denial of philosophy and of any attempt to naturalize philosophy as a discipline; 2) the denial of universals and other abstract entities as well as the type of metaphysical necessity traditionally thought to be expressed in the so-called synthetic *a priori* first truths of reason; 3) a view of living organisms as ordered aggregates with or without non-physical emergent properties instead of seeing them as substances with natures that place them in natural kinds; 4) acceptance of some version of either strict or supervenient physicalism—either way, substance dualism is anathema; 5) an assimilation of personal identity to the identity of physical artifacts with the result that persons do not possess absolute, primitive unity at or through time but, rather, are four-dimensional space-time worms; 6) an eschewal of libertarian free will and agency.

It is hard to overestimate the damage that philosophical naturalism has done to our culture. Christian philosophers need to go to work on criticizing this view and articulating alternative positions. More specifically, we need to place more efforts in defending substance dualism (either the Thomist or Cartesian version) and we need more Christian theologians and biblical scholars to follow John Cooper's lead by showing that this is, in fact, the correct biblical position instead of labeling this a Greek intrusion into biblical thought and opting for a facile Christianized physicalism.[13] The over-stated false dilemma between Hebraic holism and Greek dualism is one of the worst ideas in western thought since Descartes claimed that animals were mere machines. In fact, I think we need more work in essentialism and philosophy of biology to show that there is, in fact, a theological and philosophical contribution to our description of what is real about living things. We abandon a philosophy of nature to our own peril and then wonder why the general culture has either a diminished or superstitious set of beliefs about the afterlife. Reductionism, mechanism and physicalism are dangers for horses as much as for humans. It is interesting to note that scientists are increasingly coming to see that DNA is not the genetic blueprint for the organism but, rather, is an important physical part or tool that presupposes the organism as a whole for the existence and functioning of DNA in the first place.[14] This should come as no surprise to Christian philosophers and theologians who take the soul seriously as the fathers in the church did before us.

A second intellectual movement is *postmodernism*. For those who love truth, reason, the good life and the Christian God, postmodernism must be criticized and judged inadequate.[15] The postmodernist rejection of direct access to the mind/language/theory-independent world, the correspondence theory of truth, the paradigm independence and objectivity of rationality and justification, the objectivity and availability of authorial intent and the appropriateness of an all-encompassing meta-narrative fall short of what I believe to be the commitments entailed by evangelical faith. In a related point, I think epistemological foundationalism has been widely rejected because it came to be associated with 1) the empiricism and logical positivism that flourished in the first half of this century and 2) the need for incorrigible foundations for knowledge coupled with a view of knowledge as entailing Cartesian certainty. However, neither of these is essential to foundationalism, and, in my view, sophisticated versions of it are still the best way to describe the structure of epistemic justification and to respond to the extreme claims of certain postmodernists.[16] Whether or not you agree with me here, one thing seems clear: more work needs to be done by Christian philosophers in this area.

2. Philosophy of Religion

Three areas of philosophy of religion need more attention by philosophical apologists. First, we have Alvin Plantinga, Nicholas Wolterstorff and their friends to thank for bringing religious epistemology to the forefront of philosophical discussion.[17] However, I remain unconvinced that either the proper basicality of belief in God or epistemic externalism is the solution. I would like to see more efforts directed toward defending epistemic internalism and relating it to the philosophy of the mind. We also need to give more thought to the importance of natural theology for the justification of theistic belief. I also think that insights gained from work in moral and religious epistemology could provide defeaters for a naturalistic evolutionary view of the origin and functioning of our noetic equipment. These and other desiderata are needed areas of exploration in religious epistemology.

A second and related point is that we need to update, develop and strengthen the arguments for God's existence. William Lane Craig has already done this for the cosmological argument.[18] Currently, Phillip Johnson, Steve Meyer, Paul Nelson and Bill Dembski are heading up a group doing work on the design argument. And while we are in the neighborhood of theistic arguments, let me say that more attention needs to be given to the argument from consciousness and the moral argument.

Third, philosophers should continue to apply their craft to the clarification and defense of various Christian doctrines. Much is already being done regarding the concept, attributes and works of God, the Trinity and the hypostatic union. I also think that the issues of Christian particularism and the morality of everlasting punishment are not going to go away in the near future.[19]

3. Christianity and Science

In the last few years, a battle has been raging about the nature of science itself and how to best integrate it with Christianity. Many Christian intellectuals follow Richard Bube and Howard J. van Till who say that science must embrace methodological naturalism and that the complementarity view is the best way to integrate science and Christianity in areas of dialogue like creation and evolution.[20] I am on the other side of the divide.[21] Be that as it may, it is clear that we need to have more philosophers work on these issues because, in spite of what some Christian scientists say, the issues are largely within the purview of the history and philosophy of science.

Two other issues need to be explored more fully with an eye on integrating science and theology. First, the realism/anti-realism debate in the philosophy of science needs to be explored to develop applications from it to questions of integration. Second, as I have already said, certain views of living organisms (that they have irreducible, immaterial essences that give them their unity, their kindedness, and ground their teleological development and the functions of their parts and that are what direct the development of the organism's body and phenotypes) set easily with biblical concepts of creation, created kinds and so forth. Christians have been too frightened by the charge of vitalism—a notion that is itself grossly misunderstood—and should not abandon the philosophy of nature as a legitimate part of our search for the knowledge of true descriptions of natural living organisms.

In all of this, one thing is of paramount importance. Many today, including many Christians, think that science is the king of the hill, epistemologically speaking, and have settled on something that bears a family resemblance to fideism in the area of religious knowledge. This has contributed to the marginalization of Christianity in the culture and to a view of theology as a language game for the faithful. Whatever we do in the area of science and Christianity, we must vouchsafe a reply to this bifurcated epistemology and defend the objectivity and public assessability of Christian truth claims and the rational justification for them.

4. Ethics

Obviously, there is great need for Christians to intensify their efforts to develop articulate positions on the issues of our day. However, one word of caution is in order here. If we direct too much attention to ethics to the exclusion of metaphysics and epistemology, then we may inadvertently contribute to the cultural perspective that somehow ethics is not a field of real knowledge grounded in the way things are, but is instead an attempt to clarify and bring order to the various traditions and paradigms that, in the final analysis, are relative to individuals and communities and only involve the expression of private, subjective beliefs.

Having said this, two other things come to mind in this area. First, more work needs to be done in integrating deontological approaches to normative ethics with virtue theory. What we need is a better way of showing how moral rule-following is related to the good life of human flourishing which, in turn, is metaphysically grounded in the way we are by nature as creatures made in God's image. Second, the whole issue of human personhood is widely discussed in a way that I find inadequate. Many think that, absent God and the doctrine of creation in His image, the notion of being human is merely a biological one; anyone who thinks we are valuable because we are human is guilty of "speciesism." The locus of moral worth has come to be personhood viewed as the emergence of a set of properties on a properly structured functioning human brain that satisfy the criteria of personhood. On this view, one can be a human non-person. Some Christians have come close to accepting the spirit if not the letter of this approach. I have argued elsewhere that this is just a mistake.[22] The image of God is possessed by all human persons, who are such by nature, not by functioning. I think we need to take the image of God more seriously as a metaphysical reality and not leave definitions of being human or being a person to scientific naturalists or to Christianized appropriations of a scientistic approach to these issues.

As I said, these are my own reflections about the current state of things and I hope I have said enough to show that philosophical apologetics is critical to the vitality of the church and her mission in the world as we approach the twenty-first century. The question that remains is how we can be more effective and intentional in supporting the practice of philosophical apologetics among us.

Suggestion for Future Strategy

In light of all that has been said to this point, where do we go from here? What do we need to do as an evangelical community engaged in a culture war trying to glorify God and spread the gospel? Mark Noll wryly bemoans the fact that "[w]hen faced with a crisis situation, we evangelicals usually do one of two things. We either mount a public crusade, or we retreat into an inner pious sanctum."[23] By contrast, I suggest we rethink the role of the intellectual life, and specifically, of philosophy in that life, for the health and mission of the church. One of the most important things we can do is to reexamine the way we plan, spend our time and direct our resources in light of the following two facts. First, we are involved in a war of ideas for people's minds and hearts. This war is critical because individual and communal forms of life are governed not by mere belief, but by what people take to be known or reasonably believed. Moreover, we are living in a *Zeitgeist* that denies that religious knowledge is possible and so denies that religious claims, like most factual claims, are publicly assessable and objectively rational. Second, the evangelical community largely speaks to itself in a religiously isolated language game, most of our ministry efforts focus on "in-house" issues, and we are just not part of public discourse. In light of this, we simply must find ways to reappropriate the importance of philosophy in general and philosophical apologetics in particular. Here are some suggestions for doing this:

1. Seminaries should hire a professional philosopher for its faculty or, even better, hire a group of them to start a graduate program in philosophy and ethics. At Talbot School of Theology we started such a program three years ago, and we currently have four philosophers and ethicists on our faculty and close to seventy graduate students. Our presence has increased the spirit of intellectual depth and precision as well as students' courage to be informed activists in the culture within the seminary community. Our goal is to place 100 students in Ph.D. programs in philosophy who will become college professors in the next twenty years and to see a steady stream of philosophically trained

graduates pour into parachurch ministries or become ministers of evangelism and discipleship.

2. We need to teach pastors to start institutes for study and activism in their churches. I have already been a part of starting such an institute and I cannot go into details here about how such a center operates. But regardless of details, an institute for study and activism seeks to equip believers to think about how Christianity relates to their vocation at the level of ideas and to be able to understand and critique contemporary culture to spread Christ's influence and to win others to Christ. The standard seminary curriculum absent the chance to be trained in philosophical apologetics is simply not producing ministers who have the courage to get involved in the conflict of ideas raging all about us. People in our churches have virtually no idea how their Christian beliefs relate to ideas intrinsic to their vocations. It is well past time for us to put aside this dichotomized vision of Christian piety.

3. Parachurch ministries like Campus Crusade should designate certain staff members whose job it is to form centers of apologetical research at different sites around the country to equip their own staff and students and to penetrate the secular campuses that constitute their mission fields. It is unconscionable that the very ministries that target the citadels of learning have been so out of touch with the world of ideas.

4. Foundations need to be set up to fund evangelicals who wish to pursue Ph.D.s in philosophy or ethics. I think we need to pay special attention to these disciplines for two reasons. First, due to their very nature, these fields are absolutely foundational in mobilizing believers to be effective in getting at the bottom of systems of thought that are harming the progress of the gospel and the nurturing of the saints. The hot issues of the day are largely ethical and philosophical. Second, philosophy has a public relations problem among us and there is little effort and virtually no felt need to raise up a new generation of evangelical phi-

losophers compared to, say, Christian psychologists or biblical scholars.

5. Finally, the evangelical community has far more biblical and theological scholars than it does philosophers. Happily, however, there is a growing number of well-trained philosophers who are solid evangelicals. We need theologians and Old and New Testament scholars to take the lead in identifying crucial issues we need to address and to set up institutes, conferences or multi-authored volumes to address them. I urge us all to be sure that we bring more Christian philosophers into this networking process.

In closing, it is urgent that we rethink the importance of the intellectual life for the health of the church and the effectiveness of her outreach. When we do this, it will be obvious that philosophy is now, as it always has been in our history, a crucial component in our collective Christian concerns. We now find ourselves largely marginalized in the culture and ingrown in the issues we address, the activities we perform, the books we read and the categories in which we think and speak. Our marginalization and penchant for being ingrown are the result of several decades of academic bullying from the outside and intellectual cowardice or indifference on the inside. For some time now, with rare and notable exceptions, Christian intellectuals have largely focused their studies on religious issues within the church or on technical minutiae regarding biblical exegesis. As important as exegesis is, we do not need another commentary on Ephesians or a new book on the doctrine of salvation. Instead, we need a renaissance of evangelical statements of and defenses for what we believe about the broad issues being debated in the academy and the broader culture. We will never succeed at this if we do not give philosophical ability and training a central place in church and seminary education. If the giants of the past like Wesley and Baxter saw philosophical apologetics as crucial in this regard, we neglect this activity to our own peril.

Failure to rethink church life and seminary education in this context will only contribute to our increased marginalization and the ingrown character of our presence in an increasingly secular and alien culture.[24]

Endnotes

[1]John Wesley, "An Address to the Clergy" in *The Works of John Wesley*, 3rd ed. (Grand Rapids, MI: Baker, 1979; first ed., 1972), 481.

[2]St. Augustine, *De genesi ad litteram* 1.21.

[3]John G. Gager, *Kingdom and Community: The Social World of Early Christianity* (Englewood Cliffs, NJ: Prentice-Hall, 1975), 86-87.

[4]Does an atheist who offers good arguments for the soul (assuming as I do that Christianity teaches that souls exist) practice philosophical apologetics? Not if the latter is defined by good epistemic intentions towards Christianity. Still, such arguments have the result of increasing our justification for believing in the soul and may be counted as philosophical apologetics, at least in a secondary sense. Yet in this case would these arguments have to be used by a Christian theist to support a Christian doctrine before they would count as philosophical apologetics? I leave the matter open.

[5]See Ronald Nash, *Faith and Reason* (Grand Rapids, MI: Zondervan, 1988), 14-18.

[6]For a useful discussion of various types of defeaters, see John Pollock, *Contemporary Theories of Knowledge* (Totowa, NJ: Rowman & Littlefield, 1986), 36-39; Ralph Baergen, *Contemporary Epistemology* (Fort Worth, TX: Harcourt Brace, 1995), 119-24.

[7]Explanation can be seen as one purpose for certain types of integrative practices. But because of its importance, I make it a category of its own.

[8]For a brief typology of different aspects of integration, see William Hasker, "Faith-Learning Integration: An Overview," *Christian Scholar's Review* 21 (March 1992): 234-48.

[9]Richard Bube has complained that my characterization of complementarity is confused and is actually a description of what he calls compartmentalization. See his *Putting it All Together* (Lanham, MD: University Press of America, 1995), 168. Cf. chapters 6 and 10. For Bube, compartmentalization treats science and theology as different descriptions about different kinds of things with no common ground or possibility of conflict. Complementarity views science and theology as different descriptions of the same reality. Unfortunately, Bube is simply wrong in this complaint towards my position. What he calls compartmentalization is close to what I call the "two realms" view of integration and my description of complementarity is an accurate one. The source of Bube's confusion is revealing. I claim that the complementarity view eschews interaction between science and theology and Bube says that it embraces such interaction. However, Bube equivocates on what "interaction" means in this context. For me, it is "epistemic" interaction, roughly the same description of the same reality that can be in conflict or concord to varying degrees of strength. For Bube, interaction amounts to taking two different (non-interacting in my sense) perspectives and forming them into a whole. For example, a completely scientific description of the origin of life in natural terms could be described in theological terms as God's activity in bringing life into being. It is clear that his notion of interaction is not the one I deny in explicating complementarity. Moreover, my use of interaction is crucial in understanding the significance for scientific methodology of gaps in the natural causal fabric due to libertarian agency and primary causal activity on God's part.

[10]See Kelly James Clark, ed., *Philosophers Who Believe* (Downers Grove, IL: InterVarsity, 1993).

[11]Mark A. Noll, *The Scandal of the Evangelical Mind* (Grand Rapids, MI: Eerdmans, 1994), 236.

[12]For a clear statement of naturalism, see Reinhardt Grossmann, *The Existence of the World* (London: Routledge, 1992). Defenses of naturalism include Werner Callebaut, *Taking the Naturalistic Turn* (Chicago: University of Chicago Press, 1993) and David Papineau, *Philosophical Naturalism* (Oxford: Blackwell, 1993). A good critique of naturalism is Steven J. Wagner, Richard Warner, *Naturalism: A Critical Appraisal* (Notre Dame, IN: University of Notre Dame Press, 1993).

[13]See John W. Cooper, *Body, Soul, and Life Everlasting* (Grand Rapids, MI: Eerdmans, 1989). For the distinction between Cartesian and Thomistic Substance Dualism, see J.P. Moreland, Stan Wallace "Aquinas vs. Descartes and Locke on the Human Person and End-of-Life Ethics," *International Philosophical Quarterly* 35 (September 1995): 319-30.

[14]Cf. Jonathan Wells, "The History and Limits of Genetic Engineering," *International Journal on the Unity of the Sciences* 5 (Summer 1992): 137-50; H.F. Nijhout, "Metaphors and the Role of Genes in Development," *BioEssays* 12 (September 1990): 441-45; J.M. Barry, "Informational DNA: a useful concept?" *Trends in Biochemical Sciences* 11 (1986): 317-18.

[15]For an evangelical discussion of postmodernism, see Timothy R. Phillips, Dennis L. Okholm, *Christian Apologetics in the Postmodern World* (Downers Grove, IL: InterVarsity, 1995).

[16]See Roderick Chisholm, *Theory of Knowledge* (Englewood Cliffs, NJ: Prentice-Hall, 3rd ed., 1989); Robert Audi, *Belief, Justification, and Knowledge* (Belmont, CA: Wadsworth, 1988).

[17]See Alvin Plantinga, Nicholas Wolterstorff, *Faith and Rationality* (Notre Dame, IN: University of Notre Dame

Press, 1983); Alvin Plantinga, *Warrant: The Current Debate* (New York: Oxford, 1993); *Warrant and Proper Function* (New York: Oxford, 1993). For a response to Reformed epistemology, see Linda Zagzebski, ed., *Rational Faith: Catholic Responses to Reformed Epistemology* (Notre Dame, IN: University of Notre Dame Press, 1993).

[18]See William Lane Craig, Quentin Smith, *Theism, Atheism, and Big Bang Cosmology* (Oxford: Clarendon Press, 1993).

[19]Dennis L. Okholm, Timothy R. Phillips, eds., *More Than One Way? Four Approaches to Salvation in a Pluralistic World* (Grand Rapids, MI: Zondervan, 1995).

[20]See Howard J. Van Till, "The Character of Contemporary Natural Science," in *Portraits of Creation*, ed. by Howard J. Van Till, Robert E. Snow, John H. Stek and Davis A. Young (Grand Rapids, MI: Eerdmans, 1990), 126-65; Howard J. Van Till, Davis A. Young, Clarence Menninga, *Science Held Hostage* (Downers Grove, IL: InterVarsity, 1988); Howard J. Van Till, "Categorical Complementarity and the Creationomic Perspective," *Journal of the American Scientific Affiliation* 37 (September 1985): 149-57; Richard Bube, *Putting it All Together* (Lanham, MD: University Press of America, 1995).

[21]See J.P. Moreland, ed., *The Creation Hypothesis* (Downers Grove, IL: InterVarsity, 1994), chapters 1-2; "Creation Science and Methodological Naturalism," in *Man and Creation*, ed. by Michael Bauman (Hillsdale, MI: Hillsdale College Press, 1993), 105-139; *Christianity and the Nature of Science* (Grand Rapids, MI: Baker, 1989), chapters 1, 6; "Conceptual Problems and the Scientific Status of Creation Science," *Perspectives on Science and Christian Faith* 46 (March 1994): 2-13.

[22]J.P. Moreland, "Humanness, Personhood, and the Right to Die," *Faith and Philosophy* 12 (January 1995): 95-112; J.P. Moreland and John Mitchell, "Is the Human Person a Substance or Property-Thing?" *Ethics and Medicine* 11 (forthcoming 1995).

[23]Noll, *The Scandal of the Evangelical Mind*, 141.

[24]I wish to thank R. Douglas Geivett and John Mark Reynolds for their helpful comments on an earlier draft of this chapter.

Both/And: A Biblical Alternative to the Presuppositional/ Evidential Debate

Ronald B. Mayers

*C*hristian apologetics has been divided throughout the twentieth century, and perhaps throughout its entire history, with the same epistemological/methodological debate that featured Plato against Aristotle in the ancient world, and Descartes versus Locke in modern philosophy. The perennial question is: Are there innate ideas or principles from which we must deductively construct our world, or must we begin "where we are" and inductively construct our world piece by piece? Christian presuppositionalists argue that God is innate in the human psyche (Romans 1:19-20) and that we either start with the self-existent Creator or we end with nothing. Anselm's classic argument is philosophy's expression of this form of argumentation, even if the argument itself is not fundamental to twentieth-century evangelical presuppositionalism. Christian evidentialists, on the other hand, insist on starting "where we are" and therefore begin to build their case for the truth of Christianity via history and God's miraculous intervention that culminates in Jesus of Nazareth, the Christ. Like other historical investigations, these evangelicals begin inductively to establish the reality of God and the identity of Jesus "piece by piece." Philosophy has followed a similar path in attempting to establish the reality and necessity of God via cause and design arguments.

Must these two approaches to knowledge remain mutually exclusive, or nearly so, in Christian apologetics? While Kant's claim that "concepts without precepts are empty, precepts without concepts are blind" seemingly provides a new epistemological foundation for philosophy, philosophers of religion continue the rift; this is seen by the fact that those who most champion the cosmological (cause) and teleological (design) arguments disclaim any merit to the ontological argument of Anselm. This division is most definitively seen in evangelical apologetics in the presuppositional/evidential debate.

It is the contention of a Both/And apologetic that both evidentialism and presuppositionalism are correct. God most definitely is the self-existent Creator, but He is also the One who not only makes our history possible, but has frequently joined us. As Creator, God is certainly the presupposition of everything. Presuppositionalism is correct: there is nothing if there is not God. Evidentialism is correct also, however, because this Creator God does invade our history and we trace His historical path not only via the more abstract archeological trails that inductively support the truth of the Old Testament, but likewise establish the historic reliability of the Gospels that leave us an incarnate God/Man and not simply a fine ethical teacher, as C.S. Lewis showed in his *Mere Christianity*.

In one sense, presuppositionalism begins with God while evidentialism begins with man. They are both right! As Creator, God is primary and logically prior to all our thoughts. There is a difference, however, between logical priority and existential beginning. We are not God and thus must begin "where we are." John Calvin, I believe, knew this well and begins his *magnum opus* with these words:

> Our wisdom, in so far as it ought to be deemed true and solid wisdom, consists almost entirely of two

parts: the knowledge of God and the knowledge of ourselves. But as these are connected together by many ties, it is not easy to determine which of the two precedes, and gives birth to the other.[1]

Calvin was very sensitive to the problem of starting point. Nearly all apologetic disputes can be traced to this issue: do we start inductively from man and argue to God, or do we argue deductively from the reality of God to ourselves and everything else? Calvin was cognizant that it is not as clear or simple as many apologists of either camp have made it to appear: "It is not easy to determine which of the two precedes, and gives birth to the other." How can man *existentially* begin with God? He is man and not God. If we begin with man, there is an impelling ascension to God "because it is perfectly obvious, that the endowments which we possess cannot possibly be from ourselves."[2] These two must be held together. Though it is certain that man cannot properly know himself without knowing God, the reverse is also true. Calvin writes: "we cannot clearly and properly know God unless the knowledge of ourselves be added."[3]

This is the foundational assumption of the Both/And approach. Apologetics cannot be solely presuppositional by beginning with God to the practical exclusion of man, nor is it able to begin with supposedly agnostic man as if he is independent of God and find God by either the inductive proofs of medieval theologians or the historical evidences of contemporary evidentialists. Thus in regard to personal identity and historical reality we of necessity must begin existentially with ourselves, but in regard to ultimate meaning and eternal verities we must begin logically with God. Cornelius Van Til states this well, though I may apply it differently, when he writes that if "the human consciousness must, in the nature of the case, always be the proximate starting point, it remains true that God is always the most basic and therefore the ultimate or final reference point in human interpretation."[4]

Van Til's two-directional methodology is demanded because reality is *both* God *and* creation. The fact that we are other than God means we start with who and where we are—a God-imaged human being in the midst of His finite creation. Thus we begin inductively using the God-given means of gathering empirical data. At the same time we are always cognizant that we are God's creation and thus our meaning is derived *a priori* from God.

This biblical truth of reality being *both* God *and* creation is an answer to why there are two primary philosophic perspectives and methodologies: rationalistic idealisms and empirical naturalisms. (It must be remembered that Christian presuppositionalism and evidentialism are the methodological cousins of these philosophic orientations, even if they do not share in their ontology.) Idealisms stress the rational and logical unity and permanence of truth at the expense of the real diversity and change of the parts. Naturalisms, on the contrary, stress diversity and continuous development of the many parts of one's sense-data world to the eventual cost of the world's knowability and thus usually breed skepticism. It is the perennial philosophic problem of Being versus Becoming, or as stated above, Plato versus Aristotle. This is *not* an artificial problem in a world that is ignorant of God and creation. Biblical reality as God and creation is twofold and thus *really is* unified and permanent while being at the same time diverse and changeable. The difference between the two philosophic traditions is simply an emphasis in direction, that is, what one chooses to declare as ultimately real and thus emphasize. But we ought not choose between these emphases. Both are correct. Reality that is God and creation is *both* permanent *and* changing, *both* eternal Being *and* temporal being. Reality is *both* the inherently self-existing and absolute spirit Being of God *and* the acquired existence and relative natural being of creation. Reality is *not* monistic. Both idealisms and naturalisms are reductionistic in their respective truncated views of reality. To have either to the exclusion of the other is to have only half a loaf. Reality as we now know it (postcreation) is *both* Spirit *and* Nature. Philosophers cannot escape this creation fact as man alone participates in both dimensions, being created in the very image of God from the very dust of the ground. Similarly, presuppostionalism and evidentialism are equally correct in stressing two different starting points. They are equally in error when the former forgets that he is man and not God, and the latter forgets that all evidence is ultimately what God proclaims it to be, not what man interprets.

Further ontological clarification might be obtained by employing the distinctive between "Being" and "being." "Being" is a *tricky* word, whether we follow Parmenides' statement that "Being is, non-Being is not," or a Heideggerian analysis of the "being of nothingness." "Being" in Christian thought is neither monolithic as in Eastern frameworks, nor is God the impersonal "ground of Being" as in a Tillichian theology. While delineating the twofoldness of reality (Being), Christianity is not dualistic since one facet of reality (God) is absolute and independent and the other facet (creation) is relative and dependent. God's existence is *intrinsic*; He is self-existing. Or as He answered Moses, "I AM" (Exodus 3:13). Nothing in God's created nature exists in this manner. Heraclitus is correct if one looks only at nature—everything changes. Death is the ultimate change. My existence (being) is *extrinsic*. I cannot remember World War II as I was too young. I cannot remember the Depression because I was not here. Similarly, I am not personally anxious about the soundness of the Social Security system in the mid-twenty-first century as I will not be here. Even though made in God's image and therefore "godlike," you and I are totally dependent upon the Creator God. Our being is extrinsic. We do not exist inherently as God exists. In other words, God and creation are not equals in a Manichean dualism. Rather, God is infinite and creation is finite. God is absolutely unlimited by anything other than His own nature and will.

Creation means that God freely chose out of grace and love to have something else exist in its own right. God has, so to speak, renounced being the only existent.

Christian apologetics can neglect the ontological status of created nature only at its own peril. This does not mean the apologist must develop a natural theology, for it is impossible to build an argument from an extrinsic being to prove the existence of One whose being is intrinsic. But it does mean that *the foundation of a Christian apologetic (worldview) must be firmly based on the Christian understanding of ontology*. Given creation, the Christian apologist/theologian can no more speak adequately of God in total neglect of his creation than the secular humanist/naturalist can speak adequately of man and nature in total neglect of God. Intrinsic Being and extrinsic being must be constantly juxtaposed one with the other. This is the very foundation of a Both/And apologetic. It means that God and revelation cannot be presuppositionally emphasized apart from creation and history, and contrariwise, creation and/or history cannot be emphasized through natural theology or evidentialism apart from the distinct word of God.

Before outlining the epistemological horizons of a Both/And apologetic, something must be said of the knowing subject, man created in God's image. Genesis 1:26-27 as well as Genesis 5:1 speak of male and female being created in the image (*tselem*) and likeness (*demuth*) of God. Some theologians have denied that there is any *real* ontological likeness between God and man. Calvin himself, however, wrote that "as for myself, before I define the image of God, I would deny that it differs from His likeness."[5] Keil and Delitzsch see these words as synonymous and thus are joined for intensity, quoting Luther that it means "an image which is like us."[6] (It is noteworthy that these same two words are used of Adam and Seth in Genesis 5:3. This not only reinforces the idea of essential resemblance between God and man if we put any emphasis on verbal inspiration, but it also implies that this image of God will be universal.

Seth is a "copy" of Adam who was directly imaged and thus this becomes the basis of capital punishment in Genesis 9:6.) This "likeness" is confirmed when it is noted that *homoiosis* (LXX, "likeness") is used for both man "made in God's likeness" in James 3:9 and Christ "made in human likeness" in Philippians 2:7. While eschewing identity in either case, to be made in the image of God means that man has an essential likeness and/or similarity in a finite, relative manner to the infinite, self-existing God.

ⁱ This ontological resemblance between God and man is of extreme importance for epistemology. While it is certainly true that the image is in one sense functional, i.e., it enables man to have a relationship with God, image is not primarily relational but ontological. This resemblance of man and God in personality is indispensable for both epistemological and soteriological concerns. Only on the basis of this ontological similarity can there be the reality of a natural revelation of God *in* man; the feasibility of a propositional revelation where words can have univocal meaning and thus provide a true disclosure of God's Person and will; and lastly, the possibility of an incarnation that is not inherently contradictory. God and man thus *do have* a personal relationship *because* man is finite person in God's image. Man and God communicate via revelation and prayer because man is "wired" to think in a non-contradictory manner with unique verbal abilities absent from the rest of God's sub-human creation. Likewise, Adam can understand the initial non-contradictory verbal command from the infinite Creator because he is not only personal but moral and capable of being holy as God is (cf. Genesis 2:16, 17; Leviticus 11:44a; 1 Peter 1:16). Jesus and Paul knowingly use and argue on the basis of man's unique moral ability (John 8:9; Romans 2:15; 13:5). Lastly, man is able to create, artistically imaging God in his creation; artists are also capable of conceiving offspring in their own image and likeness even as God created in His image and likeness.

The immediate context of Genesis 1:26-27 connects man's unique creation with his being steward of God's world. He is God's vice-regent. Adam and his descendants delineate their unique relationship with God by their obedience to his moral commands. Humans are to will God's will as God's stewards.

Man, however, did not continue to will God's will as God's steward. Man's likeness to God not only gives man the God-given responsibility as steward (cultivator) of nature per se, but it also implied and demands a relationship to the One in whose image we have been made. An infinite/finite relationship, however, is one of dependence and obedience for the finite. However, the history of the divine/human relationship might be titled "the conflict of wills." From Adam to you and me, the battle has been one of autonomy, literally self-law versus God's law. In short, man desired to be "like" God absolutely instead of finitely and relatively. Like Adam, humans aspire to independence rather than dependence. Man's failure was and is the incorrect use of his God-given and God-like nature and will.

This failure sheared man of his original righteous personhood. Man's initial righteous character and innocence were as much a gift of God and the reflection of God's image as were his rational and creative abilities. Man lost this righteousness, if not his personality, in willful disobedience. Man is thus alienated from God and but dimly reflects His likeness with an image deprived of essential righteousness. Man is no longer what he was intended to be. In one sense, man is now abnormal if judged by the criteria of the original unfallen pair. We inherently misuse our rational and creative capacities by a perverted will in autonomous separation from God. This being the case, epistemological determinations, so important for apologetics, cannot but be affected. The respective starting points of presuppositionalism and evidentialism are basically determined by how seriously one understands these noetic consequences. Can a Both/And apologetic methodology find a mid-point in which man's waywardness is not denied, but God's revelation in both event and word can be objectively understood if not existentially accepted by the one to whom the Christian apologist presents the truth of the gospel?

The absolute controlling factor of Christian epistemology is special revelation. Special revelation is the activity and record of God's provision on behalf of his fallen creation. Special revelation as God's activity is the self-projection of God into our history that makes a difference. Beginning with Abraham, God's revelatory/redemptive activity is seen throughout the Old Testament, culminating in the person of Immanuel, Jesus of Nazareth, the Christ. Be it the Passover, the escape from Egypt, nationhood or captivity, God is progressively uncovering His holy Person and righteous will. This activity is neither legend nor myth, but actual history. These events need to be remembered (cf. Deuteronomy 1-33; Joshua 24) and are thus recorded as Holy Scripture. God thus provides His revelation as events in history with an absolute and definitive interpretation. Like other history, God's revelatory involvement with us must not only be recorded or it becomes lost and forgotten and thus basically meaningless, but it must also be explained or it is open to being misunderstood and misinterpreted. Scripture fulfills both purposes, recording and providing meaningful interpretation.

This twofold nature of special revelation as *both* event *and* word, similar to the twofoldedness of *both* God *and* creation for ontology, is the foundation of Christian epistemology. Special revelation is encounter *via* God's actual involvement or personal entrance into history, but it is *also* absolutely propositional. Thus evidentialism is surely correct when it desires to show us historical evidence that demonstrates the reality of God and His incarnate Son. Presuppositionalism is correct when it argues that one must deduce truth from the reality of God and His propositional revelation. The mistake of the former is that it forgets that the historical events with which it argues have only one definitive interpretation and thus they mean only what Scripture says they mean. The latter forgets that the vast majority of the propositions of Scripture are referencing and interpreting actual historical events. It is the contention of a Both/And apologetic that revelation is both event and word; that the two must never be methodologically separated can be seen in the ministries of Jesus as well as the classic sermons of Peter and Paul at Pentecost and Athens.

Jesus constantly juxtaposed his "works" (actual historical events) with his "word." For instance, in John 5:17-47 Jesus very cogently argues his equality with God on the basis of both his works and word. He claims that the "very work that the Father has given me to finish, and which I am doing, testifies that the Father has sent me" (5:36), but "since you do not believe what [Moses] wrote, how are you going to believe what I say?" (5:47). Similarly, in an even more distinctive challenge to those who rejected his claim, he states on two different occasions:

> Why then do you accuse me of blasphemy because I said, "I am God's Son"? Do not believe me unless I do what my Father does. But if I do it, even though you do not believe me, believe the miracles, that you may learn and understand that the Father is in me, and I in the Father. (John 10:36-38)

> Believe me when I say that I am in the Father and the Father is in me; or at least believe on the evidence of the miracles themselves. (John 14:11)

Jesus is certainly appealing to the actual historical events of His miraculous works to substantiate His personal claim. He is not separating His deeds from His words; the two are mutually affirming one another. He could not be doing what He is doing if He is not who He claims to be,

44

but since He is doing such, He must be who He says He is. There is no either/or here. One does not accept Jesus' word simply on the basis of who He claims to be, even if these claims be true. Evidence is demanded. But historical evidence is never sufficient on its own merit, even when first hand, as the response to the raising of Lazarus and the ascribing of Jesus' exorcism of demons to Beelzebub clearly point out. Rather rational objective evidence is a prerequisite for belief, as John implies in providing a thesis for his Gospel (John 20:31). At the same time, John understands that factual evidence alone is insufficient when he writes that "even after Jesus had done all these miraculous signs in their presence, they still would not believe in him" (John 12:37). An existential appropriation of the facts is acquired only with the penetrating arrow of a God-wrought word that convicts of sin, righteousness and judgment in light of the finished work of Christ (John 16:7-11).

Peter follows in his Master's footsteps in maintaining the indispensable unity between the revelatory Christ-event and the written Word of Scripture. Peter begins inductively from "underneath," i.e. from common knowledge of the man, Jesus of Nazareth, to his conclusion that all Israel can be assured that "God had made this Jesus, whom you crucified, both Lord and Christ" (vs. 36). Peter thus begins from the perspective of epistemology where we all must begin as men—the encounter with Jesus the man. First-century men did not begin with Jesus' divinity, but his humanity as seen by the apostles themselves when in amazement they cry out "what kind of man is this? Even the winds and the waves obey him" (Matthew 8:27). Peter, after quoting Joel which provides the interpretative word for the unique phenomena, appeals immediately to the hard empirical data of miracles (*dunamis*), wonders (*teras*) and signs (*semeion*). Peter claims that these people were able to *know* that God worked these miracles through Jesus and thus He truly was who He claimed to be. The miraculous works of Jesus are not the only positive proof of the truth

45

of God's fulfillment of His messianic word-promises in the man Jesus of Nazareth. The climactic proof is the event that separates Jesus from all other religious teachers—"God has raised this Jesus to life, and we are all witnesses of the fact" (Acts 2:32). This is the beginning both of Christ's resurrection being the central truth of Christianity (cf. 1 Corinthians 15:3-4) and the appeal to historical facts to establish that truth.

This appeal to historical facts is never outside the confines of the written Scriptures to the early Christian apologists like Peter and Paul. They are fully aware that history is the working-out of God's purposes. Therefore Peter sees the death of Christ as no simple accident of history but rather as the foreknowledge and purpose of God (Acts 2:23). Similarly, Paul in First Corinthians recognized his death and resurrection as "according to the Scriptures" (15:4). The Christian gospel rooted in the historical resurrection does not break from the Old Testament but fulfills it. This is seen in Peter's sermon by reference to David's prediction of the Messiah's resurrection in Psalm 16:8-11 and the ascension in Psalm 110:1.

Peter argues then on both evidential *and presuppositional* grounds. The empirical facts in regard to Jesus which were widely known are appealed to as evidence of his actual identity. This is not done in a vacuum, however. Joel and the Psalms are the interpretative parameters. Thus while arguing his case on the basis of recent events in Jerusalem that were undeniable, Peter understands their meaning via the limiting framework of Scripture. Word and event are not separated. Like Jesus, the events substantiate the divine word—be it spoken or written. Special revelation, then, as Peter realized in practice if not in theory, demands *both* an *a priori* methodology as in presuppositionalism by which an absolute objective meaning is delineated by God *and* an *a posteriori* methodology of evidential historiography in which the truth is presented to man.

There is more evidence than historical, however, to indicate the truth of the claims of Christian apologists. There are the ontological realities of created nature outside of man plus our inherent God-consciousness built within us because we image God (cf. Romans 1:19-20; 2:15). Paul appeals to both dimensions in his address to the Athenian philosophers, who represent the two perennial worldviews of idealism and naturalism as Stoics and Epicureans respectively. These ontological realities provide a natural revelation of God that is inescapable both without and within man. While never referencing the Old Testament directly, Paul presents an Old Testament picture of God that is absolutely faithful to the divine word. He directly argues, however, on the platform of the functional created order (Acts 17:24-28a) and the similarity of children and parents pointing to the similarity of God and ourselves (17:28b-29).

There is room here only to glance at the latter argument. In quoting the poem by Aratus of Cilicia entitled *Natural Phenomena* Paul would have been immediately understood as a Stoic monist. He does not allow this interpretation, however. From the premise "we are [God's] offspring" (17:28b), and the hidden or unspoken premise that "men are personal creatures," Paul concluded that God *could not be an impersonal Being* confined to shapes of gold, silver, or stone. God is personal—not impersonal nature as the Stoics thought. We ourselves are the proof of God's personality. Since offspring "resemble" their parents and men are personal creatures, *God must be as equally personal as His offspring are*. Paul shows that we can legitimately argue from man to God on the basis of the ontological similarity between God and man resulting from man being created in God's image. If there is no univocal dimension ontologically between God and man, then Paul's argument at Athens is fallacious.

There are obvious differences between these two snapshots of the apologies of Peter and Paul. The difference lies in their audience. Peter, presenting claims that are historically undeniable to his Jewish audience, shows that these events are the fulfillment of divine word. Paul, arguing with those who are ignorant of divine word, argues from the ontological reality of creation. Men may explicitly deny this argument, but implicitly one is always cognizant of its claims due to being an imager of God. In both apologies, different as they are, both men are Both/And apologists. Peter connects the *a priori* word with an *a posteriori* argument that Jesus is truly the Messiah he claimed to be. Paul, arguing on his *a priori* realization of the truth of theistic creation, demonstrates this reality by presenting his case inductively on the basis of man's environment and personhood. Each recognizes that while *we* must begin "where we are," be it Jerusalem or Athens, God is historically disclosed in Jesus and is the one and only Source of the reality in which we live and the personal being that we have.

I conclude with a few final thoughts regarding the possibilities of epistemology. Certainly there is no pretense of solving the many problems related to our knowing processes. However, both natural and special revelation do recognize our knowledge capabilities or they themselves are not what God claims them to be. The age-old division of knowledge into paths of rationalism, empiricism and intuition are simply false paths when proclaimed as *solitary* avenues to knowledge. Nevertheless, the ontological nature of man made in God's image and living in God's universe necessitates a natural revelation outside of man by which the visible things point to the invisible God, but also a natural revelation within man through his intuitive God-consciousness. Man does have an intuitive knowledge of the reality of the Creator because of the manner in which He has created us. This is not only shown by the religiosity of the Athenians and their altar to an "unknown god," but also by the social anthropologists who have yet to uncover a people who have no religious or transcendental aspirations. Man is truly *Homo religiosus*.

Both natural and special revelation assume the feasibility of empiricism for purposes of religious epistemology. As

Paul writes, "God's invisible qualities—his eternal power and divine nature—have been clearly seen, being understood from what has been made, so that men are without excuse" (Romans 1:20). Similarly, be it the works to which Jesus points, or the miracles, wonders and signs of Peter's reference, the possibility of acquiring legitimate knowledge by empirical means is more than implied. Jesus directs John's disciples to His true identity by telling them to "go back and report to John what you hear and see" (Matthew 11:4). Nor does he deny Thomas the evidence he requires (John 20:27). Likewise, Peter guarantees his readers that they are not following myth in his claim to be one of the empirical "eyewitnesses of his majesty" who heard "this voice that came from heaven when we were with him on the sacred mountain" (2 Peter 1:16, 18). Peter's biblical record of such a unique revelatory experience, given to only three men and then offered by one of them to a subsequent generation as historical evidence to the reality and truthfulness of the Christian message, absolutely refutes those who deny either empirical knowability or any apologetic significance to traditional Christian evidences based on original empirical perception. True, there is no presentation of "how" this occurs. This is left for philosophers and others to explain. Nevertheless, the Bible presupposes that the acquisition of knowledge through sense experience is possible and significant. It is the Lord who has made both "ears that hear and eyes that see" (Proverbs 20:12). Thus John even refutes early Christological heresies by an appeal to the empirical when he writes: "That which was from the beginning, which we have heard, which we have seen with our eyes, which we have looked at and our hands have touched—this we proclaim concerning the Word of life" (1 John 1:1).

Lastly, the very possibility that special revelation is feasible is based on the assumption that man is capable, having been made in God's image, to receive and comprehend such. The declarative sentences of the Bible presume the rules of logic/language to convey cognitive propositional revelation as truth. This does not mean that logic is ultimate and something other than God is the final reference point. Rather "logic is God-thinking." It is rooted in God and is derivatively rooted in man by the act of the gracious Creator-God. Logical (rational) thinking is inherent to us as ontological reflections of God. Logic is thus the bridge for verbal communication not only between men, but between God and men. Logic, philosophically speaking, is the epistemological prerequisite for the very possibility of revelation and Scripture.

Thus to use logic in the apologetic enterprise is not to use mere "human" criteria to judge special revelation. Rather it is to apply God-given principles to the world as He created it. If it were not for logic, we could not differentiate between *this* and *that*, be we concerned with scientific nature or God's revelation. Even worse, we could not distinguish between the voice of God and the voice of Satan without logic. As Mark Hanna writes:

> Logicians recognize that if contradiction is allowed, any proposition can be inferred; the affirmation and denial of every proposition—even the principle of noncontradiction itself—becomes possible. Hence, no absurdity can be more fundamental than the denial of the principle of noncontradiction.[7]

There is yet one final problem. If all men are made in God's image, having the same necessary capacities for logic, why do not all men accept the truth that is available in both natural and special revelation? To claim, however, that all men have the same logic *does not mean that all men have the same reasoning process*. For instance, pragmatic naturalists interpret the same world as existentialists, but "oh, do they see it differently." Similarly, man *should* reason with God as his ultimate reference point, but beginning with Adam man makes himself the final and ultimate reference point and ends up at the extremes of pragmatic optimism or existential pessimism. Man's alienation and separation from God thus affects the reasoning process if not the very ability to reason. There is not a believing and unbelieving, pagan and Christian, logic. Fallen men are still men made in God's image with the gifts of rationality, language, creativity, personality and moral—albeit self-ish—inclinations. But because of the Fall, man will not use these abilities for the purposes of God's will and glory. He will not will God's will in the universe naturally. In a self-imposed alienation his will is innately "bent" away from God in autonomous self-will. Thus while logic per se may be identical between believer and unbeliever, pagan or Christian, the actual content of one's reasoning, beginning with man's will and orientation rather than God's will and Word, will be different indeed. Thus man in this abnormal state cannot interpret the world as a God-ordained and thus a God-interpreted world. Pragmatists and existentialists are both correct in their mutually exclusive optimism and pessimism. Man is a great and highly capable being made in God's image and thus there is reason for optimism. Being alienated and separated from God, however, pessimism about man's condition is more realistically objective. Instead of seeing the double-edged being of man and the provision for such by God in Christ, fallen and unbelieving man attempts to maintain his autonomy by interpreting himself and the surrounding universe in his own metaphysical framework, be it pragmatic or existential, idealistic or naturalistic.

Both/And, a biblical alternative to the presuppositional/evidential debate, realizes that the debate in theological dress is simply the perennial philosophic dispute between *a priori* and *a posteriori* epistemologies. We should have learned from Spinoza and Hume that mutually exclusive paths are deadends. Christian apologists have more than the philosophical catastrophes of monism and skepticism to alert them to the impossibility of methodological purism, however. The Christian doctrine of creation and its implications of two unequal, but nevertheless real, *realities* absolutely deny the monisms of idealism and naturalism. From an ontological perspective, the fact that there are two realities—the infinite, self-existing God and the finite, dependent creation, including man—means that both realities must determine our apologetic framework. Because the dependent creation is defined by God, nothing exists that is not related to and interpreted by God. Therefore the debate between evidentialists and presuppositionalists over self-interpreting facts or God-interpreted facts is artificial since both sides accept and believe that this is a God-created world with a God-sanctioned history. Presuppositionalists are correct as they begin *a priori* from the ontological perspective of creation by having everything ultimately related to and interpreted by God's will and Word. Evidentialists are equally correct as they begin in an *a posteriori* fashion with the actual created and revelatory facts and argue epistemologically that the facts rightly interpreted have only one possible meaning, and in that sense carry their meaning with them in a self-interpreting manner. Presuppostionalists want to begin with God, evidentialists with ourselves; the balanced apologist says start with *both* God *and* ourselves simultaneously since these *cannot be* broken *apart*. While this apologist is probably rejected by the other two orientations as holding a theoretically uncomfortable position, both presuppositionalists and evidentialists admit that without God there is no man, and given man, "we cannot clearly and properly know God unless the knowledge of ourselves be added."[8]

Endnotes

[1]John Calvin, *The Institutes of the Christian Religion*, J.T. McNeill, ed. (Philadelphia: Westminster Press, 1960), 1.1.1.
[2]Ibid.
[3]Ibid., 1.15.1.

[4]Cornelius VanTil, *Apologetics* (Philadelphia: Westminster Theological Seminary, 1971), 45.

[5]John Calvin, *Commentaries on the First Book of Moses, called Genesis* (Grand Rapids, MI: Eerdmans, reprint 1948), 1:93.

[6]C.F. Keil and F. Delitzsch, *Commentary on the Old Testament,* vol 1: The Pentateuch (Grand Rapids, MI: Eerdmans, reprint 1968), 63.

[7]Mark Hanna, *Crucial Questions in Apologetics* (Grand Rapids, MI: Baker, 1981), 48.

[8]*The Institutes*, 1.15.1.

Apologetics through the Language of Faith

Matthew A. Cook

*E*dgar won't convert to Christianity because he has seen too many people for whom Christianity made no difference. He says, "If I convert, everybody is going to know about it."

Scott sloughs off pleas to come to church and Christ because there are more important things to do. Christ and Christianity don't have any compelling force, any attraction for him.

Owen refuses to even talk about Christianity because he has seen too many hypocrites. The people who call themselves "Christian" are further from the ideal than he is himself.

Arguing philosophical theory doesn't matter for these people. Belief is not to be argued. "The belief as formulated on the evidence can only be the last result—in which a number of ways of thinking and acting crystallize and come together."[1] Apologetics is best done through this myriad of thoughts and acts combining to produce a reason to believe. Those thoughts and acts are accumulated over a period of time of interaction with flesh-and-blood Christians—talking with them, listening to them, watching them, criticizing them. When the language of faith starts to make sense and shows its fruit to an individual, he can convert. That is apologetics through the language of faith.

I am a theologian. I have studied the great and not-so-great proofs of the faith (for some of them, they are like "spoofs of the faith"). But I am also a pastor. I have visited non-Christians at the hospital, in their home and around their grandfather's deathbed. They don't care that their worldview is epistemically unsound nor that their life philosophy is self-refuting because of internal contradiction. They care that Christianity doesn't make sense, isn't effective in life change or does not solve their intellectual, epistemological or pragmatic questions. They think Christianity does not work.

Inside the church there are many saints who vehemently assert that living without Christ is the most meaningless existence possible. Christianity is the *only* thing that works.

These two views do not contradict one another even for the common man. The deconstruction of truth has reached rural America. The fact that Christianity "works for you, but not for me" is a universal cry that we are operating in two different arenas, we are speaking two different languages. These are not incommensurable languages, but different none the less.

Suppose someone is ill and he says: "This is a punishment," and I say: "If I'm ill, I don't think of punishment at all." If you say: "Do you believe the opposite?"—you can call it believing the opposite, but it is entirely different from what we would normally call believing the opposite.

I think differently, in a different way. I say different things to myself. I have different pictures.[2] Since postmodern man accepts no meta-narratives, there can be no arbitration between the languages, no argument for superiority.

Nevertheless, apologetics through the language of faith integrates individuals into the fabric of the community of faith and teaches them the language, provides an environment where the neophyte soaks in the pictures of the faith so that a great number of ways of thinking and acting eventually crystallize in a commitment to the claims of Christ.

It is this understanding of apologetics that I will try to explain and justify in this paper.

The Grammar of Grace

Conversion consists of two elements: Repentance of one's sins and acceptance of the benefits of Christ's work through faith. I would like to suggest that no one can repent or believe until he or she understands what it means to do such a thing. I agree with those who have advocated "you have to get people to understand they are lost before they can be saved." If these people are coming from outside the Christian worldview, they have a different picture of their eternal status. Possibly they don't have any picture of heaven or hell. They just do not think that way. They will rarely be convinced to think that way on the sidewalk. Rather, we ought to insert the activity of the community as one means for individuals to learn the language of faith. They don't need only to learn pictures of heaven and hell, but how to go about repenting—knowing what words, what emotions, what actions accompany such an activity.

The community aids individuals in conversion by teaching them how to convert. The community's intervention is not a necessary condition of conversion (and certainly not a sufficient condition), because people may be taught the language by other means. God could teach them (presumably Adam and Eve were language users). They could learn it solely through reading the Bible (that is *the source* for the community's language as well).

But it is easier to learn the language of faith the same way we learn other languages—from other language users. There are three stages to this instruction: First, the potential Christian must be included in the community of faith. Second, that person will learn the "language games" of faith from the community. Third, his or her conceptual framework will change because of that linguistic change. This activity of the community is the mediated work of

57

God toward the individual so that he or she is prepared for a wholehearted adherence to the conceptual, affective and active commitments of the faith of Christianity. The work of the community paves the way toward conversion. That is apologetics in this situation.

Both children and proselytes are taught to use Christian concepts by those who already share the words of faith. These "experts" may include pastors, teachers, priests, parents and others conversant within the community of faith. The concepts are learned within the community where they have instituted ruled use.[3] To say that the use of these concepts is governed by rules is to say that they are used publicly and in such a way that any of the participants can say the concept was used correctly or incorrectly.[4] In conservative Christian language use, one cannot correctly say that "everyone is a Christian," but one can correctly say that "God is everywhere." There are sources for some of these rules (Scripture is the primary source, but also creeds and the reigning community theology) in which the learner must be instructed: "The pupils are not merely brought thereby to speak as others around them speak who are believers; they are taught to use the concepts in ruled ways."[5] We are not talking about learning "speech tracks" so that people can say things correctly. We are concerned that they learn *how* to say things correctly and *what* it means to speak the language of faith correctly. This is the grammar of the faith which must be learned before the faith *even makes sense*, that is, before the sentences of the faith make conceptual or existential sense.[6] This shows why the community plays such an important role. Imagine an atheist trying to understand the confidence a Christian has in the future which he expresses by using a word like "providence." Similarly, First Corinthians 12:3 says, ". . . no one can say, 'Jesus is Lord' except by the Holy Spirit."

> I read: "No man can say that Jesus is the Lord, but by the Holy Ghost."—And it is true: I cannot call him

Lord; because that says nothing to me. I could call him "the paragon," "God" even—or rather, I can understand it when he is called thus; but I cannot utter the word "Lord" with meaning. *Because I do not believe* that he will come to judge me; because *that* says nothing to me. And it could say something to me, only if I lived *completely* differently.[7]

A nonbeliever can utter the surface grammar; he can make the sounds come from his mouth. But the depth grammar, the meaning of the sentence, is inaccessible to him without the ruled use of the terms provided by the community mediating the work of the Spirit and a personal commitment to the meaning of that sentence (to "Jesus *as* Lord").

Learning the Language

The community teaches the faith through formal and informal means. The informal means are comprised of daily living and interacting with the potential Christian over a period of time so that she can learn how "God," "sin" and "salvation" are used in the grammar. This can happen with the child in a Christian home or the adult in the Christian community, particularly in a small group as its surrogate family—a place to learn a language—where the faith and its implications are being discussed. The grammar of faith is used throughout and informs the aspirant of appropriate uses and inappropriate uses. Other informal situations are in the church service through the singing of hymns, prayers of praise and penitence, creedal affirmations of faith, sermonic reflection and biblical readings.[8] Narrative sermons are particularly useful in this context. A whole sermon focused on painting a real-life story of someone learning the gospel and responding to it is linguistically very instructive for obeying that gospel oneself. The aspirant learns the grammar through these informal means.

Learning also occurs through formal means:

> Thus, the young students are directed to biblical stories, the words and deeds of Jesus, commands and beliefs, parables and allegories, proverbs and psalms. In addition, they are asked to memorize Scripture verses, repeat the creeds, sing songs and say prayers. Then, too, there are . . . pictures, illustrations (real or imagined), probing questions, lively anecdotes, serious admonitions, etc.[9]

Through these means the aspirant learns more than rules. She learns to speak the faith meaningfully.[10] The community has provided a language through which she can speak about God, sin and salvation. Through this language she can speak about her past and present life as well as the meaning of life with Christ. Through this repeated instruction, both formal and informal, the language of faith takes on life and meaning.

Living Linguistically

Language is connected with life. Anyone learning the language of faith would soon see hypocrisy if the words were left hanging in the air without the associated actions (2 Corinthians 13:5). The words of faith are necessarily associated with actions. That is part of their grammar. Seeing these actions and reactions of believers is one way that learners gain competence in the language of faith. They see that faith aligns the very flow of life; that is part of its grammar.

The language we use influences the concepts we understand. Concepts are linguistic. Brown is right to say that "concepts are constituted by clusters of criteria and paradigm cases."[11] People do not normally learn criteria or paradigm cases except through interaction with other language speakers. One ought to step back further and admit that there is no immediate nor intuitive grasp of a language. The young child learns to say "Daddy" when any male is around. That seems to be the first rule for applying the concept mastered by the child. Then he or she learns another rule: "Daddy is the male who lives with Mommy" or "Daddy is the one who was genetically involved in conceiving the child." Once the language is understood, concepts develop through the linguistic correction of other people. An older child, pointing to a maple tree, does not say "that is not a tree, it is a light post," because he or she has learned some of the rules for applying the concept "tree." We learn the language of our surroundings with the associated concepts.[12] This means that concepts are not inherent. Our minds are more than *tabula rasa*, because we have the ability to learn a language. I interpret Wittgenstein to say the same thing through his illustration of the shopkeeper and the five red apples.[13] It is this ability of linguistic acquisition that distinguishes those species that merely respond to a sensory flood from those that epistemically perceive and can cognitively manipulate those beliefs.[14] Understanding the concepts of religion is quite the same.

Understanding requires instruction. This teaching usually occurs over an extended period of time, but it need not be extended. The path to conversion can be quite fast, if the aspirant already understands sin, the Trinity and the nature of Christ.[15] If he or she already understands these things it is because of earlier training and experiences. Regardless of whether the process is fast or slow, individuals usually gain the concepts through language. These individuals hear others speaking and praying and worshipping according to the regulative grammar of the faith and soon learn how to do so themselves. They gain the pictures that enable them to understand the Christian world. As they begin to answer questions appropriately, participate in spiritual conversations using correct form, pray at the appropriate times and use the appropriate phrases, then it can be said that they possesses the concepts of faith.[16] One cannot merely pray once and have gotten the idea that God hears and answers. One must regularly act according to the regulative teaching one has received. Then one can say one possesses the concepts because one has demonstrated the particular capacities or skills. "Concepts *are* capacities belonging first to others and, with training, to the prospective candidate."[17] Concepts are not displayed by thinking of the content or the meaning. They are displayed through actions. Wittgenstein's argument for the use theory of meaning points to the idea that concepts are displayed through using them and acting on them according to the regulative language that gave rise to them. Indeed, the concepts, when fully inculcated, involve even reordering and redirecting one's affections. That is where the actions originate. Words, especially words of faith, have associated actions. Wittgenstein says: "How words are understood is not told by words alone," Then, in parenthesis, he adds the word "theology."[18] Wittgenstein saw that words, particularly religious words, have nonlinguistic consequences. The concepts will enable the believer to speak as well as to feel, act and respond. Possession of the concepts of the faith enables someone to convert.

The ABCs of Apologetics

Since apologetics strives to pave the way toward conversion, this approach provides an appropriate apologetic. It means inviting those hostile to the gospel into Bible studies, ladies' teas and Christian camping; it means low or *no* pressure evangelism because there is no confrontation; it means making Christian gatherings as accessible as possible to non-Christians.

The conversion that follows this type of preparation involves "a change in the way a person thinks and feels about his or her self."[19] This transformation is a qualitatively greater transformation of one's self-concept than is experienced in the mere progression of life stages (becoming an "empty nester") or circumstances (changing jobs). All these transformations result in "the creation of a new vision of who we *really* believe we are when all our social roles and self-presentations are stripped away."[20] When the person *accepts* the rules of speech and action from the community of faith, then he has changed the source of those rules from the grammatical third or second person to the first person. He is not merely following the rules and concepts, but applies them as correct. When a commitment is made, the rules no longer make him conform out of social constraint, but provide the means for transformation of the self toward the desired form of life. The personal appropriation of the language plays a transformative role. How or why one appropriates this language or, for that matter, why one converts is not humanly explicable, except to say that:

> It strikes me that a religious belief could only be something like a passionate commitment to a system of reference. Hence, although it's *belief*, it's really a way of living, or a way of assessing life. It's passionately seizing hold of *this* interpretation. Instruction in a religious faith, therefore, would have to take the form of a portrayal, a description, of that system of reference, while at the same time being an appeal to conscience. And this combination would have to result in the pupil himself, of his own accord, passionately taking hold of the system of reference. It would be as though someone were first to let me see the hopelessness of my situation and then show me the means of rescue until, of my own accord, or not at any rate led to it by my *instructor*, I ran to it and grasped it.[21]

The first-person passionate commitment to the system of reference is the key. But note that even Wittgenstein includes an idea of repentance. David Wells says, "[R]epentance and belief go hand in hand—we cannot believe without repenting, and we repent in order to believe."[22] How can the aspirant repent before he or she understands the concept of sin and the appropriate responses? How can the person repent before he or she has grasped that God is just and demands that retribution be exacted upon the guilty? Without having made those connections, there is no call for repentance, there is no reason for conversion. But once the language is in place, then the concepts and the motivation for repentance are available. One need not merely learn theology, but *how* to repent. One is not repenting only of past sins, but also of one's past system of reference. With this commitment comes a repudiation of the old pictures, the old understandings, the old system. True conversion is far more than "fire insurance."

Conclusion

I have not tried to replace orthodox talk for the work of God in conversion. Rather, I have tried to fill out the community's mediation of that work. The uniqueness of divine awareness can be discerned within the dynamics of the social interaction process.

> A mediated reality is neither separable nor reducible to those dimensions or factors through which it is mediated, any more than the tension or harmony in a work of art is insoluble from nor reducible to those particulars through which it is mediated.[23]

Conversion demands a transformation of the worldview.[24] This transformation can be mediated through interaction in the community. The final act of adopting the ruled use of language into the first person is still an act of the will which is enabled through the grace of God. It occurs along with repentance and acceptance through faith. This model does not eliminate the necessity of God's grace

(Ephesians 2:8-9) nor the responsibility of the individual to repent and believe (Mark 1:15; Acts 26:20). This model only defines more specifically the preparatory work the community and its language can perform. Repentance means that one uses the regulative concepts of the community of faith to engage in biographical reconstruction so that one sees one's past life as offensive to God. One must then turn from it. Belief is the first-person appropriation of the finished work of Christ for the individual's salvation. Relatedly, the concepts and language of the community of faith are appropriated through a passionate commitment to a new system of reference. One appropriate apologetic is through the language of faith.

Endnotes

[1] Ludwig Wittgenstein, *Lectures and Conversations on Aesthetics, Psychology and Religious Belief,* ed. Cyril Barrett (Oxford: Basil Blackwell, 1966), 56.

[2] Wittgenstein, *Lectures and Conversations,* 55.

[3] Dean M. Martin, "Learning to Become a Christian," *Religious Education* 82 (Winter 1987): 97.

[4] Cf. the account of informal controls that Middle Eastern communities exert on recounting stories in Kenneth E. Bailey, "Informal controlled oral tradition and the Synoptic Gospels," *Themelios* 20.2 (January 1995): 4-11.

[5] Dean M. Martin, "Learning to Become a Christian," 97.

[6] Wittgenstein refers to rules, grammar and other related topics in many places. For example, cf. Ludwig Wittgenstein, *Philosophical Investigations,* trans. by G.E.M. Anscombe (New York: Macmillan, 1953) Sections 31, 54, 198, 202, 206, 224-225, 371, 373 ("Theology as grammar"), 496-497; Also Ludwig Wittgenstein, *Zettel,* ed. G.E.M. Anscombe and G.H. von Wright and trans. by G.E.M. Anscombe (Berkeley and Los Angeles: University of California Press, 1967), 55, 318, 320.

[7] Ludwig Wittgenstein, *Culture and Value,* ed. G.H. von Wright in collaboration with Heikki Nyman and trans. by

Peter Winch (Oxford: Basil Blackwell, 1980), 33 (emphasis his).

[8]Martin, "Learning to Become a Christian," 98. These are the kind of things Martin says that Wittgenstein would call language games. Wittgenstein did call telling jokes, giving orders and obeying them, reporting an event, forming and testing a hypothesis, cursing, greeting, etc. language games. The term "language game" is designed to bring into prominence the fact that speaking is interwoven into the activities of life. cf. *Philosophical Investigations,* sections 7, 23, 31, 116, 563-564; 200.

[9]Martin, "Learning to Become a Christian," 97f.

[10]The later Wittgenstein is particularly known for his "use theory of meaning." That does apply here. Some passages connecting use and meaning are, *Philosophical Investigations* 43, 116, 340, 432, p. 212, 220.

[11]Harold I. Brown, *Observation and Objectivity* (Oxford: Oxford University Press, 1987), 220.

[12]Grant Gillett, "Learning to Perceive," *Philosophy and Phenomenological Research* 48 (June 1988): 608.

[13]Ludwig Wittgenstein, *Philosophical Investigations,* 3d ed., trans. G.E.M. Anscombe (New York: Basil Blackwell, 1958), sec. 1. This is one of his points anyway.

[14]For more discussion on the linguistic nature of concepts and their relationship to perception, particularly, cf. Matthew A. Cook, "A Contemporary Epistemology for Theological Prolegomena" (Ph.D. diss., Trinity Evangelical Divinity School, 1995), 96.

[15]David Wells, *Turning to God: Biblical Conversion in the Modern World* (Grand Rapids, MI: Baker, 1989), 30.

[16]"To possess the concepts of faith" is not the same as making a commitment in faith. The former paves the way for the latter.

[17]Martin, "Learning to Become a Christian," 100. cf. Paul Holmer, "Religion From an Existential Standpoint," in *Religion in Philosophical and Cultural Perspective,* ed. J. Clayton Feaver and William Horosz (Princeton, NJ: D.

Van Nostrand Co., 1967), 149-150, 168-169.

Wittgenstein, *Zettel*, 144.

Clifford L. Staples and Armand L. Mauss, "Conversion or Commitment? A Reassessment of the Snow and Machalek Approach to the Study of Conversion," *Journal for the Scientific Study of Religion* 26 (1987): 137.

Ibid.

Wittgenstein, *Culture and Value*, 64. cf. Dean M. Martin, "On Certainty and Religious Belief," *Religious Studies* 20 (1984): 609f.

Wells, *Turning to God*, 33.

Jerry Gill, "Religious Experience as Mediated," *Christian Scholar's Review* 13 (1984): 357.

Cf. John A. Gration, "Conversion in Cultural Context," *International Bulletin of Missionary Research* 7 (1983): 157-158, 160-162.

An Integrative Method of Justifying Religious Assertions

Gordon Lewis

*I*t is difficult to ignore the countless variables in different cultural contexts around the world. Human knowing is affected by a myriad of specific factors, a variety of belief systems and assorted worldviews. In spite of these kaleidoscopic influences, an analysis of meaningful human life discloses some common, non-negotiable principles.

This essay seeks *first* to discover some commonalities shared by Christian and non-Christian knowers in any global context or community. *Second*, from these points of contact, it formulates an integrative criterion of truth. *Third*, an abductive method is proposed for defense of the faith in contrast to inductive and deductive methods of reasoning.

Commonalities in Any Context

As Tom Strini said, "Bad multiculturalism promotes tribalism, the root of much of the world's meanness. Good multiculturalism underscores commonality, the footing for respect and understanding."[1]

Postmodern philosophical analysts tend to magnify the differences of social, political, sexual or religious contexts. The specific data of grammatical, historical and cultural contexts are indispensable to obtaining a writer's meaning, but an author's meaning may not necessarily be reducible to nothing but select ideas distinctive of his or her cultural context. Responsible scholarship requires that we look not only for differences in cultures, but also for similarities.

Cognitive assertions may be context-related without being context-determined. Can we not react against our situations? Do not creative people come up with ideas ahead of their times? Reducing an author's meaning to *nothing but* a limited context commits the genetic fallacy by assuming that the validity of the content of an idea is determined by the situation of its origin.

Philip D. Kenneson, in an essay titled "There's No Such Thing as Objective Truth and It's a Good Thing," emphasizes the need for authenticity in our lives and communities to give substance to Christ's Lordship. Surely existential authenticity is indispensable to witnesses for Christ, but is that enough by itself? Communicators need *logos* as well as *ethos* and *pathos*. The message conveyed by pictures without 1,000 words is often very vague. Since no community can perfectly reflect the meaning of Christ's lordship, to which religious community shall we go? Mormons and Jehovah's Witnesses seem to reflect Christ's lordship and they quote "trusted witnesses" who ought *not* therefore to be "authorized."[2]

Kenneson's communal relativism is reminiscent of the anti-enlightenment confessionalism of H. Richard Niebuhr (1894-1962). We can listen with profit to the warnings of both to avoid the dangers of absolutizing relative notions or institutions. But we cannot agree that the Bible's teaching is infinitely malleable. Niebuhr claimed, "The Bible can be read in many different contexts and will mean different things accordingly."[3] The specific *applications* of a passage may be multitudinous, but an author's intended *meaning*, if he or she did not make a mistake, is directed toward a primary objective (except in a double-entendre!). Is it not the reader's task to discover what the author expressed either in agreement with or in objection to his context?

If our basic categories are socially determined, how could one ever change religions or philosophies? And to what does a participator appeal to change a community for the better?[4] An undefined pragmatism is unsatisfactory. It is hard to know what is meant by "works" when we are asked to choose what works. And pragmatists may envision only the short run rather than the long run in time and eternity.

Do both modern and postmodern relativists overlook the soul's capacity for self-transcendence and so context-transcendence? Can we not assert things about the past, the future and some distant location in the present? Postmodernists appear to be considering their own statements to transcend their cultural contexts. But on their own showing, they cannot be regarded as meaningful for people in other than their own communities (wherever the borders may be drawn).

Consider what is essential to meaningful human life.[5] As we take a walk we may appreciate trees, birds and squirrels, but when we meet other people, what is necessary for both of us to have a meaningful life? An analysis of essentials for significantly human life indicates five commonalities in any context.

1. All everywhere ought to value each others' *inalienable rights.*[6] However different others may appear, we ought to respect their equal rights to life. Otherwise, we will not exist, let alone live meaningfully. We must also respect each other's right to liberty and equal opportunities in the pursuit of happiness. Human rights are not simply the product of legislation or social custom; they are independent grounds for judging legislation and custom. Inherent rights are the foundation, not the consequence, of freedom.[7]

Some rights are defended negatively in the Ten Commandments. Because God's image bearers have a right to life, you shall not murder. The requirements of morality, inscribed by God upon the hearts of all His image-bearers

(Romans 2:14-15), are among the nonnegotiables in any culture. One may choose freely to give up one's own rights for the kingdom of God, but no one ought to take basic human rights away from others.

2. Every person ought to relate to others with *justice*. If human relationships are to be civilized, we must necessarily relate to one another fairly. Justice is a two-edged sword requiring reciprocal fairness. We should treat others as we would be treated. "A defense of justice edifies the soul, while a defense of peevishness deteriorates it."[8] An advantage of belief in a transcendent Administrator of justice prevents the embracing of any finite system or person as absolute. And that belief does not come from "nowhere"; it comes from our Creator who is faithful and just.

Justice in academia (and elsewhere) requires allegiance to the virtue of *intellectual honesty*. Intellectual honesty is universally obligatory because it is indispensable to the mutual trust that holds schools, marriages, churches and neighborhoods together. When honesty is compromised research cannot be trusted, not even research on the injustice of oppressors.

Although appeals to the principle of justice can be misused (in taking vengeance on others), we should not do away with them in principle. If justice is the will of the stronger there is no justice. Might does not make right. Justice in law enforcement, for example, requires that suspects be handled fairly and the penalty calibrated to the heinousness of the crime.

The concept of justice may be differently applied in different cultures and be difficult to define. But when treated unjustly everyone knows what justice is. As a pragmatist, Marx edited out of all communist manuscripts he could any references to eternal justice, human equality, the rights of individuals, liberty of conscience and the fight for civilization.[9] If justice is not a transcendent principle, then relativistic tyrants can arbitrarily set their own standards of uprightness.

3. Respect for the value of persons should also yield the fruits of consideration and *love*. A customer complained to the photographer, "This picture does not do me justice." The photographer replied, "My friend, what you need is not justice, but mercy." We all do. Justice gives what is deserved. Mercy withholds deserved punishment, love bestows undeserved blessings. "Since we look for others to love us, we already know what love is; and, knowing it, we should acknowledge it."[10] An advocate of an earlier form of situational ethics, Joseph Fletcher, could not escape one universal value—the virtue of self-giving love.[11] But love ought not be isolated from other virtues such as justice. "The loving thing to do may well be more than the determination of the right thing to do; it will never be less. Love's concerns are not attained apart from the concerns of justice."[12] It is not enough to avoid hurting others. We ought to seek their well-being. We are obliged to love others as we want to be loved. What the world needs now is faithful love. It does not need a postmodern "hermeneutic of suspicion" that attempts to judge people's motives.[13] Conspiracy theories against just and loving people are difficult to put to rest. If humans on planet earth are to have meaningful life and peace, people from different religious and philosophical worldviews must be mutually accountable for respect, justice and love.

4. Whatever our label in any culture, we cannot forever refuse to face the *data* of our external and internal experience. The givens in human experience are not infinitely malleable. Is it wise to try to live in a dream castle, ignoring the realities of such diseases as cancer and AIDS?

Many maintain that we cannot refer to objective data because we always look at them from our own vantage points. But because observers report an accident differently, it does not follow that no accident occurred. There is Scripture twisting,[14] but it does not follow that there is no Scripture to twist. We call for conformity, not to first impressions as in naive realism, but to tested, relevant data, as in critical realism. Some portrayals are better informed by converging lines of data than others. Some reports of accidents are more reliable than others.

People, whether in the East or the West, ought to call contagious diseases what they are. We must rise above ethnic, state and national contexts to face the universality of data about AIDS and cancer. What diseases can do to people they do without respect of context. No amount of contextualization or relativism can delete the moral and factual givens for health.

5. Meaningful human life, furthermore, involves consistency in thought and its communication. But that is impossible if as postmoderns we give up the universal and obligatory law of noncontradiction. It is not an arbitrary Western invention. The law of noncontradiction comes from the *logos* of God whose "yes" means yes and whose "no" means no (Numbers 23:19; 1 Samuel 15:29; Matthew 5:37). If God's image bearers seek to understand each other, they cannot affirm and deny the same thing at the same time in the same respect. The principle of noncontradiction formulated by Aristotle is assumed by the prophets and presupposed in the arguments of Jesus and His apostles. It remains indispensable to any who speak or write meaningfully. If postmodern promises can mean their contradictories, trusting relationships become impossible.

Were we to delete these five values—human rights, justice, love, empirical data and logical noncontradiction—we would return to barbarism. They empower those with deep differences to think, live and debate as civilized people. They are supported to this point not by induction, deduction or abduction, but an existential analysis of what is essential for distinctively human life.

These five commonalities are givens that need to be accounted for on anyone's philosophy or theology. The third section of the paper will argue that they are most coherently accounted for, not by naturalistic or pantheistic ontologies, but by a Christian theistic worldview. If such requirements are inscribed indelibly by the Creator on the human spirit (Romans 2:14-15), we can explain their universality and necessity.

In unbelievers the ontological image of God is damaged in the Fall, but not destroyed. Unregenerate (and regenerate) people may be committed to radically antagonistic philosophies and theologies but need not fight like beasts. With this common ground members of pluralistic societies need not bomb each other's libraries. Rather, they can profitably debate their deepest presuppositional and confessional differences by appealing to logic, facts and values.

To be tolerant of the differences among us we do not need to throw over the universal values of justice, love, logic or fact. These transcendent absolutes protect us from the intolerance of temporal oppressors. All globally proposed religious, political and philosophical opinions are not morally or epistemologically equivalent. From relative perspectives on a given thing, it does not follow that we know perspectives only. The better informed are more coherent, more just and more considerate than others.

The values of common grace for every one of life's contexts need to be featured in a pluralistic world if sinners are to remain alive long enough to hear the good news of God's redemptive grace! If logic has been used to oppress, do not throw out logic; summon the oppressor to repent. If scientists have been arrogant, challenge their arrogance. Do not blame the scientific method which can be used for good as well as evil. If ethicists have failed to display justice and love, challenge them, but do not give up the normative ideals.

However much sinners suppress these ethical absolutes, we know that it is morally wrong to abuse another's human rights, flout justice, live dishonestly, be selfishly uncaring, distort facts and contradict our own word. These objective principles are not rooted in the Enlightenment, but our divine likeness to the Creator. We may learn of them from general revelation and from common grace administered in God's universal providence. They are not the production of Western oppressors or Eastern gurus. They stand in judgment upon all individuals, communities and cultures, however weak or powerful.

If we deny the universality and necessity of these foundational principles (logically, factually and axiologically) in favor of a particular confessionalism, we lose points of contact with the world. Clyde Holbrook, writing on H. Richard Niebuhr's confessionalism, asked, "What possible grounds remain for intelligible discourse between Niebuhr and his critics?"[15]

Criteria for Any Context

Even the most passionate religious language involves some cognitive assumptions that are either true to reality or not. It is either true or false that God is personal and distinct from the world but active in it. It is either true or false that Jesus is the eternal Word who became flesh. It is either true or false that we can bypass the cross and become one with God in immediate mystical experience. It is either true or false that the Bible is God's witness against us (Deuteronomy 31:19, 26) rather than merely a human witness to God. If the God of Jesus Christ and the Bible exists for one person, God exists for all persons in every context.

The crucial issue is not how people can get to God. All in every religion and philosophy will get to God—as their Judge! The issue is, how can we who are disrespectful of others, unjust and unloving, find acceptance in the immediate presence of the Holy One? How can God remain just and justify the ungodly?

To test the truth of ways to become acceptable to God (including claims to special revelation), we develop criteria from the nonnegotiable commonalities considered above. Working from the end of the previous list to its beginning, true assertions are those noncontradictory (#5) hypotheses with both empirical fit (#4) and existential authenticity (#1-3).

The post-critical epistemology of Jerry H. Gill in *On Knowing God* seeks to transcend the modern bifurcation of fact and value by stressing noncognitive, merely functional uses of language in a community. But in a later section titled "Proof and Justification," he returns to more universal guidelines for justifying religious beliefs. He writes, "A helpful way of developing the idea of the justification of religious belief is along the lines of what might be termed *experiential "adequacy" or "fit."* In that he includes: (1) comprehensive coherence, (2) internal consistency and (3) ethical fruitfulness.[16] They constitute "an integrative act." Gill explains that integrative act is "a participatory dynamic interrelationship" which not only "seeks" but also "intends meaning."

One can appreciate Gill's goal of integrating the three criteria and his use of a method of justifying religious belief that is neither inductive nor deductive. He recognizes that evidence may serve as a catalyst or juncture point for the act of integrating a whole host particulars. But I question an integrative act that allows one to read one's own agenda into another's writings. Would post-critical thinkers like conservative evangelicals to interpret their books in accord with a contradictory intention?

We do not create our own realities; we receive data from reality. One New Ager said on a talk show that in his reality there was no evil, no devil and no hell. He repeated, "That's not part of my reality." Another panelist commented, "If Jeff Dahmer came to your door, evil would enter your reality!"

Integrating three similar criteria of truth in religion and other fields, Edward John Carnell spoke of them as systematic consistency. By that he meant a logically noncontradictory account of the relevant lines of external (sensory) and internal (ethical, axiological and psychological) data. Francis Schaeffer listed them as three tests of truth: logical noncontradiction, factual adequacy and existential viability.[17] I often refer to them as "coherence" or coherence and authenticity (in contrast to hypocrisy).

The three criteria are distinguishable but interrelated. Logic continues to help clarify our views of matters of fact and value. Understanding of empirical experience needs the direction of logical and ethical principles. Ethical values ought to govern uses of logic also. Edward John Carnell's integration of logic, fact and value did not blur the distinctions between them.[18] As I have supported elsewhere, Carnell's "method of justifying beliefs integrates the emphases of Clark on logic, Van Til on the content of presuppositions, Machen on historical facts, Brightman on empirical givens, and existentialists like Niebuhr and Kierkegaard on internal data."[19]

Norman Geisler's term for Carnell's threefold criterion, "combinationalism" does not sufficiently reflect the integration of logic, fact and value required to achieve systematic consistency. Each element is adequate for the interrelated aspect of reality it is used to test. And Geisler's claim that conflicts may remain between them may reflect a lack of success in fulfilling the demands of the threefold criterion. So long as conflict remains one has not achieved systematic consistency.

Geisler even alleges that non-Christian worldviews can be as free from contradictions, discrepancies with data and hypocrisy. That is like saying that all the suspects in a murder can fit equally well all the many converging lines of evidence, motive, location, weapon, etc. Or it is like saying that the Pharisees' case as compared with that of Jesus or Paul is equally free from contradiction, equally adequate in its accounts of Jesus' life, words and miracles and equally unhypocritical in religious devotion and ethical practice.

Although Geisler does not find this threefold criterion useful *among* worldviews, he admits that it is useful for testing truth claims *within* a worldview. Why do the previous objections not apply within a philosophy? One wonders why he could use systematic consistency at all if his "leaky bucket" analogy had any relevance. Of course, analogies prove nothing; they only illustrate. And his analogy does not seem to bother him when he approves the same three-fold criterion for use *within* his worldview.

Because the criterion is drawn from the five foundational principles of general revelation (not special revelation alone) I find them of value for all human beings, outsiders as well as insiders. The argument for the five absolutes in section one of this paper did not depend on a Christian worldview. However much sinners may suppress them, they are inexcusable for breaking them. And Geisler's suggested alternative criteria for people with alternative worldviews, unaffirmability and undeniability, depend upon the validity of the logical and factual aspects of the criterion. As applications of them, they are useful.[20]

Geisler and I agree that continued freedom of religion and philosophy in pluralistic societies like that in America rests upon the foundation of common ground among all persons. Some who deny any common grace may wish to reinstate all Old Testament laws and penalties in America today. Instead, believing in common grace, Christians should be working in pluralistic societies for the consistent and factual implementation of human rights with justice and love. Intellectual freedom in public schools of pluralistic cultures calls for the presentation of a theistic *Weltanschauung* as fully as worldviews that are naturalistic and pantheistic.

A Method for Any Context

Utilizing this three-in-one criterion then, we may test any worldview or any theological, historical or scientific tenet within a worldview. But how shall we go about it? What method of research and reasoning shall we use in the twenty-first century? Although many think there are only two ways of reasoning in defense of their faith, inductive and deductive, Pascal,[21] Elton Trueblood,[22] Francis

Schaeffer[23] and Edward John Carnell proposed a third, verificational form of reasoning. In discussing these three methods of research and reasoning in this short chapter I do not imply that there are no others. In *Testing Christianity's Truth Claims* I compared six methods of reasoning and that is not exhaustive.

Although Carnell's synoptic starting point integrated the above criteria, his logical starting point began not with objective evidence or with presuppositions but with hypotheses. Carnell's "if . . . then" verificational approach acknowledges that there is subjectivity in every decision about the ultimately real and good. But it also finds that some convictions are better informed than others. The more coherent and viable proposals have greater probability than do the others."[24]

Consider how a verificational method compares and contrasts with other methods of reasoning in defense of the religious assertions at the root of all religions.

A. Inductive Evidence Insufficient

Verificational and empirical methods of reasoning concur in holding to a critical realism. There are data or givens; our experience is not wholly manufactured by ourselves or our communities. Hence for both, sensory data are important in determining truth about the physical world. We are furthermore agreed that some interpretations provide a better fit in relation to the data than others.

Differences arise, however, in regard to the starting point. Inductive reasoning, as John Locke held, begins with *tabula rasa* minds. Abductive or verificational reasoning considers that unrealistic. None of us is completely objective. Whether we come to the data of nature or Scripture we bring with us certain pre-understandings. Rather than claiming to be more objective than others, all sides should acknowledge their prescriptions for the human predicament as hypotheses to be tested.

Inductive reasoning from premises of our limited observations of some power cannot draw a valid conclusion about omnipotence. From evidence of some planning we cannot validly arrive at a conclusion about omniscience. So if there is an omnipotent, omniscient and omnipresent Lord of the universe, we finite observers could never gather sufficient evidence to establish that by inductive reasoning. And if the Bible is inerrant in all that it teaches, finite researchers could never establish that from limited evidence concerning some biblical statements. Archaeologists have confirmed many details of the biblical record but not all. Unless we start with the hypothesis that the Bible is God's witness against us (Deuteronomy 31:19, 26), life is too short to complete inductive examinations of every passage and it will always remain, in part at least, merely a fallible human witness to God.

B. Deductive Reasoning

Shall we then start with the presupposition or axiom that the God of the Bible exists independent of evidence? Is it wiser to justify our faith simply by stating unchallengeable presuppositions? Such reasoning assumes the very point to be established. However wide the circle of circular reasoning, it needs to be justified as over against alternative circles. In the philosophical arena no presuppositions are self-attesting. Our presuppositions may seem unchallengeable to us at the time, but people do change naturalistic, pantheistic and theistic axioms. The objective truth of the hypothesis is not self-authenticating for others, even though subjectively believers may be assured of its truth by the witness of the Spirit. If presuppositions are too ultimate to be supported by any data or argument, they may not tell us anything about the real world.

If an idea cannot be falsified, can it be regarded true? Presuppositions have often been confused with hypotheses, but the one is beyond confirmation or disproof, the other is subject to either confirmation or disproof. From an outreach standpoint, to ask people to be open-minded enough

81

to consider a theistic hypothesis seems more conducive to dialogue than to allege that everything is "chaos and old night" until they assume my presupposition of the God of the Bible.

In the metaphysical order, Van Til wisely emphasizes the priority of God for anything to exist. But in the order of knowing and dialogue, does it follow that an image-bearer has to acknowledge trinitarianism before math or chemistry makes sense? Rather than starting with presup-positions, people on all sides need to start with hypotheses to be tested by the integrative criteria. If true, their view will be confirmed; if false, who would want to continue as-serting them?

C. Abductive Reasoning

An abductive (critical, scientific or verificational) ap-proach starts the process of justifying religious assertions by regarding our "pre-understandings" from any philoso-phy, theology, religion or cult as hypotheses to be tested. What is the Christian hypothesis? The content is much the same as for presuppositionalists, the existence of the God disclosed in creation, in the Jesus of history and in the teaching of Scripture. *If* the Logos of the Creator of the cosmos disclosed in the Messiah and the Bible exists, *then* one should be able to account for the givens of creation such as its order and magnificence, persons and the values inscribed innately on the human heart. Second, with this hypothesis we can account for the data of first-century his-tory and any hard data from the sciences. Third, with this hypothesis we can coherently account for the phenomena related to the amazing unity and power of the Bible.

There is risk involved in an abductive approach, for any hypothesis can be disproved as well as confirmed by over-whelming evidence. At an Evangelical Theological Society meeting a number of years ago a panel on apologetic method was moderated by Carl Henry. One of the panel-ists, Gordon Clark, could not attend, and Dr. Henry asked me to take his place. I agreed to if I could represent my own perspective rather than Clark's deductive reasoning from axioms. When I mentioned the risk involved in accepting a method that involved falsifiability as a possibility, Carl Henry, the renowned first editor of *Christianity Today*, turned to me and said something like, "Gordon, do you mean that a future discovery could make you abandon your faith?" I do not recall my fumbling reply at the moment, but I wish as a young pinch-hitter I had said, "Carl, do you mean that if it were substantiated that Jesus did not rise from the dead, you would go on preaching that He did?" I do not live in fear of that. My faith in Christ, unlike the mythological Hindu and Greek gods and goddesses, is based on historical facts confirmed by many converging lines of evidence beyond reasonable doubt.

Christians do not find convincing the Latter-day Saints testimony to the self-authentication of *The Book of Mormon* by "a burning in the bosom." The witness of the Holy Spirit is not a substitute for evidence, but overcomes antagonism to the case for the gospel's truth, illumines its objective validity and persuasively assures believers of its subjective appropriation. The witness of the Spirit attests the gospel's assertions of fact (Christ died) and meaning (for our sins). And by those observed facts and revealed meanings we test the spirits (1 John 4:1-3).

Conclusions

First, postmodern thinkers cannot on Monday destroy belief in the universality and necessity of the laws of logic and morality and expect us to protect their human rights on Tuesday. Any who decry violations of human rights in another community exhibit belief in their transcultural validity. Concern for the victims of injustice also reflects the transcultural virtue of love. Furthermore, injustices must be confirmed by adequate evidence; references to them, to make sense, must be stated without contradiction. Thus the five absolutes hold like huge anchors in the sea of relativism.

2. In a world of endless, instantaneous truth claims on radio and television, we still need the critical discernment provided by the threefold criterion of truth. The coherence of logic, fact and value provides the many checks and balances needed as we hear of multiplying religious proposals. We best overcome the dualism between fact and value not by losing both in an attempt to deconstruct this world and construct another, but by integrating both fact and value with logic.

3. Although the verificationalism of positivists is passé, as Jerry Gill observes, "the spirit of the criterion continues to dominate contemporary philosophical activity."[25] Confessionalists sooner or later ask questions about the beliefs in which they were brought up. Then they need a method by which to evaluate them. Mature people in a world of many conflicting communities must determine which confession to follow. Even after choosing a Christian community one encounters conflicting interpretations of the Bible. Again, Bible interpreters should seek the interpretation of a specific biblical passage that is most coherent and viable in terms of the writer's purpose, literary genre and relevant historical and grammatical evidence. A verificational method invites people to look fairly at alternative hypotheses and test the coherence and viability of the relevant lines of data.

4. There are not just two methods of reasoning, inductive and deductive. There is a third way, that of abduction. Its starting point is not presuppositions or empirical data, but possible explanations (hypotheses) that may be falsified as well as confirmed. Because experience is more than sensory, hypotheses are tested by their coherence also with numerous converging internal lines of data such as the demand for ethical justice, the psychological need for love and the dynamic of religious experience. In other words, both an entire worldview and the doctrines within it are

verified when they offer a coherent and viable account of the relevant data (of general and special revelation).

Because we are finite and sinful, a verificational method of reasoning does not yield absolute intellectual certainty. Nevertheless, a sensible person accepts the view with the fewest difficulties. Probability is an indication that one is dealing in philosophical theology with such realities as history, science and law. But a well-informed view that is without contradiction provides psychological certitude and moral responsibility.

5. As exhibited elsewhere, a Carnellian approach integrates the values of five other apologetic methods: the data of the inductive reasoning (of J. Oliver Buswell, John Gerstner, John Warwick Montgomery, etc.), the logical noncontradiction of a rational empiricist like Stuart Hackett and a rationalist like Gordon Clark, and the content of Cornelius Van Til's presupposition of the God of the Bible. It incorporates also the personal witness of immediate experiences of conversion to Christ and existential authenticity in life and ministry.[26] In spite of the real strategic differences of our different mentors, they are all merely human servants. We can learn from all who are of Christ, as Paul emphasized, "all are yours!" (1 Corinthians 3:22).

Personal Challenge

Being able to look back upon fifty years of preparation, pastoral work and teaching, may I be permitted a further observation? In the first half of the twentieth century, modernism dominated the major schools, missions, denominations and publications. Imagine being without *Christianity Today* (and other recent evangelical publications) and finding few accredited colleges or seminaries! But in the last half of the twentieth century evangelicals have flourished in ways I could not have thought during my college and seminary days in the 1940s. Gordon Clark,

Carl Henry, Cornelius Van Til, Billy Graham, Vernon Grounds and Edward John Carnell (with many others) passed to my generation a distinctively evangelical commitment to the plenary inerrancy of Scripture.

Those of us who learned from such stalwarts commit to the next generation the treasured heritage of universal and necessary moral laws and so the universal need for the inerrant message of God's mercy and grace in Christ once-for-all. I pray that the coming generation will make the most of this, the greatest era of evangelical opportunity in history. God forbid that any should return to the totalistic relativism from which, at such great cost, evangelical schools, churches and publications were so recently delivered!

Endnotes

[1] Tom Strini, PBS Series "Dance as a Link Between Cultures, a Human Mirror," *Milwaukee Journal* 9 May 1993. Cited by Gene E. Veith, Jr., *Postmodern Times* (Wheaton, IL: Crossway, 1994), 155.

[2] Philip D. Kenneson, "There's No Such Thing As Objective Truth, and It's a Good Thing, Too," ed. Timothy R. Philipps and Dennis L. Okholm, *Christian Apologetics in the Postmodern World* (Downers Grove, IL: InterVarsity Press, 1995), 166.

[3] H. Richard Niebuhr, *The Meaning of Revelation* (New York: Macmillan, 1942), 38.

[4] For additional evaluation of confessionalism see Gordon R. Lewis, "The Niebuhrs' Relativism, Relationalism and Contextualization" ed. by Gordon R. Lewis and Bruce A. Demarest, *Challenges to Inerrancy: A Theological Response* (Chicago: Moody, 1984), 145-173.

[5] The suggestion of Edward John Carnell in *Christian Commitment* (New York: Macmillan, 1957), 34-35.

[6] Ibid., 86-91.

[7] Ronald Dworkin, *Taking Rights Seriously* (Cambridge, MA: Harvard University Press, 1977), 177, 205, 269.

[8] Ibid., 90.

[9]Michael Polanyi, *Personal Knowledge: Towards a Post-Critical Philosophy* (Chicago: University of Chicago Press, 1962), 228.

[10]Carnell, *Christian Commitment*, 210.

[11]Joseph Fletcher, *Situation Ethics* (Philadelphia: Westminster Press, 1966).

[12]Hugh A. Koops, "Pressing the Claims, Interpreting the Cries," ed. Allen O. Miller, *Christian Declaration on Human Rights* (Grand Rapids, MI: Eerdmans, 1977), 59.

[13]Gene Edward Veith, Jr., *Postmodern Times* (Wheaton, IL: Crossway, 1994), 54.

[14]James Sire, *Scripture Twisting* (Downers Grove, IL: InterVarsity Press, 1980).

[15]Clyde A. Holbrook, "H. Richard Niebuhr" in Dean G. Peerman and Martin E. Marty, eds., *A Handbook of Christian Theologians* (New York: World, 1965), 392-393.

[16]Jerry H. Gill, *On Knowing God* (Philadelphia: Westminster, 1981), 143-144.

[17]For documentation see Gordon R. Lewis, "Schaeffer's Apologetic Method," Ronald W. Ruegsegger, ed., *Reflections on Francis Schaeffer* (Grand Rapids, MI: Academie Books, 1986), 69-104.

[18]Carnell majored on logic and fact in *An Introduction to Christian Apologetics* (Grand Rapids, MI: Eerdmans, 1948) and on values in *A Philosophy of the Christian Religion* (Grand Rapids, MI: Eerdmans, 1952).

[19]Gordon R. Lewis, "Edward John Carnell," ed. Walter Elwell, *Handbook of Evangelical Theologians* (Grand Rapids, MI: Baker, 1993), 325.

[20]Norman Geisler, *Christian Apologetics* (Grand Rapids, MI: Baker, 1976), 121-132, 141-147.

[21]See Douglas Groothuis, "Deposed Royalty: Pascal's Anthropological Argument," *Premise,* vol. 3, no. 4, 6.

[22]D. Elton Trueblood, *Philosophy of Religion* (New York: Harper & Brothers, 1957).

[23]For justification of the claim that Schaeffer used a verificational method versus those who regarded Schaeffer an

empiricist or a presuppositionalist, see Gordon R. Lewis, "Francis Schaeffer's Apologetic Method," ed. Ronald W. Ruegsegger, *Reflections on Francis Schaeffer* (Grand Rapids, MI: Academie, 1986), 69-104.

[24]"Edward John Carnell," *Handbook of Evangelical Theologians*, 325.

[25]Jerry Gill, *On Knowing God*, 36.

[26]Gordon R. Lewis, *Testing Christianity's Truth Claims* (rpr. Lanham, MD: University Press of America, 1990).

Part II

Defending the Faith Historically

Philosophy of History, Historical Relativism and History As Evidence

Gary R. Habermas

There is little challenge to the general assertion that history is crucial to the Judeo-Christian faith. But what history is or how this discipline should be implemented is, for some, another matter altogether. This is especially the case when one discusses the apologetic use of history, even if one is limiting the discussion to evangelicals.

In this essay, we confine ourselves to an overview of history as a means of defending the Christian faith, including several strengths and weaknesses of evangelical historical apologetics. This will also involve entering the broader fields of historiography and philosophy of history. Our purpose is to move from a sense of where we have been to some areas that we might pursue in the future.

Many years ago while writing my dissertation, I attempted to address certain methodological issues in historiography. A history professor responded to my survey of contemporary definitions with the remark: "Don't tell me what history *is*," he directed, "because no one agrees, anyway. Just tell me what concept you are going to *use*." Briefly, I will include at least two indispensable notions that figure prominently in by far the majority of such discussions. History includes (1) those events that have occurred in the past as well as (2) the interpretation and recording of them. Additional elements are surely significant as well,[1] but need not detain us at this juncture.

When I speak of defending the faith historically, I am referring to what might broadly be called historical apologetics. Here we need to differentiate at least two aspects: factual evidences and answering various detractors that seek to undermine the Christian faith. In other words, we will pursue here both evidence and apologetic avenues.[2]

I think that, in spite of certain differences, especially in methodology, there is a growing evangelical consensus on many of the crucial issues in this field. I will comment, in order, on some of the positive strides achieved by recent efforts in evangelical historical apologetics and on some weaknesses that need to be remedied. Then I will provide an example of the latter by surveying a major discussion in the philosophy of history. Last, I will conclude with some specific suggestions for the future. My recommendations will concern not only theoretical matters, but will also be oriented toward certain practical items that can be immediately applied. I make this last point because I think that apologetics has often ignored or underemphasized several areas, and we are long overdue for excellence in *both* theory *and* practice. Each is absolutely indispensable.

Areas of Agreement in Evangelical Historical Apologetics

One of my main concerns is that historical apologetics in the evangelical tradition usually operates in a rather piecemeal fashion. In this sense we do not take a holistic approach to the subject matter of history, but tend to extract only what we want, picking and choosing those aspects of historiography that best suit our needs. Still, while gathering data to confirm one's position may only be a small piece of the historical pie, such endeavors remain exceptionally crucial. So beyond this important caveat that needs to be explored in the next section, we can still enumerate some areas of harmony that are, at the same time, strengths in the evangelical focus.

The current literature indicates more agreement in evangelical apologetics today than there has been for several decades. This consensus permeates different areas too, including theoretical, methodological and practical concerns. One example where this has been more apparent in recent years is the increasing recognition concerning the presence of presuppositions in one's thinking, whether by believers or unbelievers. Distinctions between different forms of presupposition notwithstanding,[3] it must be recognized that all sorts of assumptions are inherent in historical (or other) inductive research. Personal biases, prejudices and even preferences can affect substantially our conclusions, as can more weighty areas such as our worldviews, including our moral values.[4]

Although there is a wide range of thoughts on the type, strength and influence of our presuppositions, evangelicals seem to be in extensive agreement that our assumptions do affect our views. Therefore, we should not build our systems on so-called brute, self-interpreting facts. In order to report the data of the past, we must interact with it in personal ways, although we dare not stop there.

A second multifaceted theme on which evangelicals express widespread agreement is not only the importance of historical evidences, but a general sense concerning the type of research that should be accomplished in these areas.[5] Even apologetic methodology does not separate us as much as it has in the past. Once believed to be an area of great disagreement, recent efforts have cleared some previously muddied waters. If my play on words will be forgiven, there is increasing room here for "common ground" even between apologists![6]

A third area of historical apologetics that has found extensive acceptance among evangelicals is also methodological in nature: the usefulness of public debates. For whatever reasons, evangelicals frequently seem to do exceptionally well in these endeavors. However, since this is not to argue that the ends justify the means, we must offer some caveats here. Debates need to be done under the right conditions and require the exhibition of proper attitudes. A haughty tone or other encouragement to one's pride can equally well produce an opposite effect.

Largely due to recent adjustments, the application of apologetics to practical concerns has also changed. Accordingly, a fourth sphere of considerable agreement is an expanded sense of how historical apologetics may be applied to ministry. For instance, it is widely recognized by commentators that the Book of Acts exhibits numerous evangelistic and church-planting efforts that are based on the facts of fulfilled prophecy and the resurrection of Jesus.[7] Furthermore, there are multiple examples in the New Testament of the truth of the resurrection being related to a variety of other doctrines and practical applications.[8]

It should also be realized that such public displays are exercises in spiritual warfare and ought to be treated as such. But when done in the power of the Holy Spirit and with the appropriate attitude, debates can provide a powerful witness to the gospel for the sort of audience that may not otherwise hear it. It was that way in Paul's day where he made the proper use of such methods,[9] and remains a possibility today.

A fifth area of agreement in evangelical apologetics is the recognition that, while this discipline is correctly taken to provide evidence for the truthfulness of Christianity, and the gospel in particular, it is not necessarily synonymous with the work of the Holy Spirit. For example, individuals are never argued into the kingdom of God by sheer force and our power of persuasion; such a task can only be accomplished by the Spirit of God. Further, as we just said, dialogue can be conducted in other than an edifying manner. Neither is apologetics the same as the witness of the Holy Spirit.[10] We also need to note the differences between the facts of the gospel and evidences *for* them, since they are not synonymous. At least in our more lucid moments, evangelicals do make such important distinctions.

These are some of the areas where there appears to be a large measure of agreement among believers. These matters also signal some important contributions made by the proper use of historical apologetics.

Some Weaknesses in Evangelical Historical Apologetics

Besides these more positive trends, however, there are also some points on which evangelicals need to do a better job. I will mention three such areas. Each of these topics is implied by matters that we have already mentioned.

I have said that our historical endeavors tend to be overly one-dimensional. This tendency includes at least two problems.

First, while we concentrate almost exclusively on historical evidences, even here some curious neglect is manifest. For instance, while evangelicals generally do much better on the resurrection of Jesus, and while we have been growing in sophistication in our defense of the Scriptures, we tend not to venture very far beyond these select areas.

To illustrate, in the majority of our latest apologetics texts, it seems we have forfeited Paul's other favorite topic—messianic prophecy. Bernard Ramm posed this same challenge a generation ago, although the trend appears to continue.[11] Are there sufficient reasons for this, or, as I prefer, do we need to amend our methodology and address critical concerns without surrendering the topic itself?[12] We also need to pursue historical defenses of essential doctrines like the virgin birth and the incarnation.[13] To be honest, sometimes it seems that we give in prematurely to critical challenges and occasionally buckle to peer pressure.

Even on the topics that *do* receive stronger treatment, one often has the sense that evangelicals depend too much on quoting others and too little on original research. It will no doubt be protested that this situation is often due to the popular nature of many of our writings, and this point certainly has merit. However, it does not excuse the tendency to fight bygone battles instead of being informed of the latest areas of attack.

For example, some recent critical questions about the historicity of the resurrection frequently go unnoticed. On other occasions, we respond only after a new trend has gained far too much ground; sometimes, devastatingly, the losses even affect our own ranks before we take notice.

Further, we continue to repeat points that sometimes appear to be mistaken. For example, one frequently repeated comment in evangelical apologetic literature is that there is far too little time from Jesus' life to the New Testament documents to allow for myth to creep into the text. Frequently, the studies of historian A.N. Sherwin-White are cited in order to justify the comment. However, Sherwin-White did not say that myth could never make its way into the text in such a short time, but that two generations is an insufficient interval to allow myth to *destroy* the core of the historical material.[14] Moreover, a few studies have shown that myth sometimes has accompanied religious persons even during their lifetimes and shortly afterward.[15]

Now this does not mean that the essential apologetic point being made about the absence of mythology in the Gospels is ultimately incorrect. But perhaps we need to arrive at this conclusion more carefully. The means of establishing such an important detail is not to issue a preemptive edict that appears contrary to certain data. Rather, if Sherwin-White's observations are accurate, we can utilize them as part of a case to establish another crucial assertion—that the essence of the Gospel reports is historical. Then we need to address differently the question of whether *any* myth is present in these texts.

At any rate, my initial suggestion is that evangelicals be more aware of simplistic, one-dimensional approaches within the field of historical apologetics. We need to plug some holes by expanding into areas that evangelicals sometimes neglect, by pursuing original research whenever possible, by not overemphasizing battles that are no longer quite as relevant and by patching up weaker areas of argumentation. We need historical research, not theologizing *about* history. These recommendations will also help us to set an apologetic agenda that will have more influence for the cause of Jesus Christ.

Second, there are also some major theoretical areas in the broader discipline of historical studies that comparatively few evangelicals have addressed. This is especially inexplicable when they impinge on the crucial task of apologetics. This appears to me to be a very strange stance for evangelicals, for whom history is of central importance.[16]

One such example is a definition of history. What kind of progress can be made on this preliminary enterprise? Which of several angles should one take? How is the subject approached by those of differing schools of thought?[17]

An even broader and more crucial area is the philosophy of history, which is frequently addressed under two general divisions: speculative and critical. While the wide-ranging interpretive schemas of speculative philosophers of history are much less popular in recent decades, the work of Bruce Mazlish is an indication that it is not entirely obsolete.[18] Perhaps the chief concern here, and one that has a bearing on a Christian worldview, is whether one can identify broad, interpretive schemes pervading the course of history that can also be argued from the historical data rather than theologically.

On the other hand, critical philosophy of history addresses numerous issues that are perhaps more particularly relevant to evangelical interests. Many sub-categories could occupy our attention here.[19]

One such topic is that of historiography. How do we actually *do* history? What are the historian's tools and how do we employ them? Are all data on equal footing? If not, how

are they to be weighed? What kinds of criticism are appropriate and how do we apply them both to our sources and
to the results of our own research? British philosopher-
historian Robin Collingwood reminds us that one cannot
simply take the word of one's authorities at face value.[20]

Then there is the more technical area of the epistemology of history. What standards of evidence are applicable to
historical research? Is there any such thing as inductive
proof or must we speak strictly in terms of probabilities?
Are probabilities rather specific or must we be satisfied
with more vagueness? How does one know when one's conclusions have been demonstrated according to the appropriate standards of the discipline?[21] Making this aspect
more complicated is David Fischer's observation: "Specific
canons of historical proof are neither widely observed nor
generally agreed upon."[22] Yet Fischer still provides seven
guidelines for determining historical truth.[23]

Further, we dare not ignore the significance of historical
hermeneutics. What is the relation between historical facts
and their interpretation? Is the former subject to the latter?
Must all interpretation, by its very nature, be subjective?
Can the historian in any sense relive the past or enter the
world of those who recorded the data in question? Another
British philosopher-historian, W.H. Walsh, comments that
"historians have conspicuously failed to develop . . . a set of
agreed canons of interpretation which all who work at the
subject would be ready to acknowledge."[24]

I think evangelicals need to respond in detail to each of
these critical issues in the philosophy of history. But I want
to concentrate on the one that may have received the most
attention from philosophers and historians, as well as being exceptionally relevant to our topic today. Can the past
be known objectively, or are we limited to subjective standards?[25] Philosophers and historians have been enmeshed
in a lengthy controversy over this topic, a discussion that
foreshadows our own important questions on this precise
theme.

Additionally, there are some very significant parallels here to certain current trends toward relativism, such as some of those found in deconstruction. We may recall the popular saying that those who ignore history are bound to repeat it, yet it is amazing that this historical debate began more than one hundred years ago! In fact, some reasons for the emerging consensus among historical scholars could help in the larger question of relativism.

I think this issue is important enough to develop in the next section, as a more detailed example of our second point. A critical evaluation of these decades of dialogue may prove to be instructive for all those who attempt to defend the faith historically. Working out such details definitely has a bearing, for instance, on how we investigate the resurrection of Jesus. Such studies of specific facts ought not be done in a vacuum.

Before turning to a brief treatment of historical relativism, a third weakness in evangelical historical apologetics needs to be mentioned. While we often acknowledge the application of historical apologetics to the practical Christian life, we have frequently been a bit slow to address the actual implementation of our studies. But we need some explicit ways to "drive home" our conclusions.

For example, what is the relationship between apologetics and the work of the Holy Spirit? Is there a modern counterpart to Paul's use of historical evidences as his chief means of planting churches (Acts 17:2)? What is the "power of his resurrection" (Philippians 3:10) and how does it apply to the daily Christian life? What does Paul mean by his suggestion that the truth of Jesus' resurrection and its message of immortality should be applied to our work ethic, including assisting poor believers (1 Corinthians 15:58-16:3)? How does the resurrection both provide a glimpse of heaven and give us a new perspective on life's struggles (1 Peter 1:3-6)? What about the relation between apologetics and the spiritual disciplines? And how can we do our best in discipling the next generation of apologists?

Evangelicals sometimes appear, for whatever reasons, to isolate apologetics and treat it almost as a separate, stand-alone discipline. Yet we need to move more aggressively from our best theoretical research to equally serious, full-length works on application. Until we do so, we are not taking our apologetics to its proper conclusion, thereby not bringing all our weapons to bear on the practical Christian life. As much as the more speculative work is absolutely required, and as much as some of us might enjoy doing it, we all need to acknowledge that our Lord likewise commands us to cultivate our personal walk with Him. The field of apologetics has much to contribute to our commitment.

In sum, evangelicals tend to be too single-dimensional in their own treatment of historical apologetics, leaving important gaps even in evidential matters. We also neglect the more theoretical aspects of the philosophy of history, such as historiography, the epistemology of history and historical hermeneutics. In so doing, we miss significant chances to buttress our work in crucial areas. Further, we neglect to build bridges between historical apologetics and Christian practice, thus failing to fully implement our studies.

The Objectivity of Our Knowledge of the Past

Here we shall briefly outline certain features of a vital issue in the philosophy of history—the objectivity of historical knowledge. Several lessons relative to historical apologetics will hopefully emerge as a result.

During the mid-nineteenth century, German historian Leopold von Ranke (1795-1886) championed a method of research later identified as historical positivism. It was the dominant view in Western European and American historiography over the remainder of the century. This approach emphasized thorough, painstaking analysis that was believed to yield the discovery of the cold, hard facts of history. Such research was said to be capable of objectively discovering the data of the past as it actually occurred, which could be reconstructed in an unbiased fashion, just as in the other sciences.

In fact, history was viewed as a science, employing scientific methodology. Many of these scholars held that there were universal laws governing history and other disciplines just as there were laws that operated in nature. French philosopher Auguste Comte (1798-1857) believed that such laws applied to all areas of knowledge. He thought that he had properly traced these natural ordinances through the disciplines of history and sociology, in particular, just as others had made major inroads by recognizing these laws in science. German philosopher Karl Marx (1818-1883) also shared the view that the scientific study of history would reveal the natural laws that governed societal development. British historian Henry Buckle (1821-1862) thought that history was subject to the universal laws of nature, which could be discovered by scientific methodology.

By employing the inductive method and properly delineating and applying these universal laws, it was thought that the past could be reconstructed in exact terms. It was deemed possible to discover the pattern of history without any interference from prejudice or other subjective biases.

By the end of the nineteenth century, however, a relativistic tendency began to gain momentum in historical studies, in strict opposition to this objectivisitic trend. Over against positivism, this latter emphasis is usually associated with idealistic philosophy, often in the traditions of Immanuel Kant and G.W.F. Hegel. In the next few decades the more recent movement continued to level criticisms against the view that history was a science, employing the same methodological techniques.

Wilhelm Dilthey (1833-1911) was an early proponent of the emerging idealistic position. Although he separated the historical method from that of the natural sciences, he still thought that historical facts were empirically derived and objectively known. Yet true knowledge of the past was said to be gained according to the influential idea that one could be projected through "lively visualization" back "into a work or person," allowing one to "relive" the past.[26]

In contrast to positivism, the new outlook not only enumerated differences between historical and scientific techniques, but emphasized the more subjective role of the historian. W.H. Walsh includes the contributing factors under four categories: the researcher's personal preferences, group prejudices, differing concepts of historical interpretation, and philosophical conflicts pertaining to one's worldview. Such influences were said to contribute much more to the writing of history than was previously believed.[27]

While even these idealistic historians thought that the past could often be reconstructed in factual terms, especially where historians of differing views agreed, interpreting these events was taken as the chief realm where the subjective tendencies were paramount. One prominent trend among historians such as Benedetto Croce (1866-1952) and Robin Collingwood (1889-1943) was to view all history as contemporary, to be relived in the modern historian's thoughts.[28] While Collingwood was not as extreme as Croce,[29] he would still conclude: "The history of thought, and therefore all history, is the re-enactment of past thought in the historian's own mind."[30]

Since the middle of this century, much synthesis has taken place, with historians both pursuing the facts of the past by utilizing the more objective tools of historical research on the one hand, while attempting to take seriously the limitations imposed by various sorts of subjective factors on the other. Thus, while recognizing the influence of considerations that restrict us, we still have at our disposal significant historical means of researching the past and deciding what occurred.[31]

Why do so many contemporary historians opt for a synthesis between discovering objective facts even while subjective limitations are taken seriously, rather than opting for relativism? There is no question that personal biases can and do distort data and affect one's research. Yet to hold that these elements are so serious that they must nullify all historical conclusions is to stumble into a host of errors. Historians and philosophers alike have noted numerous problems with relativistic hypotheses, which in more recent times have "suffered a decline in status."[32]

First, to argue that subjective preferences must nullify objective standards is a *non sequitur*. Morton White contends that "The mere fact that historians are biased is no argument against the existence of impersonal standards." To argue otherwise is fallacious, just as it is to assert that a physician's feelings about a patient's sickness preclude the physician from making a proper diagnosis.[33] Ernest Nagel adds: "the bare fact that inquiry is selective (is) no valid ground for doubting the objectively warranted character of its conclusions."[34]

Second, and more devastating, the claim that all historical knowledge is relative is self-contradictory. Nagel argues that, if such a claim is made, then at least one objective conclusion *is* known, so there could well be others.[35] Christopher Blake expands the criticism: "[E]ither Relativism is wrong or, if it is correct, then it is itself only a relative verdict."[36]

Incredibly, Charles Beard (often identified as the "foremost spokesman" for historical relativism[37]) fully admits this criticism. It could scarcely be said in any stronger terms than his:

> Contemporary criticism shows that the apostle of relativity is destined to be destroyed by the child of his own brain. If all historical conceptions are merely relative to passing events . . . then the conception of relativity is itself relative. When absolutes in history are rejected the absolutism of relativity is also rejected. . . . [T]he conception of relativity will also pass, as previous conceptions and interpretations of events have passed. . . . [T]he skeptic of relativity will

disappear in due course. . . . [T]he apostle of relativity will surely be executed by his own logic.[38]

Third, another confusion comes from historians who engage in relativistic comments on the one hand, even while, in their own research, they pursue the writing of actual history. White is critical of Beard's skeptical approach which, thankfully, he says did not affect Beard's "own scientific work" on "the essence of history."[39] For example, Beard thought that his work on an economic understanding of the Constitution[40] "was objective and factual."[41] Meyerhoff agrees that "Beard never reached a satisfactory middle ground" between objective and subjective elements in historiography.[42]

Fourth, and stated negatively, although prejudice is present, it can be recognized and handled. Nagel points out that "The very fact that biased thinking may be detected and its sources investigated shows that the case for objective explanations in history is not necessarily hopeless."[43] A historian can avoid the crippling affects of partiality. Even though bias can never totally be uprooted, Walsh still notes that "every reputable historian acknowledges the need for some sort of objectivity and impartiality in his work" in order to separate history from propaganda, feelings and personal preconceptions.[44]

Fifth, and more positively, historiography employs normal inductive measures that render knowable conclusions. Although he reaches a moderate resolution of this issue, Walsh explains: "Historical conclusions must be backed by evidence just as scientific conclusions must."[45] Beard even adds: "The historian . . . sees the doctrine of relativity crumble in the cold light of historical knowledge."[46]

Interestingly enough, the historians who are often categorized as relativists agree at this point on the reality of obtaining knowledge of the past.[47] Karl Mannheim, whom Gardiner calls "[p]erhaps the most forthright proponent of historical relativism in recent times,"[48] still points out that the presence of subjective concerns "does not imply renunciation of the postulate of objectivity and the possibility of arriving at decisions in factual disputes."[49] Arguing for objective data, Blake remarks that there is a large amount of historical research that is acceptable to the entire historical community.[50]

Relativistic approaches to historiography have also been severely criticized for other shortcomings as well.[51] These critiques have been offered for two reasons. This serves as an example of how investigating a neglected aspect of philosophy of history actually serves as an important, component part of a historical apologetic. In this case, we are defending Christianity against detractors that, if true, would undermine the Christian faith on the central topic of history. Further, critiques such as these can, and should be, applied to recent trends (such as deconstruction) that make similar claims against the objectivity of historical knowledge. As we have said, if we had done better homework the first time, we would have been more prepared for similar challenges.

This leads us directly to a few cognate issues in the epistemology of history that we need to address briefly. Given that subjective factors often take their toll on researchers even though we can determine facts about the past, in what sense do we have *objective* historical truth? Blake maintains that the chief "criterion of objectivity" might be a notion that "entails reporting accurately, together with some vaguer notion of neutrality."[52] One goal here would be the agreement of others who have studied the relevant issues. Blake explains that "working canons of historians are standards for determining the accuracy or reliability of sources—standards that are corporately applied."[53] Berlin agrees, using the term "objective" to indicate the common ground between historians as they assemble, as much as is possible, "the fragments of the past."[54]

What about the incompleteness of the data? Both Berlin and Blake agree that even the best research will still have to be open to correction, but this does not preclude the notion of objectivity. Although this sense of the term is a bit ambiguous and fluid, Berlin points out that it still remains "within limits recognized by normal usage."[55]

Nagel sums up very nicely the issue of objectivity:

> In brief, therefore, although the historian is undoubtedly selective in the conduct of his inquiries, and although personal and social bias frequently color his judgment and control what conclusions he accepts, none of these facts precludes the possibility of warranted explanations for the events he studies.[56]

I refer to historical objectivity as indicating at least that the historian has accurately performed his investigation, applied the appropriate standards of criticism and determined the outcome according to accepted canons of reliability. Then the scholar needs to be open to additional critique, entailing defense and/or adjustment.

This also raises the issue of certainty.[57] The best-established historical events are those that are confirmed by careful research, especially when they have repeatedly withstood the eye of critical scrutiny. These occurrences are supported by the relevant data, with no viable contrary evidence. Future reevaluation may periodically have to be done, but this does not preclude present certainty. After all, we cannot hold in abeyance all of history, in the constant fear that something may be challenged![58]

Now we have come full circle to one of our earlier points by understanding some of the reasons for the widespread agreement among evangelicals that a totally neutral approach to historical evidence is impossible, as well as why "brute facts" are not just sitting "out there" in the past, ready to be discovered. Even though historical data do exist in some objective sense, they still must be ascertained through human research and writing. Human finiteness and fallenness need to be factored in as well.

It will no doubt occur to some that our conclusion so far

has had very little to do with the possibility of God's intervention in history via particular acts. In addition, most historians will resist this subject altogether. All we can say here is that, regardless of the views of current historians, evangelicals should continue to hold to the historical method, investigating all the data that we have at our disposal.

However, others (often friends) think that the historical method, by its very nature, does not allow any analysis of the supernatural. It must be admitted that the notion of miracle does involve complicated philosophical issues such as the existence and activity of God. Yet it must be insisted that historians are still free to examine *at least* the historical side of the *claim* that some particular act *A* occurred in history. In other words, if believers say that God intervened in history at such-and-such a time and place, some will contend that God's direct actions cannot be checked by human means. However, if the event actually intersected time-space history at all, we can, *at a minimum*, inspect that particular mundane, this-worldly aspect of the claim. Thus, the *historical portion* is open to investigation.

For the objector to continue past this point would seem to involve some version of *a priori* dismissal of the supernatural. But we simply do not know in advance and without viewing the data whether or not something happened in history.

Interestingly, two Oxford historians have helped support this conclusion. Walsh raises the question of religious beliefs being a part of the prejudice that historians bring to their work. He concludes that the only supportable beliefs in religion or politics are those "they can justify on rational grounds, or they must be extruded from their history." If religious beliefs are such that are "a matter of rational conviction" then it is "not only inevitable but perfectly proper that they should exert an influence on the historian's thinking."[59]

William Wand addresses this subject as well:

It would seem then that the right attitude to adopt in historical matters is neither that of total doubt nor of total credulity, but of caution. In particular where history impinges on the sphere of religion, we shall not be overdisposed to accept a supernatural explanation just because it is supernatural, nor to reject it just because we dislike the supernatural anyway. . . . [The historian] must be as openminded as he can.[60]

Wand later charges that anyone who is unwilling to even look at the evidence "is not functioning as a historian at all." In fact,

a critical historian can [only] decide on the evidence before him—unless indeed he already holds some secret which will invalidate in advance any evidence that can be brought in favour of the phenomenon in question.[61]

Suggestions for the Future

We have outlined both some strengths and a number of weaknesses in evangelical historical apologetics. Where do we go from here? I will close with some suggestions for the future, in the hope that we may begin to move in a few directions that will help to facilitate some needed change.

Evangelicals need to correct single-faceted historical apologetics by filling both internal and external gaps. Internally, we need more depth and balance in our studies. Suggestions involve developing neglected evidences and defending central doctrines, as well as utilizing careful research techniques and accurate reporting.

Externally, we need to broaden our mastery of the crucial discipline of history, especially in aspects of the philosophy of history like epistemology, historiography and hermeneutics. It is critical that we know *why* there is an objective basis for history. By deciphering the latest trends when they occur, we can avoid having to repeat the past. Such efforts will further enhance our ability to provide the best in both factual evidences and answering detractors.

Throughout these enterprises, we need to do more than just *simply respond* to our critics. We have, for too long, taught ourselves to *react* to subjects that critics initiate. I think that this is so much the case that we seldom venture beyond defensive modes. To give but one example, too infrequently do we challenge unbelievers to provide the grounds for *their* beliefs and assertions. The time has come for believers to state their positions in ways that will cause our critics to respond to us. This will, of course, mean that we will need to do a better job both in the products we produce, as well as in the avenues we take to make them available to those who hold other positions.

Evangelicals also need to devote more attention to the application of apologetics. Here I would like to elaborate on two examples of how this might be done.

First, we need to develop better ways to use historical evidences with unbelievers. It seems that evangelicals do very well in public debates, in writing for others of like faith, and in occasional witnessing to non-Christians. Perhaps we could also expand creatively into other sorts of ministries. Long-term, significant friendships with unbelievers are often very productive and can be carried out by a variety of means. For example, home discussions where Christians and non-Christians alike can openly examine questions and challenges are an excellent way to apply historical evidences. So are coffeehouse situations where times are set up specifically to invite such dialogue. Extended letter-writing or phone calls are two other ways for private interaction that can be carried on indefinitely and on a very personal level.

Another means of prolonged, private exchange comes from taking advantage of the latest computer technology, like on-line forums for public debate and discussion. This opens a new realm of interaction with unbelievers who actually *seek* such discussions! Can we do less than cooperate?

We also need to pursue much more rigorously the proclamation of our ideas in non-evangelical forums like publishing houses, journals and magazines. This includes both attending and reading papers at professional society meetings.

What would the Apostle Paul do if he had all of these contemporary opportunities to continue discussions with the Athenian philosophers he engaged in the marketplace and later in his Areopagus meeting? In the witnessing situations in Acts 13-19, Paul used a wide variety of techniques to air his message. It is difficult for me to imagine him turning down such modern opportunities, especially when the other person is initiating the dialogue.

Second, we have a distinct duty to disciple the next generation of Christian apologists. Who will "carry the ball" for us? Which Scripture scholars will continue to defend the text? Which apologists will formulate arguments for the resurrection to meet the next wave of challenges? Which theologians will defend the cardinal doctrines of the Christian faith? Which historians will be prepared to step into the arena of the philosophy of history and answer the tough questions? Which philosophers will pay the price to spar with those who degrade our worldview? Which campus leaders will challenge their universities? And which preachers and missionaries will carry these same messages to the congregations of the world?

Who will take the time to train others for the tough but exciting days ahead? In whom will we invest our resources? How can we best facilitate this ministry? Will apologists be willing to sacrifice in terms of personal research and experience?

Defending the faith historically is not just for the intellectually elite. The philosophy of history is more than a separate, stand-alone discipline for professional philosophers and historians. Gaining expertise in these areas is more than learning for the sake of knowledge or exhibition. We must remember that we are not just apologists, but evangelicals. Beyond the theoretical aspects that we dare never minimize, historical apologetics also must be applied to real lives in a fallen world. Like the rest of Christianity, our ultimate goal is eternal: the making and maturing of believers in Jesus Christ by the power of the Holy Spirit.

Endnotes

[1]A helpful introductory discussion, including a very useful chart, in provided in Earle E. Cairns, *God and Man in Time: A Christian Approach to Historiography* (Grand Rapids, MI: Baker, 1979), 12-15.

[2]For one popular way to distinguish between evidences and apologetics, see Cornelius van Til, *Apologetics* (Phillipsburg, NJ: Presbyterian and Reformed Publishing Company, 1980), 1. I think van Til is right that this distinction can only be one of emphasis, but never separation.

[3]See John Warwick Montgomery, *The Shape of the Past* (Minneapolis, MN: Bethany Fellowship, Inc., 1975), 140-141; Clark H. Pinnock, *Live Now, Brother* (Chicago: Moody, 1972), 44.

[4]For agreement on this point from two non-presuppositionalist apologists, see Norman L. Geisler, *Christian Apologetics* (Grand Rapids, MI: Baker, 1976), 94-98 and ch. 15; A.J. Hoover, *The Case for Christian Theism: An Introduction to Apologetics* (Grand Rapids, MI: Baker, 1976), 47-53.

[5]For a noteworthy presuppositionalist approach to apologetics, see Ronald H. Nash, *Faith and Reason: Searching for a Rational Faith* (Grand Rapids, MI: Zondervan, 1988).

[6]There are many important contributions on this subject. For some recent examples from presuppositionalists, see John Frame, "Epistemological Perspectives and Evangelical Apologetics," *Bulletin of the Evangelical Philosophical Society*, 7 (1984), 6-7; Cornelius van Til, *The Defense of the*

Faith (Phillipsburg, NJ: Presbyterian and Reformed Publishing Company, 1980), 199; Thom Notaro, *Van Til and the Use of Evidence* (Phillipsburg, NJ: Presbyterian and Reformed Publishing Company, 1980), chs. 1, 2 and 9. For an eclectic approach that is also in broad agreement here, see Ronald B. Mayers, *Both/And: A Balanced Apologetic* (Chicago: Moody, 1984), 49-53, 152-158.

[7]One such example is F.F. Bruce, *The Defence of the Gospel in the New Testament* (Grand Rapids, MI: Eerdmans, 1959), 9-21 in particular.

[8]More than 300 verses in the New Testament are concerned with the subject of Jesus' resurrection. This occurrence is not only a sign for unbelievers (Matthew 12:38-40; cf. John 20:24-29), but is also the answer for the believer's doubt (Luke 24:36ff.; John 21:12). It guarantees that Jesus' teachings are truthful (Acts 2:22-24; Romans 1:3-4; 1 Corinthians 15:12-20) and is the very center of the gospel (Romans 4:24-25; 10:9; 1 Corinthians 15:1-4). Further, the resurrection is the catalyst for evangelism (Matthew 28:18-20; Acts 10:39-43), the key to the believer's power to live the Christian life (Romans 6:4-14; 8:9-11; Philippians 3:10) and the reason we are to live committed lives (Romans 7:4; 1 Corinthians 15:57-58). The resurrection effectively answers the fear of death (John 11:25; 1 Corinthians 15:54-58; cf. Hebrews 2:14-15) and is connected to Jesus' Second Coming (Acts 1:11; Revelation 1:7). Perhaps most of all, this event is the model for the believer's bodily resurrection (Acts 4:2; 1 Corinthians 6:14; 1 John 3:2) and supplies a foretaste of heaven (1 Peter 1:3-5; Philippians 3:20-21). See Gary R. Habermas, *The Centrality of the Resurrection*, forthcoming, for a treatment addressing these and other such aspects.

[9]See Acts 17:2, 17; 18:4, 19; 19:8-9.

[10]See Romans 8:16; Galatians 4:6-7; 1 John 3:24; 4:16. For a stimulating treatment of this subject, see Bernard Ramm, *The Witness of the Spirit* (Grand Rapids, MI: Eerdmans, 1959).

[11]Bernard Ramm, "The Evidence of Prophecy and Miracle," in *Revelation and the Bible*, ed. Carl F.H. Henry (Grand Rapids, MI: Baker, 1958), 253-263.

[12]I have long thought that a case that is built on a small number of well-established prophecies is the best way to proceed. Three themes for such an endeavor would be instances of messianic, city/nation and land of Israel prophecies that provide superior answers to the critical concerns. For two good overviews that address various critical issues, see Robert C. Newman, ed., *The Evidence of Prophecy: Fulfilled Prediction as a Testimony to the Truth of Christianity* (Hatfield, PA: Interdisciplinary Biblical Research Institute, 1988) and the appropriate chapters on prophecy in John Warwick Montgomery, ed., *Evidence for Faith: Deciding the God Question* (Dallas, TX: Probe Books, Word Books, 1991). For a more systematic treatment, see Kenny Barfield, *The Prophet Motive: Examining the Reliability of the Biblical Prophets* (Nashville, TN: Gospel Advocate Company, 1995). Stuart Hackett offers some wise words on some of the evidential aspects of fulfilled prophecy in *The Reconstruction of the Christian Revelation Claim* (Grand Rapids, MI: Baker, 1984), 326-329.

[13]There have been some highly significant, sophisticated defenses of orthodox doctrine from various members of the Society of Christian Philosophers. Most notable is Thomas V. Morris, *The Logic of God Incarnate* (Ithaca, NY: Cornell University Press, 1986). But we also need to move into some of these areas in mainline evangelical publications. One good start is John Feinberg, "The Incarnation of Jesus Christ," in *Miracles: Has God Acted in History?*, ed. R. Douglas Geivett and Gary R. Habermas (Downers Grove, IL: InterVarsity, 1996).

[14]Sherwin-White states: "Herodotus enables us to test the tempo of myth-making, and the tests suggest that even two generations are too short a span to allow the mythical tendency *to prevail* over the hard historic core of the oral tradition." Then, addressing the Gospel writer's "passion-

ate interest in the story of Christ," Sherwin-White asserts that the concern for teaching their beliefs would still not lead them "to *pervert* and *utterly destroy* the historical kernel of their material" (my emphases). See *Roman Society and Roman Law in the New Testament* (Oxford: Oxford University Press, 1963; Grand Rapids, MI: Baker, 1978), 190.

[15]Robert M. Price, "Is there a Place for Historical Criticism?" *Religious Studies*, 27 (1991), especially 373-377.

[16]This does not mean that evangelicals have completely ignored these issues. Ronald Nash edited a noteworthy anthology, *Ideas of History*, 2 vols. (New York: E.P. Dutton, 1969). See also Nash's *Christian Faith and Historical Understanding* (Grand Rapids, MI: Zondervan Publishing House, 1984). For some helpful introductions to historical methodology, see Cairns, *God and Man in Time* and Winfried Corduan, "Back to the Past," in *Reasonable Faith: Christian Apologetics* (Nashville, TN: Broadman and Holman, 1993).

[17]Cairns provides an overview of several definitions of history (pp. 11-15).

[18]For example, Bruce Mazlish, *The Riddle of History: The Great Speculators from Vico to Freud* (New York: Harper and Row, 1966), 1-3.

[19]One influential topic not addressed here is the relation between history and the natural sciences. Another is the part history plays in the broader panorama of a philosophy of the social sciences.

[20]R.G. Collingwood, "The Historical Imagination" in Hans Meyerhoff, ed., *The Philosophy of History in Our Time: An Anthology* (New York: Doubleday and Company, 1959), 73-75.

[21]For a detailed introduction to some of these issues, see Gary R. Habermas, "Probability Calculus, Proof and Christian Apologetics," *The Simon Greenleaf Review of Law and Religion,* vol. 8 (1988-1989), 57-88.

[22]David Hackett Fischer, *Historian's Fallacies: Toward a Logic of Historical Thought* (New York: Harper and Row, 1970), 62.

[23]Ibid., 62-63.

[24]W.H. Walsh, *Philosophy of History: An Introduction* (New York: Harper and Brothers, 1960), 20.

[25]Evangelicals have most frequently dealt with the issue of the objectivity of historical knowledge. See William Lane Craig, "The Problem of Historical Knowledge," in *Apologetics: An Introduction* (Chicago: Moody, 1984) and Norman L. Geisler, "Objectivism and History," in *Christian Apologetics* (Grand Rapids, IL: Baker, 1976). On this same subject, compare the following articles: the dialogue between Ronald Nash (*Christian Scholar's Review*, vol. 1, no. 3 [Spring 1971]) and Paul Feinberg (*Christian Scholars' Review*, vol. 1, no. 4 [Summer 1971]) and the lively, prolonged discussion between Ronald VanderMolen (*Fides et Historia*, 3, no. 1 [Fall, 1970]), William Speck, John Warwick Montgomery and James Moore (*Fides et Historia*, vol. 4, no. 1 [Fall 1971]), Steven Hein (*Fides et Historia*, vol. 4, no. 2 [Spring 1972]), W. Stanford Reid, William Speck, Ronald VanderMolen and Earl William Kennedy (*Fides et Historia* vol. 5, nos. 1-2 [Spring 1973]).

[26]Wilhelm Dilthey, "The Understanding of Other Persons and their Life-Experiences," in Patrick Gardiner, ed., *Theories of History* (New York: Macmillan, 1959), 220-222 in particular.

[27]Walsh in Meyerhoff, 216-224.

[28]Several excellent anthologies provide perhaps the best way to gain an overview of this debate. For example, contributions by Dilthey, Croce and Collingwood can be found in both Meyerhoff, sec. 1 and Gardiner, pt. 1.

[29]See the critique of Croce in Robin Collingwood, *Essays in the Philosophy of History*, ed. William Debbins (New York: McGraw-Hill, 1965), ch. 1.

[30]Collingwood in Gardiner, 253. Further comments by Collingwood confirm this emphasis: "If we raise the question, Of what can there be historical knowledge? the answer is, Of that which can be re-enacted in the historian's mind" (257). "Of everything other than thought, there can

be no history" (258). We will not be able to address here this aspect of idealistic historiography. For a critical evaluation of what the author calls an "absurd" view, see Morton White, *Foundations of Historical Knowledge* (New York: Harper and Row, 1965), 147-151.

[31] For the later dialogue, see especially the essays by Carl Becker, Charles Beard, Morton White, Ernest Nagel and W.H. Walsh in Meyerhoff, sec. 2; and the selections by Walsh, White, Isaiah Berlin, Christopher Blake, and William Dray in Gardiner, pt. 2. Compare, in particular, the contributions by Walsh and J.A. Passmore in William H. Dray, ed., *Philosophical Analysis and History* (New York: Harper and Row, 1966).

[32] So comments Meyerhoff (119), discussing the views of Carl Becker and Charles Beard.

[33] White in Meyerhoff, 194-195. White (199) borrows the analogy of the physician from Sidney Hook.

[34] Nagel in Meyerhoff, 210.

[35] Nagel in Meyerhoff, 214.

[36] Blake in Gardiner, 332; cf. 335, 343; Fischer, 42-43.

[37] Meyerhoff, 138.

[38] Beard in Meyerhoff, 147.

[39] White in Meyerhoff, 200-201.

[40] Charles Beard, *An Economic Interpretation of the Constitution* (New York: Macmillan, 1935).

[41] White in Meyerhoff, 190-196, 200-201. Further, White charges Beard with contradicting himself on whether or not history can be done in a neutral manner (196-197).

[42] Meyerhoff, 138.

[43] Nagel in Meyerhoff, 213.

[44] Walsh, *Philosophy of History*, 19; cf. other comments by Walsh in Meyerhoff, 217, 222, 224; in Dray, 60-61, 74; in Gardiner, 60-61, 74.

[45] Walsh in Gardiner, 301. Most historians agree with this point. See Fischer, 42-43; Passmore in Dray, 79-80, 88; Berlin in Gardiner, 324-329; Blake in Gardiner, 331-332, 339; White in Gardiner, 365.

[46]Beard in Meyerhoff, 148.

[47]Some impressive examples can be found in Dilthey (in Gardiner, 224), Croce (in Gardiner, 228 and in Meyerhoff, 47), Collingwood (in *Essays in the Philosophy of History*, 102-103 and in Meyerhoff, 79-84), Beard (in *An Economic Interpretation of the Constitution* and in Meyerhoff, 141, 149) and Becker (in Meyerhoff, 122-128, 134, 136; cf. Carl L. Becker, *The Heavenly City of the Eighteenth-Century Philosophers* [New Haven: Yale University Press, 1932; reprint 1969], chs. 1-2). It should be carefully noted that it is precisely for this reason that the label "relativists" is somewhat of a misnomer for these idealistic historians.

[48]Gardiner, 269.

[49]See Karl Mannheim in Gardiner, 244, 247.

[50]Blake in Gardiner, 331.

[51]Isaiah Berlin charges that terms such as "relative" and "subjective" either "need correlatives, or else they turn out to be without meaning themselves." In other words, what is the standard for comparison? (See Berlin in Gardiner, 324, 328.) Blake agrees, complaining that there is otherwise "no alternative recognisable sense" of meaning. (See Blake in Gardiner, 335). Fischer thinks that relativists confuse knowledge itself with the **means** by which knowledge is obtained (Fischer, 44-45). This is what White calls "a confusion which is typical in the philosophy of history, the confusion between the psychology of historical interpretation and its logic." (See White in Meyerhoff, 199.) It might also be complained that although relativists recognize that objectively knowable facts exist and are necessary, these are still underemphasized in light of the role of interpretation. (For an insightful comparison here, contrast Collingwood's treatment [in Gardiner, 251-258] of what he terms an investigation of both the "outside" and the "inside" of an event.)

[52]Blake in Gardiner, 335.

[53]Ibid., 331.

[54]Berlin in Gardiner, 328.

[55]Berlin, 325, 328; cf. Blake, 338.

[56]Nagel in Meyerhoff, 215.

[57]Some researchers even refer to historical or inductive "proof." See Habermas, "Probability Calculus, Proof and Christian Apologetics," 62-67.

[58]For further details on these issues, see Gary R. Habermas, "Historical Methodology and Miracle-Claims," in *Ancient Evidence for the Life of Jesus: Historical Records of His Death and Resurrection* (Nashville, TN: Thomas Nelson, 1984), ch. 1; cf. Gary R. Habermas, "History and Evidence" in *Why Believe? God Exists!* (Joplin, MO: College Press, 1993), ch. 24.

[59]Walsh in Meyerhoff, 218.

[60]William Wand, *Christianity: A Historical Religion?* (Valley Forge, PA: Judson Press, 1972), 29-30.

[61]Ibid., 70-71.

Neglected Apologetic Styles:
The Juridical and the Literary

John Warwick Montgomery

The late Edward John Carnell once remarked, "There are as many apologetics as there are facts in the world."[1] However, traditional Christian apologetics has overwhelmingly limited itself to the philosophical, scientific and historical realms. While in no way undervaluing the contributions made in these areas, one must recognize—especially in regard to philosophical apologetics—that the interminable attempts to baptize and rehabilitate Aristotle's traditional proofs for God's existence, justify Anselm's ontological argument and refute Kant's critical philosophy have led many moderns to conclude that apologetics as such is an arid and irrelevant activity.

The present essay endeavors to introduce its audience to two apologetic approaches of a different character. The one, legal or juridical apologetics, like most traditional defense of the faith, appeals to William James's "tough-minded" personality, in that it deals with objective evidence for Christian truth; but it goes beyond them by employing the canons of evidence developed in the courts, thus benefiting from the most sophisticated criteria for resolving intractable disputes which civilized societies have developed. The other apologetic approach, the literary, provides a method with the "tender-minded" individual who, though serious in his or her search for ultimate reality, sees life primarily in subjective, existential terms and thus is little interested in the apologetic force of the Second Law of Thermodynamics or the question of whether the notions of Time and Creation are technically compatible or incompatible.

Juridical Apologetics

The apostle exhorts Christians: "Always be prepared to give an answer to everyone who asks you to give the reason for the hope that you have" (1 Peter 3:15). The word translated "answer" here is the Greek *apologia*, "defense."

Worth emphasizing is the legal flavor of the word *apologia*: the apostle consciously employed a technical term of ancient Greek law, having reference to the answer given by a defendant before a tribunal. One should not therefore be surprised to discover that the Law of Evidence offers innumerable valuable insights for the defense of historic Christian faith.

Our expectations in this regard are particularly heightened when we consider that the evidential machinery of the law has been developed, as the 1975 *Federal Rules of Evidence* state, "to the end that the truth may be ascertained."[2] All societies, whether civilized or primitive, require legal techniques for getting at the truth when disputes arise, and these techniques are refined through experience until they reach a level of sophistication satisfying to litigants who otherwise would breach the peace to settle their conflicts. Small wonder that philosopher Stephen Toulmin argues that philosophical inquiry itself could be considerably improved if it would look to legal reasoning as a model.[3]

Early Christianity based its case for divine truth on the deity of Jesus Christ, and its claim to His deity on His resurrection from the dead (1 Corinthians 15). The Law of Evidence well sustains this argumentation as will be seen from the application of several specific evidential rules.

1. Decisions on questions of fact must be made by the

trier of fact on the basis of the weight of relevant evidence, defined by the *Federal Rules* as "evidence having any tendency to make the existence of any fact that is of consequence to the determination of the action more probable or less probable than it would be without the evidence."[4] Christians are therefore precisely on the right track when they defend their position in terms of the weight of factual evidence for Christ's deity. A disputed question of religious truth must not be prejudged in a presuppositional manner: no one can expect that judicial notice will be taken for or against Christian truth, since "a judicially noticed fact must be one not subject to reasonable dispute."[5] The outcome of the case will depend, rather, on evidential probability.[6] And probability has to do with the weight of evidence for the particular claim at issue, without reference to general or collateral considerations. Thus just as "evidence of a person's character or a trait of his character is not admissible for the purpose of proving that he acted in conformity therewith on a particular occasion,"[7] so the non-Christian will be prevented from arguing against Christ's resurrection on the ground that regular events in general make a particular miracle too "improbable" to consider. The law refuses to obscure concrete evidence of the particular by the introduction of collateral generalities, for it recognizes that "there are too many differences to insure that what holds true in one case will apply in the other."[8]

2. "The common law system of proof," writes McCormick in his standard treatise on evidence,

> is exacting in its insistence upon the most reliable sources of information. This policy is apparent in the Opinion rule, the Hearsay rule and the Documentary Originals rule. One of the earliest and most pervasive manifestations of this attitude is the rule requiring that a witness who testifies to a fact which can be perceived by the senses must have had an opportunity to observe, and must have actually observed the fact.

In strict conformity to these requirements, the Christian properly focuses attention on the New Testament documents relating to the life of Christ as the best evidence concerning Him, since these can be shown to be primary sources—either written by those, such as Matthew and John who had immediate firsthand eyewitness contact with Jesus, or by others (Mark, Luke, Paul) who were intimately acquainted with the original apostolic circle. Moreover, as Simon Greenleaf of Harvard, author of the nineteenth century classic on evidence, stressed, any common-law court would favor the New Testament writings with a presumption of authenticity as ancient documents regular on their face and preserved through the centuries in a place of natural custody. The burden of proof thus rests upon the unbeliever to disprove the testimonial value of these apostolic books, not upon the Christian to build up support for documents already having *prima facie* legal authenticity.[9]

3. Where direct evidence is not available, the law allows circumstantial evidence and also proof by *res ipsa loquitur*. The latter is often resorted to in negligence cases where no one directly observed the act in question but where, by process of elimination, only the defendant was in a position to have done it.[10] Likewise, no one was present at the moment of Christ's resurrection, but the events surrounding it were testified to by careful eyewitnesses (Jesus was in fact put to death by crucifixion; Jesus afterwards made numerous physical post-resurrection appearances over a forty-day period).

Res ipsa loquitur in typical negligence case:

1. Accident does not normally occur in the absence of negligence.

2. Instrumentality causing injury was under the defendant's exclusive control.

3. Plaintiff did not himself contribute to the injury.

Therefore, defendant negligent: "the event speaks for itself."

Res ipsa loquitur as applied to Christ's resurrection:

1. Dead bodies do not leave tombs in the absence of some agency effecting the removal.

2. The tomb was under God's exclusive control, for it had been sealed, and Jesus, the sole occupant of it, was dead.

3. The Romans and the Jewish religious leaders did not contribute to the removal of the body (they had been responsible for sealing and guarding the tomb to prevent anyone from stealing the body), and the disciples would not have stolen it, then prevaricated and finally died for what they knew to be untrue.

Therefore, only God was in a position to empty the tomb, which He did, as Jesus Himself had predicted, by raising Him from the dead: "the event speaks for itself."

This reasoning process has close affinities with the method of *reductio ad absurdum*, which Professor Daube has shown to have been common in Greek and Roman law: supporting a case "by showing the alternative to be in striking contrast to the declared specific objective of the enterprise."[11] If the object of examining the primary-source documentary evidence for Christian claims is to determine what in fact happened, one cannot arrive at an "explanation" of the resurrection which entirely contradicts what these documents have to say about the historical circumstances and about the personalities and motivations of the people involved in them.[12]

And here, in contact with Greco-Roman jurisprudence, we see that the Law of Evidence is not a self-serving technique developed by common-law jurists in subtle support of Christian theology! The fundamental canons of evidence which we have employed in defense of biblical faith are found with remarkable consistency in all legal systems—from primitive to civilized, from ancient to modern. Max Gluckman writes of the Lozi people of Northern Rhodesia: "The Lozi distinguish between different kinds of evidence as hearsay, circumstantial, and direct, and attach different degrees of cogency to these and different degrees of credibility to various witnesses."[13] The ancient Persian *Digest of a Thousand Points of Law* begins with a detailed chapter on the Law of Evidence, insisting, as does the common law, on "independent and convincing proof" to support allegations, and setting forth detailed criteria for distinguishing reliable from unreliable testimony (declarations against interest as opposed to self-serving declarations, etc.).[14] In Roman law,

> when the witnesses for the parties gave conflicting testimony on any point, it was the duty of the judge, not to count the number on each side, but to consider which of them were entitled to the greatest credit, according to the well-known rule, "Testimonia ponderanda sunt, non numeranda." It rarely happens that the evidence is so nicely balanced as not to preponderate on one side or the other. But questions of fact may be supported and opposed by every degree of evidence, and sometimes by that degree of evidence of which the proper effect is to leave the mind in a state of doubt, or in an equipoise between two conclusions. Where such a case occurred, the Roman law provided that the benefit of the doubt should be given to the defendant rather than to the plaintiff.[15]

Where unsatisfactory or bizarre evidential standards have been developed in a society, these have generally been due to religious influences of an unfortunate kind. Thus among the Muslims one finds not only severe deficiencies in substantive law (e.g., the inferior legal position of women) but also sad procedural standards:

> One of the most serious limitations upon the practical efficiency of the Shari'a courts lay in the rigid system of procedure and evidence, applicable both in

124

civil and criminal cases, by which they were bound. The burden of proof was strict, and the party who bore it, usually the plaintiff, was obliged to produce two male, adult, Muslim witnesses, whose moral integrity and religious probity were unimpeachable, to testify orally to their direct knowledge of the truth of his claim. If the plaintiff or prosecution failed to discharge this burden of proof the defendant or accused was offered the oath of denial. Properly sworn on the *Qur'an*, such an oath secured judgment in his favor; if he failed to take it, judgment would be given for the plaintiff or prosecution, provided, in some circumstances, this side in turn took the oath. Such a system of procedure and evidence may have reflected the religious idealism of the scholars: but it was largely because of the often impractical burden of proof that was imposed upon a plaintiff, and the corresponding ease with which unscrupulous defendants might avoid a civil or criminal liability which reason declared to exist, that the Shari'a courts proved an unsatisfactory organ for the administration of certain spheres of the law.[16]

It is almost universally agreed that to solve disputes over truth questions in society, factual evidence—not mere sincerity—must carry the day. In the words of the pre-Christian Roman dramatist Plautus,

> One eyewitness is worth more than ten purveyors of
>   hearsay;
> Those who only hear about things say what they've
>   heard,
> but those who see know the score![17]

The Christian faith, alone among the religious claims of history, is able to stand in the dock and be vindicated evidentially.[18] For only Christianity rests its case on the divine life, sacrificial death, and miraculous resurrection of the Incarnate God—events witnessed to by those who had direct contact with them and who in consequence "knew the score" (Acts 1:1-3; 2 Peter 1:16-18).

Literary Apologetics

The ongoing, self-perpetuating juggernaut of scientific technology has alienated many in our society from the ideals of scientific objectivity. Objectivity seems for them (irrationally, but after all, they are trying to run from rationality!) the source of pollution, depersonalization and a culture that will spend billions on a moon shot and quibble about appropriations to clean up the ghetto. Young people in particular drop out and freak out as a protest against such hyper-objectifying of life and its values. They seek another kind of answer—an answer perhaps hidden in the subjective depths of their own souls.

But what key will unlock this hidden treasure? Some go the whole experiential route: sex, drugs, masochism, satanic occultism. Others seek salvation in the inward-focused Eastern religions. But the path of drugs and the occult is strewn with the wrecked lives of those who have given themselves to these false gods.[19] And, as Arthur Koestler has so definitively shown in the account of his frustrating pilgrimage in search of Eastern wisdom, the ambiguities of the Tantristic religions open them to the most immoral, destructive and demonic possibilities.[20]

Might literary creativity offer a way through this labyrinth? Can literature perhaps succeed where these deceptive paths have failed?

"A drainless shower/Of light is poesy: 'tis the supreme of power," declared Keats in *Sleep and Poetry*. As a dream while asleep can touch the depths of our being, could not the literature of wakefulness shower with light and supreme power the landscape of religious concern and provide the subjective attestation of Christian truth for which men long?

Suppose that the fallen race had kept a primordial realization of its separation from God through sinful self-centeredness and of its specific need for redemption through the divine-human conquest of the evil powers arrayed against it. Suppose within each human heart this realization were etched beyond effacement. The sinner would of course repress this knowledge, for his sin would be too painful to bear and his egotism would not want to face redemption apart from his own works-righteousness. Though "God's invisible qualities . . . have been clearly seen," so that men are "without excuse, . . . their thinking became futile and their foolish hearts were darkened" (Romans 1:20-21). This darkening of the heart would quite naturally take the form of a repression of the natural knowledge of God's redemptive plan to the subconscious level, where it would be ignored consciously; but its eradication from the psyche could never occur.

Under these circumstances, redemptive knowledge would surface not in a direct fashion but by way of symbolic patterns—visible not only to the sensitive psychoanalyst, but also to the folklorist whose material "bubbles up" collectively from the subconscious of the race. Literature in this special sense could therefore reflect the Christian story in an objective sense and trigger conscious acceptance of it. Is this perhaps the background of Paul's literary appeal on the Areopagus: "As some of your own poets have said, 'We are his offspring' " (Acts 17:28)?

Jungian analytical psychotherapy has indeed identified such redemptive "archetypes," or fundamental and universal symbolic patterns, which appear equally in the physical liturgies of ancient alchemists and in the dreams of contemporary business men. Religious phenomenologists—the greatest being Mircea Eliade—have discovered these motifs in the most widely diversified primitive and sophisticated religions. Concludes Eliade after examining one of the most basic archetypal themes:

At the "beginning" as well as at the "end" of the religious history of Man, we find the same yearning for Paradise. If we take into account the fact that the "yearning for Paradise" is equally discernible in the general religious attitude of early man we have the right to assume that the mystical memory of a blessedness without history haunts man from the moment he becomes aware of his situation in the cosmos.[21]

Thus does the great universal literary tradition of Utopia point back, with inexpressible longings, to the Garden. And thus consciously-produced modern literary endeavors can appeal to a yearning in every human heart. One thinks of James Hilton's *Lost Horizon*—or the captivating Lerner-Loewe musical, *Brigadoon*. In that Edenic town, the people are redemptively protected from witches when they sleep by a vicarious act of their pastor; as they sleep, one hundred years wondrously pass.

> Tommy: But at night when you go to sleep; what's it like?
>
> Mr. Lundie: Well, for me, 'tis like being carried on shadowy arms to some far-off cloud an there I float till mornin'. An yet, sometimes I think I hear strange voices.
>
> Tommy: Voices?
>
> Mr. Lundie: Aye. They say no words I can remember. But they're voices filled with a fearful longin'; and often they seem to be callin' me back. I've pondered it when I'm awake; and I think—I have a feelin' I'm hearin' the outside world. There must be lots of folk out there who'd like a Brigadoon.[22]

Mythology and folktale are especially pregnant with archetypal significance. In an important study on "Recurrent Themes in Myths and Mythmaking," Kluckhohn provides rigorous attestation of anthropologist Levi-Strauss's contention that there is an "astounding similarity between myths collected in widely different regions" of the world.[23] Kluckhohn and Moench used Murdock's "world ethnographic sample"[24] to analyze recurrent mythical themes in fifty cultures, "distributed about evenly among Murdock's six major regions" (Circum-Mediterranean, Negro Africa, East Eurasia, Insular Pacific, North America, South America). Two of the most prominent recurrent themes are the Flood ("a universal or near-universal theme in mythology" which "hardly seems plausible to attribute to Jewish-Christian sources")[25] and the "Slaying of Monsters": "This theme appears in thirty-seven of our fifty cultures, and here the distribution approaches equality save for a slightly greater frequency in North America and the Insular Pacific. . . . In Bantu Africa (and beyond) a hero is born to a woman who survives after a monster has eaten her spouse (and everyone else). The son immediately turns into a man, slays a monster or monsters, restores his people."[26]

Does not this "slaying of a monster" have a familiar ring to it (our pun on Tolkien's One Ring is not unintentional!)? Gustaf Aulén has demonstrated the centrality of the *Christus Victor* motif to the entire New Testament message: Jesus, born of a woman, is in fact the Divine Christ who conquers the Evil Power that has brought the race into bondage, and thereby restores mankind.[27] From such universal—and therefore impressively objective—archetypal motifs can the Christian literary apologist draw his themes and patterns, thereby creating stories that, if sensitively and artistically executed, are sure to strike to the deep reaches of man's being and point him toward the Christ who fulfilled the myths and legends of the world. This, to be sure, is precisely what such contemporary Christian writers as C.S. Lewis (the Narnian Chronicles) and J.R.R. Tolkien (*The Lord of the Rings*) have done—with tremendous positive impact for the cause of Christ.[28]

Let us, then, conclude with Lewis' confessions of mythopoeic faith—the first, from his spiritual autobiography,

Surprised by Joy, in a passage perceptively anthologized by Edmund Fuller; the second from his seminal essay, "Myth Became Fact":

I was by now too experienced in literary criticism to regard the Gospels as myths. They had not the mythical taste. And yet the very matter which they set down in their artless, historical fashion—those narrow, unattractive Jews, too blind to the mythical wealth of the Pagan world around them—was precisely the matter of the great myths. If ever a myth had become fact, had been incarnated, it would be just like this. Myths were like it in one way. Histories were like it in another. But nothing was simply like it. And no person was like the Person it depicted; as real, as recognizable, through all that depth of time, as Plato's Socrates or Boswell's Johnson (ten times more so than Eckermann's Goethe or Lockhart's Scott), yet also numinous, lit by a light from beyond the world, a god. But if a god—we are no longer polytheists—then not a god, but God. Here and here only in all time the myth must become a fact; the Word, flesh; God, Man. This is not "a religion," nor "a philosophy." It is the summing up and actuality of them all.[29]

We must not be ashamed of the mythical radiance resting on our theology. We must not be nervous about "parallels" and "Pagan Christs": they *ought* to be there—it would be a stumbling block if they weren't. We must not, in false spirituality, withhold our imaginative welcome. If God chooses to be mythopoeic—and is not the sky itself a myth?—shall we refuse to be *mythopatic?* For this is the marriage of heaven and earth: Perfect Myth and Perfect Fact: claiming not only our love and our obedience, but also our wonder and delight, addressed to the savage, the child and the poet in each one of us no less than to the moralist, the scholar and the philosopher.[30]

Endnotes

Citations related to the juridicial section of the paper (endnotes 1-18 follow the Harvard Law Review *style.*

[1]In personal conversation with the essayist.

[2]*Fed. R. Evid.* 102; on the new *Rules* in general, see *ALI-ABA Federal Rules of Evidence Resource Materials, with October 1975 Supplement* (1975).

[3]S.E. Toulmin, *The Uses of Argument* (1958); cf. J.W. Montgomery, *The Law Above the Law* 84-90 (1975).

[4]*Fed. R. Evid.* 401. This definition of relevant evidence derives from Professor Thayer's classic *Preliminary Treatise on Evidence* (1898).

[5]*Fed. R. Evid.* 201. Indeed, statutes undertaking to establish conclusive presumptions with respect to material facts are held unconstitutional—on the ground that they deprive the accused of due process of law (Caroline Products Co. v. McLaughlin, 365 IL 62).

[6]Cf. V.C. Ball, "The Moment of Truth: Probability Theory and Standards of Proof," in *Essays on Procedure and Evidence* 84-107 (T.G. Roady and R.N. Covington, ed., 1961).

[7]*Fed. R. Evid.* 404.

[8]H.P. Chandler and S.D. Hirschl, "Evidence," 11 *American Law and Procedure* 21 (1910, rev. ed. 1955).

[9]Professor Greenleaf makes this important point in his *Testimony of the Evangelists*, now reprinted in J.W. Montgomery, *The Law Above the Law* 91-140, 149-63 (1975). On the historical soundness of the New Testament writings, see F.F. Bruce, *The New Testament Documents: Are They Reliable?* (5th ed. 1960), and cf. J.A.T. Robinson, *Redating the New Testament* (1977).

[10]M. Shain, Res Ipsa Loquitur, *Presumptions and Burden of Proof* (1945).

[11]D. Daube, *Roman Law: Linguistic, Social and Philosophical Aspects* 180 (1969).

[12]J.W. Montgomery, *History and Christianity* (1965).

[13]M. Gluckman, *The Judicial Process Among the Barotse of Northern Rhodesia* 82 (1955).

[14]*The Laws of the Ancient Persians* pt. 1, 12, 26-27 (S.J. Bulsara ed. 1937).

[15]Lord Mackenzie, *Studies in Roman Law, with Comparative Views of the Laws of France, England, and Scotland* 382 (7th ed. J. Kirkpatrick 1911). Cf. H.F. Jolowicz, *Roman Foundations of Modern Law* 102 (1957).

[16]N.J. Coulson, "Islamic Law," in *An Introduction to Legal Systems* 67-68 (J.D.M. Derrett, ed., 1968). For an expanded treatment of the same subject, see N.J. Coulson, *A History of Islamic Law* 124-27 (1964).

[17]Plautus, *Truculentus* Act ii, sc. 6, 11. 8-9 (our translation).

[18]Cf. C.S. Lewis, *God in the Dock* (W. Hooper, ed., 1970). Also: J.W. Montgomery, *Law and Gospel* (1978), *Human Rights and Human Dignity* (1986), *Evidence for Faith* (1991), *Law and Morality* (1994).

[19]Montgomery, *Principalities and Powers: The World of the Occult* (Minneapolis, MN: Bethany Fellowship, 1973), especially 121-50 ("The Land of Mordor") and 188-90 ("The Gospel according to LSD").

[20]Arthur Koestler, *The Lotus and the Robot* (New York: Macmillan, 1961), especially 236-41, 268-75.

[21]Mircea Eliade, "The Yearning for Paradise in Primitive Tradition," in *Myth and Mythmaking*, Henry A. Murray, ed. (New York: George Braziller, 1960), 73.

[22]Alan Jay Lerner, *Brigadoon* (New York: Coward-McCann, 1947), 88-89. This musical first opened in the Ziegfeld Theatre in New York City in March 1947—soon after the end of World War II, when America's utopian longings were revivified.

[23]Claude Levi-Strauss, "The Structural Study of Myth," *Journal of American Folklore*, 68 (1955): 428-45; cf. the same author's "Structure et dialectique" in the Festschrift for Roman Jakobson, ed. Morris Halle (The Hague: Mouton,

1957), 289-94.

[24]G.P. Murdock, "World Ethnographic Sample," *American Anthropologist*, 59 (1957): 664-88.

[25]Cf. Montgomery, *The Quest for Noah's Ark* (Minneapolis, MN: Bethany Fellowship, 1972), *passim*.

[26]Clyde Kluckhohn, "Recurrent Themes in Myths and Mythmaking," in *Myth and Mythmaking*, 51.

[27]Gustaf Aulén, *Christus Victor*, trans. A. G. Hebert (New York: Macmillan, 1956); cf. my "Short Critique of Gustaf Aulen's *Christus Victor*," printed as an appendix in my *Chytraeus on Sacrifice* (St. Louis, MO: Concordia, 1962).

[28]See Montgomery, *Myth, Allegory and Gospel* (Minneapolis, MN: Bethany Fellowship, 1974), *passim*.

[29]Edmund Fuller, ed., *Affirmations of God and Man* (New York: Association Press, 1967), 37.

[30]C.S. Lewis, "Myth Became Fact," in his *God in the Dock*, 67. Cf. the chapter on myth in Lewis's *An Experiment in Criticism* (Cambridge, England: Cambridge University Press, 1961), 40-49.

Historicity As Apologetic:
The Cutting Edge

Michael A. Harbin

A number of years ago, I listened as a respected evangelical biblicist was criticized for "not being on the cutting edge of theology." As I analyzed the diagnosis and the particular issues which generated it, I came to realize that the critic, who styled himself an evangelical scholar, was denigrating the fact that his colleague was more involved in demonstrating the validity of biblical claims than engaging in current hot-button theological debates.

Since that time I have tried to evaluate what it means to be on the cutting edge of theology. I have come to the conclusion that apologetics should be given the honor of that position since it not only involves the defense of the faith, but validates that on which Christians stake both life and eternity. Within apologetics, I would suggest that historicity be our primary focus, as I will develop below.

First, we should evaluate the concept of the "cutting edge." It is quite fashionable to describe some leader in a particular field as being "on the cutting edge." This figure is used to designate pioneers in a number of academic disciplines. As an image of one who leads in his or her field, this designation is generally appropriate. However, what is not clear (and seldom addressed) is whether these new paradigms truly advance or are illusory.

When we come to the cutting edge of theology, the concept is especially nebulous and controversial. In essence, the phrase describes thinking which anticipates general trends of theological discussion and debate. As such, the phrase tends to reflect the most recent theological fad, which usually springs from radical presuppositions regarding the Bible and its claims. If this is true, then our "cutting edge" is actually that which hacks and tears away. The image that comes to mind is a machete. As an evangelical I would like to think that what is being hacked and torn away is the undergrowth and weeds—the extraneous issues which obscure the way of true progress. Given the presuppositions of much of today's biblical studies and the history of theological trends, it is more likely that what is being torn away is really what we are trying to cultivate, i.e., the body of data which constitutes historic Christianity. Thus, a person desiring to be on the "cutting edge of theology" may well be failing to discern where his work is leading.

However, machetes are not the only cutting edges we encounter. Another analogy is that of a scalpel used by a skilled surgeon to cut away cancerous growths. The assumption here, naturally, is that the growth which is being cut away is detrimental to the body, and not a natural growth of the body.

Of course, one of the big questions we face is, how do we verify that we are using a scalpel and not a machete? Or that the material we are attacking is a cancerous growth and not a natural growth of the Christian faith? Or, to put the question another way, as we think of the "cutting edge of theology," how do we ensure that we do not abdicate real issues for the trumpery of academic acceptability?

With this question in mind, we must ask, what are the real issues of Christianity? Clearly, one of the most critical, as evidenced by the theme of this book, would be that of apologetics—the defense of the faith.

There are several views on the best way to defend our faith, as evidenced by a casual survey of any apologetics text as well as the presentations at this conference. Probably the most notable are philosophical and historical. The dominant approach today, however, seems to be philosophical, i.e., first inductively demonstrate the existence of God (or begin with God as a stated assumption) and then deduce Christianity. Francis Schaeffer used this approach in his work in Switzerland and has affected many.[1] Schaeffer and others were strongly influenced by Cornelius Van Til, who appealed to Scripture as a "self-attesting unit," i.e., a book which authenticates itself.[2] More recently, Tony Campolo has argued for a system which appeals to reason while virtually ignoring the historical evidence.[3] Some systematic apologists take a similar approach, although they do note a place for historicity.[4]

In some ways, this philosophical approach may be an accommodation to modern radical theology.[5] Many issues being debated today reflect distinctions of interpretation which are in reality based on extremely disparate presuppositions. If evangelical theology appropriates these presuppositions, its "cutting edge" (or even its intellectual vitality) could be dictated by outsiders. More than this, the very foundational issues are often clouded, as is demonstrated in a very recent article by C. Stephen Evans. "The new Jesus" explored by the Jesus Seminar and other recent attacks on historic Christianity permit two sources of knowledge about Jesus (i.e., the basis of our faith). Evans states:

> One story, traditionally emphasized by the Roman Catholic church, . . . stresses that the knowledge the ordinary person needs to have about Jesus is grounded in the testimony of the church. The other story, which one might call the Reformed story . . . lays great stress on what is termed "the inner testimony of the Holy Spirit."[6]

In other words, the source and defense of our faith is either the church or a subjective feeling.

I would suggest, however, that the primary issue we should be addressing is the historicity of the resurrection event. There are three key reasons I propose this. First, it is the testimony of comparative religion. Second, it is the testimony of the apostolic church. Third, it is the foundation for Christian theology and doctrine.

Historicity and Comparative Religion

First, let us consider the testimony of comparative religion. When I began research on my history of religion, *To Serve Other Gods*,[7] two startling points caught my attention. The first was the significance of the sixth century B.C. During this one century, approximately 800 years after the founding of Judaism, the entire scope of world religion was reshaped. Gautama the Buddha (c. 563-c. 483 B.C.) appeared in the Ganges River region of India.[8] Attempting to reform Brahmanism he rather produced Buddhism.[9] Zoroaster (c. 618-c. 541 B.C.) appeared in what is modern Uzbekistan. He expounded a dualistic philosophy which became Zoroastrianism.[10] In China, two other contemporaries also advocated religious reform. Confucius (c. 551-c. 479 B.C.) advocated a return to the worship of the ancestor spirits in order to produce a stable society.[11] This became the philosophical religion Confucianism. Lao Tzu (c. 604-c. 517 B.C.) developed the concepts of Taoism.[12] At the same time in India, composition of the Upanishads began, marking the transition from Brahmanism to Classical Hinduism.[13] Likewise, in Greece, the foundations of Greek philosophy were laid.[14] During this one century, virtually all the major world religions were founded. The most notable exceptions are Judaism, Christianity and Islam. Clearly, Judaism and Christianity share a common source and thread. A careful study of Islam, however, suggests that it too is of this strain. Apparently Mohammed attempted to reconcile Judaism and Christianity while rejecting both God's special relationship with the Jews and the Messiahship of Jesus.[15]

How do we bring this all together? I suggest in *To Serve Other Gods*, that the timing of this religious-philosophical proliferation of the sixth century B.C. is not accidental but reflects an effort on Satan's part to produce counterfeits during the time the nation of Israel was in exile in Babylon.[16]

While important, this proliferation is secondary to another point which I noted in my research. Studying the writings of these various religious leaders and their followers, I discovered a very sharp contrast in the authority foundations. Most religions, including all those founded in the sixth century B.C., base their authority on the teachings of their founder. The historicity of the founding events is secondary at best. In some cases the actual existence of the founder can be and has been questioned without detriment to the religion.

This is clearly the case for Buddhism. For example, Phra Khantipalo states, "Lord Buddha taught methods which one might apply to one's own life and speedily come to see the benefits of their practice here and now."[17] Khantipalo's explanation of Buddhism shows clearly that it is perceived as a body of teaching which anyone may adapt without reference to its founder. Even biographies of Gautama suggest that he perceived this teaching to be the real issue, and his personal life of no consequence.[18]

This is also true of Confucianism. Confucianism has often been touted as a philosophical system, rather than a religion. However, Confucian thought began with a premise of ancestor worship. The people venerated their deceased ancestors who were deemed to have joined the behind-the-scenes spiritual hierarchy which was the true world government according to Chinese thought. According to this perspective, after his death, Confucius joined this group of ancestors and thus became a focus of worship.[19] Still, the real value of the person Confucius has been as a teacher. James R. Ware describes him as "The First Teacher, The Sagest of the Sage."[20]

The same is true of his contemporary, Lao Tzu. Kaltenmark observes that the debate about whether Lao Tzu actually existed is totally irrelevant. The real point of discussion is the work attributed to him, *Tao Te Ching*, a collection of mystic poetry which teaches right living.[21]

To this group we may also add Islam. While Islam dates its founding on the *Hijara*, Mohammed's flight from Mecca to Medina where he was welcomed as the Messiah anticipated by the Jews,[22] the religious foundation is clearly the *Qur'an*. The very name means either "the lecture" or "the reading." As Muhammad M. Pickthall states in his introduction to the edition of the *Qur'an* distributed by the World Muslim League,

> The words which came to him when in a state of trance are held sacred by the Muslims and are never confounded with those which he uttered when no physical change was apparent in him. The former are the Sacred Book.[23]

In contrast, Judaism and Christianity both base their existence and authority on historical events, the Exodus and the Resurrection, respectively. This brings us to our second point, i.e., that historicity is the testimony of the apostolic church. I place this point second only because of the sharp authority base distinctions between the Judeo-Christian heritage and other world religions.[24] As we look at the situation, however, we need to begin with Judaism to clearly understand the unity and developmental relationship between it and Christianity.

Historicity and Judaism

Judaism is clearly based on the Exodus. This event incorporates the series of plagues on Egypt, the Passover and the actual Exodus. This is demonstrated by the references to the Exodus event throughout the Old Testament.[25] Historically, all national events flow from it. More than this, it became the national authority base, that is, all law was predicated on the reality of this event.

When the newly evacuated masses of Israel were camped at Mt. Sinai preparing to become organized into a nation, the table of commandments in the book of Exodus was both prefaced by and based on the declaration, "I am the LORD your God who brought you out of the land of Egypt, out of the house of slavery" (20:2, NASB). While the statement is not related grammatically to the following injunctions or "words" we call the Ten Commandments by any of the expected Hebrew particles, the stark disjunction virtually demands a cause and effect relationship, i.e., "because I brought you out of Egypt, you will have no other gods before me." This is especially true as we have begun to understand the literary genre of both Exodus and Deuteronomy as developing a covenant between God and the nation.[26]

These passages clearly show that this historical incident was the authoritative foundation for the relationship God was establishing with Israel.[27] Moreover, by bringing the nation out of Egypt, God demonstrated that the Exodus was more than just a historical incident: He, Yahweh, was the Deity who intervened in space-time history to affect the flow of events. Further, because of His intervention, God expected certain actions to be performed by the people whom He had redeemed. These actions are set forth not only in the Ten Commandments, but also in the following more specific stipulations in Exodus, Leviticus, Numbers and Deuteronomy.

Thus, the historical Exodus became the foundation for God's future expectations of the nation. The phrase, "I am the LORD your God who brought you out of the land of Egypt," appears in this sense approximately seventy-five times in the Old Testament, almost evenly divided between the Pentateuch and the rest of the Old Testament. Additionally, there are approximately sixty further references to the Exodus event in both the Old Testament and the New

141

Testament.[28] These expectations included issues of national destiny (the most significant of which was the Messiah), social-economic functions, judicial procedures and standards, and of course the matter of worship, which ultimately developed into modern Judaism.[29] The Exodus event also became the authoritative foundation for God's judgment on the nation when it failed to live up to the standards He presented. For example, Leviticus 11:45 concludes a series of commandments on clean and unclean foods with the following declaration: "For I am the LORD, who brought you up from the land of Egypt, to be your God; thus you shall be holy for I am holy" (NASB).[30] This is a regular pattern: the declaration of an expected action coupled with a variation of the phrase "for I am the LORD who brought you up from the land of Egypt to be your God." Its frequency demonstrates that this event is the authority base for God's relationship to Israel.

This is evident also in prophetic literature, which tends to follow a motif of anticipated future judgment interspersed with anticipated future blessing, both designed to change actions.[31] Both aspects of the motif find their focus in a person who came to be called the Messiah.[32] Yet it is at this exact point that the prophets stressed the issue of the Exodus. For example, in the Messianic prophecy of Isaiah 11:11, God declares that this future event will be an event comparable to the Exodus (". . . the Lord will again recover the second time with His hand the remnant of His people," NASB).[33]

The same Exodus declaration is used in the New Testament at least six times. We note that Paul uses it as part of his demonstration that Jesus was the Messiah in his proclamation of the gospel to the Jews in the synagogue in Antioch of Pisidia (Acts 13:17).[34] Paul's argument here apparently demonstrates the methodology of the early church. The logic of his argument runs like this: God demonstrated His power and authority through Moses and the events of the Exodus. However, the people disobeyed God.

After recounting the failure of the judges and the kings, Paul asserts that Jesus is the heir of David and the fulfillment of the prophets "which are read every Sabbath" (13:27-29, NASB). The position of Jesus as Heir and Messiah was demonstrated by His resurrection, attested by eyewitnesses, i.e., a historical event (13:30-31).

Historicity and Apostolic Christianity

Judaism parted from Christianity on this very issue. Christianity dates its foundation to the resurrection of Jesus Christ. Of course, while we correctly view these two as separate religions, in reality the issue that divides the two is the question of the second event, i.e., was Jesus resurrected from the dead? If He was, does this not demonstrate Him to be the Messiah the Jews looked for? This example suggests that the writers in the New Testament do not refer frequently to the Exodus event because their greater concern is with the more telling Resurrection event. In the New Testament the Exodus event is used merely to verify the authority of the writers who prophetically point to the Messiah. This is the Messiah whom the apostles and others have observed as having risen.

The driving issue of the Gospels is, "Who was Jesus?"[35] As presented there, He claimed to be the Messiah. This Old Testament prophetic term reflected a coming individual who would fulfill certain eschatological expectations and provide a national restoration and salvation.

Whereas the Exodus validated God's redemption of the nation from Egypt, the Resurrection validated God's salvation not only of the nation but of all people. While adhering to the historicity of the earlier event, clearly the apostles viewed the resurrection of Jesus as the historical foundation on which they operated. This explains the paucity of references to the Exodus event, as evident in Peter's sermon in Acts 2, especially in verses 24 and 32. Immediately after the outpouring of the Holy Spirit on Pentecost,

Peter cites the Joel text as one that anticipated this event (2:17-21). He then immediately switches to the person of Jesus and declares His resurrection (2:24). Given the circumstances of His death and burial, it is likely that many rumors about what had happened to Jesus circulated during the previous seven weeks; but Peter contextualizes these rumors by tying the event to Old Testament anticipation. He hammers this point home by citing Psalm 16 and reiterating the fact of the Resurrection and the testimony that he and all those with him[36] were witnesses. The fact of the Resurrection was the foundation of his authority to declare the way of salvation.

This is the pattern which prevails throughout Acts. Peter's second sermon begins with the healing of a lame man (Acts 3:1 ff). When the crowd gathers, Peter points to the greater event, that of the Resurrection, to which he and those with him were witnesses.

On at least ten occasions in the book of Acts the Resurrection is presented by the apostles and early disciples as a historical fact.[37] More than this, as in the case of the Exodus and God's expectations for the nation, the Resurrection is presented as the foundation of this apostolic authority as well as the authority of the message they preach, including its implications for lifestyle.

What we normally call historical facts are actually recorded eyewitness accounts.[38] This is an expansion of a basic understanding of historical research and a correction of a common misconception: e.g., an empty tomb is not a historical fact, but a physical, corroborating datum (or to use the legal term, evidence).[39] Further, I have attempted to demonstrate that the validity of historical data is based on a foundation as secure as scientific data.[40]

The key analogy I use is the assassination of John F. Kennedy. Virtually no one disputes that Kennedy was shot. Some might question (and have) whether he is really dead. The real controversy, however, lies in the issue of who was involved in the assassination and whether there was a cover-up. Is the assassination of John F. Kennedy accepted as a historical fact? I would submit that it is. The question is, why would we label the shooting of John F. Kennedy a historical fact? It is primarily because of eyewitness accounts, both of the shooting and the dead body.[41] Do some of these eyewitness accounts conflict in details? Yes they do. Is it possible that there was some attempt at a cover-up? Yes, it is possible. How, then, do we determine what really happened?

This is the process of historical-legal research. A competent investigator procures as much data as possible and postulates a coherent hypothesis regarding the scenario. Other competent investigators then evaluate the hypothesis. But the issue always returns to the question: What is the evidence? In the case of unique events occurring in space-time history, the primary answer is always eyewitness accounts.[42]

This is very similar to the methods of science, especially the field sciences.[43] The scientist or observer collects data. But science is far more than collecting data. The observer must also explain the *why* of the data. This is the process of logical inference based on the observations of credible observers or eyewitness accounts.[44] Like the scientist, the historian makes logical inferences based on observations of credible observers or eyewitness accounts.

The critical point is this: The eyewitness accounts are the data collected and thus equivalent to scientific data. As such, they may also be reviewed by numerous scholars to evaluate the validity of the conclusions reached by others. Thus, the two fields are much closer in both process and validity than is often supposed.

Given the claims of the biblical documents, greater emphasis from a scholarly perspective must be given to evaluating the nature of the historical events. Several recent works have begun this approach. I note the works of Craig Blomberg,[45] Paul Barnett,[46] V. Philips Long[47] and William Lane Craig[48] as positive steps. Over the years, a number of writers besides these have evaluated the claims of Jesus from a historical perspective, including Josh McDowell, John Warwick Montgomery and J.N.D. Anderson, all of whom have had a profound influence in my own studies.

Still, there is much work to be done. In terms of apologetics, we need to enhance our understanding of what historicity means in terms of both Old and New Testament documents.[49] As we realize that the eyewitness accounts that have been preserved over the centuries are not only our primary evidence, but valid historical evidence, we need to adjust our argumentation accordingly. I will address this more fully momentarily.

Historicity and Theology

Historicity not only affects apologetics, but our entire system of theology. This brings us to our third point: historicity is the foundation of Christian theology and doctrine.

As already mentioned, on at least ten occasions in the book of Acts the resurrection is set forth as the authority of the apostles. Interestingly, in eight of those references, God is the subject of the action—"God raised Him from the dead."[50] This statement transcends the observation of the fact of the resurrection and begins to develop implications and consequences.

Especially significant is Acts 17:31, where Paul addresses the philosophers of Athens. He argues that the Resurrection is God's proof that He is going to judge the world in righteousness through Jesus. This begins the process of using the Resurrection to validate logical conclusions based on the teachings of Jesus.

The Resurrection as authority is also evident in other New Testament writings. The prime example is the well-known passage in First Corinthians 15 where Paul demonstrates the historicity of the Resurrection by citing a number of witnesses.[51] After this litany of witnesses, he hastens on to his point which is a logical deduction. If Jesus has been resurrected, then we can be assured of a yet future resurrection, as well as a future reign of Jesus and judgment of all those who oppose God (1 Corinthians 15:20-28).

Developing and validating logical conclusions is the historical process which produced church doctrine and theology. For example, Berkhof cites Irenaeus as having "a superior Christology" because he "takes as his real starting-point the historically revealed Son of God."[52]

The beginning premise of theology is, as Berkhof states, that "[r]eligious doctrines are found in Scriptures, though not in finished forms. . . ."[53] The finished form is the result of a developmental process, usually in terms of a controversy, i.e., when individuals or groups begin teaching conclusions denied by the eyewitnesses or their successors.

This process began early in the history of the church. Paul warned the Galatians, "But even though we, or an angel from heaven, should preach to you a gospel contrary to that which we have preached to you, let him be accursed" (Galatians 1:8, NASB).

Even as we look at issues today there is a strong correlation between one's view on the historicity of these key events and the theological viewpoints one holds. This is evident in terms of soteriology. One who does not hold to the historicity of the Resurrection cannot subscribe to exclusivist claims of salvation through the central figure of the Resurrection. In contrast, one who accepts the historicity of the Resurrection is almost forced to accept that claim.[54] Similarly, other theological issues are evaluated on the basis of these basic conclusions and their logical extensions.[55]

As touched on above, and developed more fully elsewhere,[56] this historic intervention of God into space-time history, evident primarily in the Exodus and the Resurrection, is the authoritative foundation for biblical revelation. That it was designed to be so is demonstrated by the basic criteria of evaluating a prophet: a true prophet is one who demonstrates his ability to give revelation from God by means of supernormal historical manifestations[57] and a coherence with previously validated revelation.[58]

As we consider this process, we are brought face to face with a critical issue. Geivett argues that our position on the nature of Jesus (the Jesus question) derives from our beliefs in God (the God question).[59] However, he also admits that our concept of God derives from our conceptual framework, which is largely presuppositional.[60] As such, one would never be able to use logic to convince a naturalistic atheist that Jesus rose from the grave. McKnight notes, however, "Jesus saw his miraculous cures and marvelous acts as evidence that he, Jesus of Galilee, was bringing the kingdom of God to bear on the people who responded to his message and mission."[61]

In terms of apologetics, I would suggest that the issues are reversed: the Jesus question should precede the God question. The processes of both scientific and historical-legal proof begin from the known and work to the unknown. That indeed is the premise of traditional apologetics, but usually that process is an argument of inference from the physical universe (or some aspect of it) to God, which then proceeds deductively to the truth of Christianity.[62] If we demonstrate that the presentation of Jesus is indeed historical, then logically we need to develop a concept that explains the data at hand, including most notably the various supernormal manifestations up to and including the Resurrection.[63]

Ideally, that does not necessarily assume an acceptance of the reality of these supernormal manifestations. It does require the willingness to include their possibility as an option to be evaluated, which theoretically should be the scholarly attitude.[64]

Unfortunately, many approach the data with certain predispositions which preclude an objective evaluation. That brings us to a hurdle that we must keep in mind in our approach to the entire issue of apologetics: the Bible testifies to the reality of spiritual warfare, and the obstacles to a reasoned apologetic far exceed objective evaluation and logical arguments. Dealing with those obstacles is far beyond the scope of my paper, however.

The Future of Historicity in Apologetics

I raise one final question in conclusion: "Where do we go from here?" If historicity is the cutting edge, where should we focus our attention? In terms of further work, may I suggest the following possible areas of exploration.

First, as scholars, we need to focus on validating historicity. As already mentioned, several others are already working in this direction, and if I might say so, are truly on the cutting edge. There is still much to do. There are many details that need to be nailed down, issues which, while perhaps on the periphery, would help clarify the picture. For example, earlier this year Philip Comfort and Carsten Thiede both published articles on three New Testament manuscripts, p4, p64, and p67. Both have concluded that p64 and p67 are portions of Matthew from the same codex and, based on paleography, argue for a first-century date.[65] If valid, of course, this has tremendous implications for New Testament studies. Less noticed has been the observation both have made that p4 seems to be a portion of Luke written by the same scribe, although probably not the same codex. Both of these issues affect historicity.

As we continue to probe this issue we need to challenge critical scholars who deny historicity as a matter of course. I recognize that this is really much easier to state than to carry out, for, to be honest, it is evident that critical scholars do not appear to read, let alone interact with, those who do not share their basic assumptions. Craig expresses it well when he comments on Crossan's work:

> You can imagine my sense of disappointment when, consulting Crossan's works, I found that he had no

particular evidence, much less compelling evidence, for his allegation; rather it was just his hunch as to what happened to the body of Jesus.[66]

Second, as theologians, we need to continue the process of developing systematically the logical conclusions of the historical data. We cannot rely on tradition, but must continually evaluate the edifices we have built in terms of theological systems. I do not mean that we must keep reinventing the wheel regarding theological concepts such as the Deity of Christ, but we cannot assume that the theological systems of the reformers are sacrosanct.[67] The dispensational study group of this conference seems to be an area where this is, or should be, happening.

Third, as academicians, we need to provide input into other fields, especially with respect to evaluating their assumptions. For example, it is not enough to accept "the conclusions of science," when these conclusions are solely a result of naturalistic presuppositions. We need to challenge the issue of how science reaches those conclusions. We especially need to join the debate of historicity and the process of doing history, for if our claim of historicity is correct, then the events recorded in both Testaments that took place in the Middle East from approximately two to four thousand years ago fit into an overall fabric of space-time history, not as a patch, but as an integral part of the structure.

Endnotes

[1] Edith Schaeffer, *L'Abri*, 2nd ed. (Wheaton, IL: Tyndale, 1970), 13-14, 26-28. Cf. Francis Schaeffer, *The God Who Is There* (Downers Grove, IL: InterVarsity, 1968), 88-104.

[2] Cornelius Van Til, *A Christian Theory of Knowledge* (Nutley, NJ: Presbyterian and Reformed Publishing, 1977), 30.

[3] Tony Campolo, *A Reasonable Faith* (Waco, TX: Word Books, 1983).

[4]E.g., Peter Kreeft and Ronald K. Tacelli, *Handbook of Christian Apologetics* (Downers Grove, IL: InterVarsity, 1994) relegate the historical foundation to chapters 8 and 9 in their development as they primarily appeal to reason. Likewise, J.P. Moreland, *Scaling the Secular City: A Defense of Christianity* (Grand Rapids, MI: Baker, 1987) waits until chapters 5 and 6 to explore the issue of historicity, although he then gives an extensive development.

[5]In this light, one of the tension points I observed as I began looking at the issue in light of this conference was the intended audience of our apologetics. The theme of the meeting is "Defending the Faith in a Non-Christian World." This leads me to evaluate the issue in terms of attacks from proponents of other religions. However, much of the work done in this field recently seems addressed to a person within the Judeo-Christian tradition who denies the traditional or orthodox perspectives on Jesus Christ. To be very blunt, although we are careful not to say so in our scholarly circles, we are addressing heretics. The extreme differences between these two groups may necessitate different apologetic approaches, but both should be based on historicity.

[6]C. Stephen Evans, "Can the New Jesus Save Us?" (*Books and Culture: A Christian Review* 1:2 [November/December 1995]), 7.

[7]Michael A. Harbin, *To Serve Other Gods: An Evangelical History of Religion* (Lanham, MD: University Press of America, 1994).

[8]H.W. Schumann, *The Historical Buddha* (London: Arkana, 1989), 10-13.

[9]Gautama was just one of several reformers of the same period, although his movement was the most profound. Vardhamana was another who founded the movement known today as the Jains. Cf. Harbin, 135, n. 3.

[10]Harbin, 154, n. 2.

[11]D. Howard Smith, *Confucius* (New York: Charles Scribner's Sons, 1973), 62-63.

[12]Max Kaltenmark, *Lao Tzu and Taoism* (Stanford, CA: Stanford University Press, 1969), 13-15.

[13]Exact dates for their composition is uncertain, but most scholars place it during the sixth century B.C. Cf. Kenneth W. Morgan, ed., *The Religion of the Hindus: Interpreted by Hindus* (New York: The Ronald Press, 1953), 30-32.

[14]Gordon H. Clark, *Thales to Dewey: A History of Philosophy* (Grand Rapids, MI: Baker, reprint 1980), 4, dates the founding of Greek philosophy to the prediction of a solar eclipse in May of 585. The noted key Greek philosophers appear a century or so later (e.g., Socrates [c. 470-399 B.C.] and Plato [c. 428-c. 348 B.C.]).

[15]Harbin, 179, n. 7.

[16]Harbin, 227.

[17]Phra Khantipalo, *Buddhism Explained: An Introduction to the Teachings of Lord Buddha* (Bangkok: Mahamkut Rajavidyalaya Press, 1989), 3.

[18]For example, cf. W. Woodville Rockhill, trans., *The Life of the Buddha and the Early History of His Order,* (Petaling Jaya, Malaysia: Mandala Trading, repr. ed., 1987), 37-38. This section recounts the traditional account of the conversion of Gautama's first five disciples as follows: "He [Gautama] imported his doctrine to two of the Five (sic) in the morning, for the three others had gone to the city to beg, and in the evening he taught the latter while the other two went to collect alms. . . . When he had finished speaking, he turned to the oldest of the five, Kaundinya and said, 'Kaundinya, hast thou thoroughly understood the *doctrine*?' " (italics added).

[19]Harbin, 147-50.

[20]James R. Ware, *The Sayings of Confucius* (New York: The New American Library, 1955), 7.

[21]Kaltenmark, 5.

[22]There is debate whether this view of him as Messiah was initially accepted by the Jews (so Robert Payne, *The History of Islam* [New York: Dorset Press, 1959, repr. ed.,

1990], 23 ff), or whether just by Arabs to spite the Jews (so Mohammed Husayn Haykal, *The Life of Mohammed* [Delhi: Crescent Publishing Co., 1976], 153 ff. Clearly, the Jews controlled Medina at the time, and as such had a significant role in the invitation for Mohammed to move there.

[23]Muhammad M. Pickthall, *The Meaning of the Glorious Qur'an* (Mecca: Muslim World League, 1977), v.

[24]Cf. Michael Harbin, "Authority Bases and Hermeneutical Principles," paper presented at the Evangelical Theological Society national meeting, 19 November 1994.

[25]It is referenced approximately 135 times in the Old Testament. Specific references are listed in footnote 28.

[26]R. Alan Cole argues that this sentence is the "self-proclamation" of the great king who declares what "he has done for his prospective vassal" (*Exodus: An Introduction and Commentary* [Downers Grove IL: Inter-Varsity Press, 1973], 152-153). If so, the entire sense then is that the "prospective vassal" is entering this position because of the stated act of the "great king." The fuller development of the treaty form in the parallel account in Deuteronomy, which uses virtually identical language, might raise some question on this issue which requires further work. However, the basic premise still stands.

[27]Childs seems to understand it in this sense when he states: "The formula identifies the authority and right of God to make known his will because he has already graciously acted on Israel's behalf," although he focuses on what he adopts from Zimmerli as the "introduction formula," i.e., "I am Yahweh your God. . . ." As such, for Childs the basis of God's authority is who He is. (Brevard Childs, *The Book of Exodus* [Philadelphia: The Westminster Press, 1974], 401).

[28]It is cited in this manner approximately thirty-seven instances in the Pentateuch, and thirty-nine times in the rest of the Old Testament. Similar phrases, such as "the Lord your God redeemed you from [Egypt]" (Deuteronomy 24:24) or "you came out of Egypt," are noted in fifty-

eight other passages. In addition, there are several passages which refer to the event elliptically such as Psalm 105. The specific citations include Exodus 13:3, 9, 14, 16; 16:6, 32; 18:1; 20:2; 23:15; 34:18; 29:46; Leviticus 11:45; 19:36; 22:33; 23:43; 25:38; 25:42; 25:55; 26:13; 26:45; Numbers 3:13; 8:17; 15:41; 20: 16; 23:22; 24:8; Deuteronomy 1:27; 4:37; 5:6, 15; 6:12, 21; 7:8, 18; 8:14-15; 9:26; 11:3; 13:5, 10; 15:15; 16:1, 6; 20:1; 23:4; 24:9, 22; 26:8; 29:25; 34:11; Joshua 2:10; 5:6; 9:9, 24:5, 17, 32; Judges 2:1, 12; 6:8, 13; 11:16; 19:30; 1 Samuel 2:27; 8:8; 10:18; 12:6, 8; 15:2; 2 Samuel 7:6, 23; 1 Kings 6:1; 8:9, 21, 51, 53; 9:9; 2 Kings 17:7, 36; 21:15; 1 Chronicles 17:5, 21; 2 Chronicles 5:10; 6:5; 7:22; 20:10; Nehemiah 9:9, 18; Psalm 78:12, 43; 80:8; 81:10; 85:1; 105; 106; 114:1; 135:8; 136:11; Isaiah 11:11, 16; 52:4; Jeremiah 2:6; 7:22; 11:4, 7; 16:14; 23:7; 31:32; 32:20-21; 34:13; Ezekiel 20:5-6; 23:27; Daniel 9:15; Hosea 2:15; 11:1; 12:9, 13; 13:4; Amos 2:10; 3:1; 9:7; Micah 6:4; 7:15; Haggai 2:5; Acts 7:36; 13:17; Hebrews 3:16; 8:9; 11:26-29; Jude 5.

[29]I argue in *To Serve Other Gods* that Judaism dates from the revelation of God given to Moses at Sinai which can be dated to approximately 1446 B.C. What we term modern Judaism is a result of debate beginning with Ezra and Nehemiah regarding what specific acts were required to obey the Old Testament law. After the fall of Jerusalem, this debate was committed to writing in the Mishnah and then supplemented by the Gemara. The two constitute the Talmud, the foundation of modern Judaism (cf. Isidore Epstein, *Judaism: A Historical Presentation* (London: Penguin Books, 1950), 114-119.

[30]We have already noted how this is demonstrated by Exodus 20:2 and Deuteronomy 5:6, where it introduces the so-called Ten Commandments, and Leviticus 19:36 where it is presented as the foundation of justice. Joshua uses it as the foundation of his exhortation to obey the law and turn from idolatry (Joshua 24:5), and the writer of the Judges uses it as a justification for the judgement cycles which

came upon the country (Judges 2:12). The writer of Kings uses it as a foundation for upcoming national rejection in the case of the Northern Kingdom (1 Kings 9:9), as also does Hosea (Hosea 11:1). Jeremiah uses it as a warning in the case of the Southern Kingdom (Jeremiah 11:4). Jeremiah also uses this as an anticipation of a future historical event which will transcend the Exodus—the restoration of the nation and a new covenant (Jeremiah 16:14 and 31:32 et al.). Nehemiah uses it after the exile as a foundation for the confession and repentance (Nehemiah 9:18).

[31]Cf. Gary V. Smith, *An Introduction to the Hebrew Prophets as Preachers* (Nashville, TN: Broadman and Holman, 1994), 5-24.

[32]Cf. J. Alec Motyer, *The Prophecy of Isaiah* (Downers Grove, IL: InterVarsity, 1993), 13-16.

[33]Motyer, 125-126.

[34]In addition to Paul's use in Acts 13:17, Stephen uses the phrase similarly in Acts 7:36. However, Stephen is unable to complete his argument, which is designed to demonstrate that Jesus is the Messiah, because the Jews cover their ears in anger and rush him out of town to be executed. The writer of Hebrews refers to the Exodus three times, once in reference to the new covenant (Hebrews 8:9), and Jude also mentions it in connection with God's judgment.

[35]This very basic observation may provide some direction for the discussion on the nature or identity of a "gospel." Cf. Craig Blomberg, *The Historical Reliability of the Gospels* (Downers Grove, IL: Intervarsity Press, 1987), 236-240.

[36]The number of witnesses included in this phrase must include at a minimum the apostles about him. It is also possible that he is declaring that everyone in his hearing was also a witness to the fact that the grave was empty, and thus intuitively a witness to the resurrection. Alford suggests that it includes the twelve and other believers (Henry Alford, *Alford's Greek Testament*, 7th ed., vol 2 (London:

Rivingtons, 1877; repr. ed., Grand Rapids, IL: Baker, 1980), 2:25.

[37]These ten occasions occur in thirteen references which include Acts 2:24, 32; 3:15; 4:10, 33; 5:30; 10:40; 13:30, 34; 17:3, 31; 25:19; 26:23. These do not include all of the methods of addressing the issue. When Philip met the Ethiopian eunuch, it is said "he preached Jesus to him" (Acts 8:35, NASB). When Paul was converted, his first proclamation was that Jesus was "the Son of God" (9:20). Later, he was "proving that this Jesus is the Christ" (9:22, NASB). However, the overall pattern is that these all tie together with the Resurrection—the decisive demonstrating point.

[38]Maurice Mandelbaum develops this concept philosophically as a foundation for all historical research in *The Problem of Historical Knowledge* (New York: Harper and Row, 1967 edition), 181.

[39]For example, Gustavson states, "Since the historian is writing about events that *someone else* saw or heard, the writing of history is necessarily a cooperative effort. He is largely dependent upon those original witnesses for their accuracy of observation and truthful reporting" (Carl G. Gustavson, *A Preface to History* [New York: McGraw-Hill, 1955], 170 [italics in original]). This is expanded by Mandelbaum, 177-191.

[40]Harbin, "Authority Bases and Hermeneutical Principles," 8-12.

[41]Some might suggest that we view this as a fact because we have film footage. Unfortunately, film footage, like all other documentation, is subject to forgery and alteration. The recent movie *Forrest Gump* very clearly demonstrates the point that there can be a serious problem even with photographic evidence. Incidentally, this point is one of the contentions of those who would argue that the holocaust was a sham. Cf. Collingwood, 251.

[42]Pieces of physical evidence aid in corroborating aspects of the event. In the case of Kennedy, ballistic tests deter-

mined that a given bullet was fired by a given gun. Finger-prints on the gun point to a person who had handled it. But physical evidence without a verbal account from a witness is problematical at best. While laboratory tests could demonstrate that the bullet which killed Kennedy likely came from a specific rifle and Lee Harvey Oswald had apparently handled that rifle, they could not prove that Oswald pulled the trigger for that particular shot. Logic would strongly suggest so, but this is still a less strong case than an eye-witness account, as evidenced by the recent O.J. Simpson trial. For historians the basic raw material consists of eyewitness accounts, as imperfect as they may be (R.G. Collingwood, *The Idea of History* [London: Oxford University Press, 1946; repr. ed. 1977], 252). That is why history is characterized as the period *after* writing was invented (cf. S.N. Kramer, *History Begins at Sumer*, 3rd ed. [Philadelphia: University of Pennsylvania Press, 1981]).

This would seem to suggest that historical-legal "facts" are suspicious at best. Actually, all facts, whether they are historical-legal or scientific are subject to the limitations of the observer. As Jay Rosenberg suggests, natural science is the process of explaining appearance (observations of individuals) on the basis of a theoretical reality, and a process that constantly needs updating because of new perceptions (or new observations of individuals) (J.F. Rosenberg, "Science and the Epistemic Authority of Logical Analysis," in *Reason and Rationality in Natural Science*, ed. Nicholas Rescher [Lanham, MD: University Press of America, 1985], 9-16).

[43]Here Craig, in his otherwise excellent essay, misstates the comparison when he states "the scientist then tests his proposed theory by performing various experiments." Cf. William Lane Craig, "Did Jesus Rise from the Dead?" in *Jesus Under Fire*, ed. Michael J. Wilkins and J.P. Moreland (Grand Rapids, MI: Zondervan, 1995), 143. Field science follows exactly the same method as the historian: "the scientist-historian tests his historical reconstruction by

157

seeing how well it elucidates the evidence." We might amplify this by observing that other historians then evaluate the reconstruction to determine if any evidence has been overlooked or misinterpreted.

[44]Rosenberg, 12.

[45]Craig Blomberg *The Historical Reliability of the Gospels* (Downers Grove, IL: InterVarsity, 1987).

[46]Paul Barnett, *Is The New Testament Reliable?* (Downers Grove, IL: InterVarsity, 1986).

[47]V. Philips Long, *The Art of Biblical History*, (Grand Rapids, MI: Zondervan, 1994).

[48]William Lane Craig, *The Historical Argument for the Resurrection of Jesus*, Texts and Studies in Religion 23 (Lewiston, NY: Edwin Mellen, 1985), and *Assessing the New Testament Evidence for the Historicity of the Resurrection of Jesus*, Studies in the Bible and Early Christianity 16 (Lewiston, NY: Edwin Mellen, 1989).

[49]This is not only an epistemological question, but one very basic in terms of the philosophy of history. This is evidenced by Mandlebaum when he states:

> And the truth of a historical work consists in the truth of its statements, not in the fact that the author judged as he did on such-and-such grounds. To consider historical truth, therefore, as a function of the conditions on which the historian judged the statements which he made to be true, is a totally irrelevant procedure. It arises out of a confusion of statements with judgments, which is one of the basic errors committed by the historical relativists. (Mandlebaum, 183)

This is supported by the argument of David Hacket Fischer, *Historians' Fallacies: Toward a Logic of Historical Thought* (New York: Harper and Row, Publishers, 1970), 40. Likewise Blomberg condenses these arguments into a concise statement, ". . . relativism confuses facts with their interpretations" (Blomberg, 55).

[50]The ten references include Acts 2:24, 32; 3:15; 4:10, 33; 5:30; 10:40; 13:30, 34; 17:31; and 26:23. Of these, 4:33 and 26:23 merely state that Jesus was resurrected. The rest cite God as the source of the action.

[51]Other instances include Romans 1:4, 4:24, 6:4, 7:4 (this passage especially uses the Resurrection as an authority for righteous living), 8:11; 1 Corinthians 6:14; 2 Corinthians 4:14; Galatians 1:1; Ephesians 1:20; Colossians 2:12; 1 Thessalonians 1:10; 2 Timothy 2:8; Hebrews 6:2 (here, however, the Resurrection is presented as a very basic teaching, suggesting that it is foundational and thus authoritative); 1 Peter 1:3 and 21.

[52]Louis Berkhof, *The History of Christian Doctrines*, (Grand Rapids, MI: Eerdmans, 1937; repr. ed., Grand Rapids, MI: Baker, 1975), 64-65.

[53]Berkhof, 16.

[54]R. Douglas Geivett, "Is Jesus the Only Way?" in *Jesus Under Fire*, 178-9, 189-90. This assumes a certain amount of logical consistency, which is not always evident.

[55]Charles Hodge, *Systematic Theology* (Grand Rapids, MI: Eerdmans, repr. ed., 1973), vol. 1:9-17. Cf. Charles C. Ryrie, *Basic Theology* (Wheaton, IL: Scripture Press, 1986), 13-15.

[56]Harbin, "Authority Bases and Hermeneutical Principles," 16-18.

[57]Two problems exist in the issue of what I call "supernormal manifestations," more popularly known as "miracles." The first is an inadequate understanding of "miracles." The second is an improper understanding of scientific "law." By definition, a "miracle" is a historical event which transcends the normal cause-and-effect relationships which we term scientific "law." Likewise, by definition, scientific law is a logical induction based on copious collected observations of nature. For example, every experiment demonstrates that a item dropped falls. The logical induction of this is the law of gravity. This does not necessarily mean that miracles violate laws. For example, healings might be greatly accelerated natural processes.

However, if spiritual beings which exist beyond our space-time limitations are introduced, their intervention may well run counter to what is observed as law. Thus, an item suspended by a spiritual being otherwise unobserved would appear to violate the law of gravity. Spiritual beings are likewise evidenced both by historical testimony and by the logical induction of observed data (cf. *Jesus Under Fire*, 164).

[58]We have already examined how historical events demonstrated God's authority. Isaiah, among others, is very clear that God sets forth predictive prophecy as the demonstration of His uniqueness, thus underlining His authority (cf. Isaiah 42:9, 43:19; and 48:6). Further, short-term prophecies and supernormal events are used as "signs" to validate specific declarations (cf. 1 Samuel 9:19-20 and 1 Kings 22:28).

[59]Geivett in *Jesus Under Fire*, 179.

[60]Geivett in ibid., 187. Craig points to the issue that God is a logically inducted explanation of observed phenomena, much as the scientifically inducted supposition of entities such as quarks and black holes (Craig in ibid., 164).

[61]Scot McKnight, "Who Is Jesus? An Introduction to Jesus Studies," ibid., 64.

[62]Cf. Kreeft and Tacelli, 150-74. They begin with the standard arguments for the existence of God, then argue the divinity of Jesus Christ in chapter 7, and *then* address the issue of the resurrection in chapter 8 and follow that with an evaluation of the historicity of the Bible.

[63]Gary R. Habermas, "Did Jesus Perform Miracles?" in *Jesus Under Fire*, 125-33. Of course, in the case of one who acknowledges the existence of God, this step is not necessary.

[64]Craig, ibid., 144.

[65]Philip W. Comfort, "Exploring the Common Identification of Three New Testament Manuscripts: p4, p64, and p67" (*Tyndale Bulletin* 46.1, 1995), 43-54. Carsten Philip Thiede, "Papyrus Magdalen Greek 17 (Gregory-

Aland p64): A Reappraisal" (*Tyndale Bulletin* 46.1, 1995), 29-42.

[66]William Lane Craig, "Did Jesus Rise from the Dead?" in *Jesus Under Fire*, 142.

[67]Such as Mark Noll does in his *The Scandal of the Evangelical Mind* (Grand Rapids, MI: Eerdmans, 1994). After beginning with the challenging premise that evangelical thinking has deteriorated, he then makes one of his main arguments a declaration that anyone who holds to certain theological positions which he does not hold (most specifically, premillennialism or abrupt appearance in terms of origins) is immediately viewed as nonintellectual. Not only is this an *ad hominem* argument, but it makes at least two critical mistakes. First, it assumes that certain theological constructs which the reformers brought out of medieval Roman Catholicism and never evaluated are inviolate because they were held by certain reformers. Second, it assumes that hypothetical scientific constructs which are being increasingly criticized by secular scientists are to be viewed as authoritative for biblical interpretation.

Part III

Defending the Faith Scientifically

DNA: A New Argument
from Design[1]

Charles B. Thaxton

Generations of philosophers and theologians have taught the design argument for God's existence. The classical design argument called people to look at order or pattern in the world and to conclude that some designing intelligence called God must have caused it. Archdeacon William Paley in the nineteenth century refined the argument and put it in its most eloquent and persuasive form. Paley looked at the order of human artifacts and compared it to the order in living beings. Since human intellect is responsible for artifacts, reasoned Paley, then some intelligent power similar to and greater than human intellect must have produced living beings.[2]

As convincing as that argument has been for many people, for most of the educated world it has lost its appeal and persuasive power. Belief in design has declined with the acceptance of the scientific world picture. Three centuries after Newton's *Principia*,[3] with its mechanically operating universe, the official and widely accepted scientific view is that the heavens have been swept clean of any intelligent influence. Most educated people today see the notion of design in nature as anachronistic and consider anyone who dredges up the design argument as uninformed. More than a century after Darwin the culturally accepted view is that people and all living beings are the products of physical forces at work on earth and throughout the cosmos. According to the widely accepted scientific story today, living beings were not the result of anyone's plan or purpose. In the words of Richard Dawkins of Oxford, living beings are only "complicated things that give the *appearance* of having been designed for a purpose"[4] (my emphasis).

Our culture's repudiation of design is based on last century's science. Major scientific discoveries in the twentieth century provide the basis for dramatically changing our views about design. But these changes have occurred faster than they have been culturally assimilated. Einstein's relativity revolution, quantum theory, DNA (deoxyribonucleic acid) and the process of heredity, spinoff discoveries in molecular medicine and the great computer revolution, which spawned internet and cyberspace—the larger implications of these great developments have only barely been sensed by the culture as a whole.

Today we are beginning to hear prominent scientists again speaking favorably about design in the universe. Paul Davies, a quantum physicist who received the 1995 Templeton Prize for Progress in Religion, stated his enthusiasm about design in the universe.[5] But Davies is not the only current scientist referring to design in such glowing terms. Numerous books discuss the amazing design features of the universe: *The Grand Design*,[6] *God and the New Physics*,[7] *Disturbing the Universe*,[8] *The Anthropic Cosmological Principle*,[9] *The Symbiotic Universe*,[10] *Perfect Symmetry*,[11] *The Cosmic Code*.[12] The topic of design in the universe is turning into a veritable industry.

Astronomers and physicists of the late twentieth century may be using the term design, but most, like Davies, mean only *apparent* design, giving credit to natural laws for the observed pattern that impresses them. The best that can be said is that these scientists are vague on the point of whether there is a designer behind the natural laws, and they often give the impression that there is not.

Breakthrough discoveries in mathematics and biology

are every bit as noteworthy and exciting as those in physics and astronomy. As I shall show, these discoveries in mathematics and biology are making way for design *with* a designer, even though few dare to draw this implication from their work.

The new argument from design in biology and mathematics is not as well known as the one from astronomy and physics. Even so, it is perhaps more important. If the argument developed here can be shown to indicate a designer, then it may be used fairly as a basis for clarifying the vague impression on this point obtained in astronomy and physics. It is this new argument from design that I plan to focus on today. My remarks will come under the following headings:

> The Method of Abductive Inference
> The Disappearance of Intelligent Causes from
> Natural Science
> Order, Complexity and Information
> The New Argument from Design
> Answers to Common Objections
> Summary and Conclusion

The Method of Abductive Inference

Reasoning from experience and linking cause to effect developed over several centuries and became a recognized scientific method of causal inference. It has been a part of science since the Scientific Revolution, which culminated in the great synthesis of Isaac Newton in the seventeenth century. Over the course of the development of modern experimental science, Western culture learned to rely on sensory experience to gain knowledge about natural phenomena.[13] By following experience, scientists learned to infer causes from effects, i.e., to work backward from the character of the effects to the cause. A cause is that necessary and sufficient condition that alone can give rise to the occurrence of a given event. And it does not matter if the cause is natural or intelligent. David Hume gave a formal analysis of this approach: "From causes which appear *similar* we expect similar effects" (emphasis his). Later in the same book he added, "the same rule holds, whether the cause assigned be brute unconscious matter, or a rational intelligent being."[14] The inferential methods we usually learn in school are deductive, i.e., inference from the general to the particular, and inductive, i.e., inference from the particular to the general. There has always been a third method of inference, although not clearly described and formally analyzed until the 1870s, this being abductive, i.e., inference from experience.[15] The method of abductive inference is particularly important in the historical sciences, reasoning backward from phenomena to the cause.

Let us apply the method of abductive inference to a few examples. Strolling along a wave-swept beach we notice ripple patterns in the sand. The first time it may seem mysterious, but after repeated experiences, we associate the ripple patterns with the waves. We are so accustomed to making this assignment of cause that seeing photographs of similar ripple patterns in sediments that geologists had dated as three billion years old, we would infer water as the natural cause. Likewise deep channels or rills on the Martian surface are so similar to what we know by experience to be the result of running water, that we would associate the natural cause of the channels with water—even if there is no water on Mars today. Thus scientists at NASA (National Aeronautics and Space Administration) have concluded that water must have been on Mars sometime in the past.[16]

On the other hand, were we to hike in the Black Hills of South Dakota and come upon granite cliffs bearing the likenesses of four United States Presidents, we would quickly identify Mount Rushmore as the work of artisans instead of a product of wind and erosion. Our accumulated reservoir of experience enables us to discriminate types of effects we see and to distinguish a natural process from an intelligent cause. Walking farther along and finding "John loves Mary" etched on a rock, what do we conclude? Again from experience, we infer that someone, perhaps John or Mary, left this sign of his or her affection. We would not conclude it to be the work of erosional forces, since we are able to discriminate causes. This ability is what led anthropologists to eventually change their judgment regarding eoliths. Eoliths are chipped flints that, for a time, had been considered indicators of early man. Later it was discovered that such chips and scars on rocks can result from tumbling in a stream. This change in the assignment of cause was on the basis of additional experience.[17]

The abductive method gives us a way to approach phenomena and be completely open to either natural or intelligent causes. The assignment of causal category depends on the character of the effects. To illustrate the method, suppose we are detectives investigating someone's death. Is this a case of death by natural causes (accident) or death by design (murder or suicide)? We do not know the answer in advance. We must investigate and find out. If we announced before beginning our investigation that death *must* have been accidental (natural), others would be justified in objecting that we had illegitimately restricted the field of possible causes. An important purpose of the investigation is to determine whether this was a case of intelligent cause (murder or suicide) or natural death. We need a method that is open to either possibility. The abductive method of reasoning backward from the effects considers and evaluates various candidates' natural and intelligent cause hypotheses and eliminates those that do not agree with experience. Such openness to the full spectrum of natural and intelligent cause scenarios gives confidence that the abductive inference does yield the *best* explanation.[18]

Despite the above explanation, some people, especially among scientists, suggest that science may not entertain intelligent causes. This notion is certainly mistaken. The abductive inference is very much at home in modern science. Retrospective causal reasoning is routinely used by NASA scientists as they explore the heavens looking for signs of intelligence in their SETI (Search for Extra-Terrestrial Intelligence) program. If signals from space conveyed artificial electromagnetic pulses sent in code to give, for example, the first thousand digits in the transcendental number *pi* (3.14159 . . .), this would be considered so improbable an occurrence that we concur that intelligence had sent it. If scientists ever receive radio signals that are distinguished from noise and have the *indicia* of intelligence, we can surely expect a jubilant announcement from Washington.

The Planetary Society has initiated its Billion Channel Extraterrestrial Assay (BETA) survey of the heavens using the world's largest receiver, an eighty-four-foot radio telescope set up in Harvard, Massachusetts.[19] The goal of this heavenly scan is to receive intelligent messages that some advanced civilization could be beaming our way. It is a program within the borders of legitimate science. It is safe to put the objection aside that modern science is opposed *in principle* to the notion of intelligent cause.

The Disappearance of Intelligent Causes from Natural Science

Despite the fact that intelligent causes are a legitimate part of the search for extraterrestrials (and a legitimate part of archeology, anthropology and forensic science), the notion of intelligent cause has disappeared from natural science. It is important to understand why this has happened.

Most of the history of western civilization has been characterized by belief in design. Despite the successes of Newtonian physics and the emerging chemical sciences, all of which relied on experience to associate recurring phenomena with natural causes, this was clearly in the context of exploring the ongoing operation of nature. These scientists accepted an ordered world as a given, a *designed* given. According to Whitehead, these were not "the explicit beliefs of a few individuals," but rather "the impress on the European mind arising from the unquestioned faith of centuries." It was thus an "instinctive tone of thought and not a mere creed of words."[20] In this context of faith the scientific quest involved discovering the laws describing the world's patterned behavior, reducing an apparent chaos to order. These scientists and the larger culture had an implicit belief structure that behind the order lay the great ordering intelligence of God.

So deep was this impress on the European mind that few scientists, even well into the nineteenth century, disagreed with Isaac Newton who had written: "This most beautiful system of the sun, planets, and comets, could only proceed from the counsel and dominion of an intelligent and powerful Being."[21] Because of the cultural conviction of a created and designed universe, including earth and life upon it, it was very widely appreciated, from the early days of seventeenth-century science onward until the time of Darwin, that science is not concerned with the question of origins. Why, they must have thought, would we want to scientifically pursue an answer we already possess? The world is created and designed; science seeks laws that describe the regular patterns we observe. A newspaper article in the days of the Darwin controversy expressed the predominant cultural view, including that of most scientists, when it said, "we look to men of Science rather for observation than for imagination."[22]

Yet out of view there was an undercurrent of variant opinion as the scientific naturalists were marching to a different drummer. The culture and most scientists were so enamored with nature's many regularities and confirmations of their underlying beliefs that they hardly noticed when the scientific naturalists inferred from these regularities absolute natural laws which even God (if He existed) *must* obey. For the naturalists nature had replaced God. The external signs of religious orthodoxy remained, but a mental dislocation had occurred in the intellectual world, which represented a radical shift from theism to naturalism.[23]

Implicit within naturalism is the denial of a creation distinct from its Creator. It logically developed, therefore, that naturalists sought to answer the great origin questions without reference to a Creator. A new intellectual regime (naturalism) was taking over the culture, even if it was not recognized by the majority for what it was. It had no clerical trappings, no shrines, no symbols, no places of worship reserved for it alone. It was fitting, therefore, that origin questions would be answered by appealing to the new deity, natural law.

A particularly important speculative foray into explaining origins by natural law was Laplace's nebular hypothesis for the origin of the solar system.[24] There were also speculative naturalistic explanations offered in the area of biology, especially the evocative popular work by Chambers.[25]

Despite naturalistic speculation, professional biologists and the culture maintained their conviction that life owed its presence on earth to a great designing intelligence.

It is not immediately obvious to most readers today just how nineteenth-century biologists made their appeal to intelligent cause. If you pick up many books on biology before 1859, it may not be obvious that it is arguing for intelligent design. Yet, if you know the code words you can readily recognize it. To pre-Darwinian biologists, if an organism could be shown to be adapted to its environment, or if some structure could be shown adapted to function, that was tantamount to showing that it was purposefully designed, and hence the result of intelligent creation.[26]

Charles Darwin pioneered in the development of scientific methodology that seeks to answer origin questions.[27] Until Darwin it seemed to everyone that design required a designer. Intelligent design was finally removed from biology with the triumph of Darwin, who argued that the power of natural selection produces only *apparent* design in organisms.[28]

Laboratory demonstrations

Why then do scientists no longer accept intelligent design in nature? The short answer is that a naturalistic culture needs a naturalistic answer, and scientists can show many examples of natural processes producing order. Whether the beautiful patterns in crystals, the soapy swirl down the drain or the order evident in a spiral nebula, natural forces of physics have been demonstrated which produce order.[29]

An easy kitchen demonstration to show the power of natural causes in generating order is to put a round flat-bottom glass container of oil on a well regulated hot plate and to slowly heat it from below. Soon hexagonal patterns will spontaneously appear on the oil surface. The generalization drawn from this is that energy passing through a physical system is all that is required to generate order.[30]

According to the scientific picture, even if we consider the total universe as a thermodynamically isolated system,[31] one where energy will eventually run down, there are still pockets within the total system of the universe where energy flow may sustain order over long periods. That is all the defense that materialists needed in order to satisfy themselves against the classic order-means-design and design-means-a-designer argument. Because these scientists are no longer persuaded by the design argument, many of the larger educated community are judging these objections valid, and they too are rejecting design.

For nineteen hundred years of Western history, the prevailing view was that the presence of order requires an ordering intelligence to account for it. The dominant view of the past century in Western culture is that an ordering intelligence is no longer needed. Natural processes have been demonstrated to account for many examples of order in the world, and it is assumed that natural processes will be found to account for all the examples of order that remain.

Order, Complexity and Information

Then the unexpected happened. Just when it seemed that natural causes might suffice to account for all natural phenomena, there were breakthrough discoveries in both mathematics and biology. These gave the basis for a dramatic change in the way of describing living organisms and in answering questions about their origin.[32]

We begin with biology.[33] Most people today are familiar with deoxyribonucleic acid, DNA, the double helical molecule of heredity. It is like a long ladder twisted into a spiral. The sides of the ladder are composed of sugar and phosphate molecules. Its "rungs" are made of the four bases— adenine (A), guanine (G), cytosine (C) and thymine (T). A nucleotide consists of a base linked to a sugar linked to a phosphate. A polynucleotide is many nucleotides linked together, phosphate to sugar, like freight cars in a long train. During replication inside the cell, the two sides of the "ladder" split, and each half attracts a new set of nucleotides from the surrounding cytoplasm (the part of the cell outside the nucleus) in order to replace the missing half. The sequence of nucleotides making up the DNA chain runs from a few million in bacteria to three billion in human beings. Not only is the length important; their specific sequence is too.

DNA is called an informational molecule because its unique structure functions as the central part of an elaborate communication system within the cell. This code aspect was hinted at by Francis Crick and James Watson in their modest announcement of the famous double helix structure of DNA.[34] An early written statement of this idea was recorded in a letter that Crick wrote on March 19, 1953 to his son Michael: "Now we believe that the D.N.A. *is* a code. That is, the order of bases (the letters) makes one gene different from another gene (just as one page of print is different from another)."[35]

A second group of informational molecules is proteins. They are long chain-like molecules composed of amino acids linked together end to end, which fold up into very complicated shapes. The specific sequence of amino acids in a protein is what determines its overall three-dimensional shape and function.

DNA, with its alphabet of four bases, and protein, with an alphabet of twenty amino acids, represent two different languages related by a code. When the cell constructs proteins, a translation takes place between one language and the other; the sequence in DNA codes for and determines the sequence in protein.

Information theory is a special branch of mathematics that has developed a way to measure information. In brief, the information content of a structure is the minimum number of instructions required to describe or specify it, whether that structure is a rock or a rocket ship, a pile of leaves or a living organism. The more complex a structure is, the more instructions are needed to describe it.[36]

Order: periodic and specified

The development of information theory provides a tool for distinguishing between order and complexity. Examples of ordered structures are a repeating wallpaper or floor tile pattern, the hexagonal pattern appearing on the surface of heated oil, the single structure repeated over and over in a crystal and a sequence of alphabetical letters such as ABABABABAB. The characteristic feature of an ordered structure is the *periodic and specified* arrangement of its constituent parts. That means the parts are arranged in a highly repetitious and specific fashion. Such structures have a low information content and require only a few instructions to specify them. As an example, if you want to tell a chemist how to make a crystal, you need only two instructions. First, specify the substance you want and the way you want the molecules packed together. Second, tell the chemist, "Now do it again." Repeat until the crystal is made. The structural information has to be given only once because a crystal has a regular pattern. To tell your computer's printer to make a page of "Hello Bob!" will take only two instructions: 1. "Print 'H-e-l-l-o B-o-b-!' " and 2. "Do it again," until the page is filled.

Complexity: aperiodic and unspecified

On the other hand, aperiodic structures, i.e., structures that lack periodicity, are called "complex." Complex structures are of two types. The simplest type of complexity is a random structure. A random structure has no order, but, like an ordered structure, it has little information because few instructions are needed to specify it. By definition random structures are *aperiodic and unspecified*, such as a lump of granite, a pile of leaves, a random polymer or a sequence of letters drawn at random. A pile of leaves is random and can be specified with just two instructions: 1. "Select any type of leaf and drop it on the pile" and 2. "Do it again." To write a series of random letters, you also need only two instructions: 1. "Select at random a letter from A to Z and write it down" and 2. "Do it again." This way you can make as long a random sequence as you want.

Information: aperiodic and specified

It is the second type of complexity, however, that is most relevant for biology. Written messages, artifacts, DNA and proteins are all examples of specified complexity. By definition structures characterized by specified complexity are those whose constituent parts are arranged in an *aperiodic and specified* manner. Such structures have a high information content, which means that many instructions are needed to specify them. As an example, if you wanted to print out a copy of Lincoln's Gettysburg Address that begins, "Fourscore and seven years ago . . . ," you could not find any brief set of instructions to give your computer.

Your instructions would be as long as the famous address itself. You must specify every letter, one at a time, in the correct sequence. There are no shortcuts.

It would be quite impossible to give a chemist a set of few instructions to synthesize the DNA of even the simplest bacterium. The instructions would have to include every chemical letter, one by one. That would be several million of them. Rather than a few sentences of instructions, there would be enough to fill a large book.

Now we have a clear and mathematically defined distinction between order and complexity. Experience shows that natural processes produce ordered structures like ripples in sand, hexagonal patterns on a heated oil surface and crystals. Natural processes are also known by experience to produce a random distribution of leaves in autumn and the random polymers in the reported origin of life experiments.[37] Experience also shows many examples of specified complexity, e.g., books, paintings, artifacts—all produced by intelligence and none produced by natural processes. Living organisms are characterized not by order but by specified complexity, i.e., information. This dramatic development has profound implications for the design argument.

The New Argument from Design

As we have seen, the abductive method of inferring backward from the effects has shown that natural processes suffice to produce order and an ordering intelligence is not needed (except perhaps in the remote sense of an intelligence standing behind the natural process, which is the view of many theists). But with the discovery of informational molecules, DNA and protein, which are characterized by specified complexity instead of order, the situation has changed dramatically.[38]

DNA and protein and, of course, living beings are rich in information. Other structures that are characterized by specified complexity are linguistic messages, bridges,

177

paintings, computer programs and, in general, human artifacts.

A structural identity has been discovered between the genetic messages on DNA and the written messages of a human language. This discovery opened the way for the application of information theory to biology. Information theory applies to any symbol system, regardless of the elements of that system. The so-called Shannon information laws apply equally well to human language, Morse code and the genetic code. Hubert P. Yockey notes in the *Journal of Theoretical Biology*:

> It is important to understand that we are not reasoning by analogy. The sequence hypothesis [that the exact order of symbols records the information] applies directly to the protein and the genetic text as well as to written language and therefore the treatment is mathematically identical.[39]

There is an identity of structure between DNA (and protein) and written linguistic messages. Because we know by experience that intelligence produces written messages, and no other cause is known, the implication, according to the abductive method, is that intelligent cause produced DNA and protein. The significance of this result lies in the security of it, for it is much stronger than if the structures were merely similar. We are not dealing with anything like a superficial resemblance between DNA and a written text. We are not saying DNA is *like* a message. Rather, DNA *is* a message. True design thus returns to biology.

Answers to Common Objections

A straightforward application of the abductive method of inference to the genetic text implies that DNA had an intelligent cause. Yet few scientists acknowledge the result. Why not? Why would scientists (and large segments of our culture) not abide by this method in this one instance of DNA (and protein)? As we have seen from the acceptance within science of the search for extraterrestrial intelligence and also of the general methodology of forensic science, neither the scientists nor the culture are opposed in principle to the notion of intelligent cause.

We must, therefore, look for the source of the opposition elsewhere, in something that is very widespread and pervasive throughout the culture. Were it due to something exclusively within science itself, it is doubtful the opposition would be culture-wide or that it would have so thoroughly pervaded all other branches of science which have little professional interest in the subject of DNA.

I have sought the explanation for this culture-wide opposition to intelligent cause for DNA and provide three primary objections: philosophical, methodological and psychological.

Philosophical

The first objection to intelligent design of DNA is philosophical. Most scientists come into discussions of science, particularly origins, already with a natural/supernatural way of thinking. It is easy, therefore, for these scientists to conclude that the notion of intelligent cause is a ruse, that it is really the supernatural without the courage of the one promoting it saying so. And because we do not incorporate the supernatural into science, the objection continues, the only way to proceed in the investigation of any natural phenomenon is to assume a natural cause.[40]

It is easy to see how the critic might think intelligent cause is a ruse, for surely the cause might be supernatural. The problem is that we do not know from the inference we make from experience of DNA (and protein) whether the intelligence is beyond the cosmos, or within it. These prepositions *beyond* and *within* make all the difference. Because we do not know from the inference itself which preposition truly represents the case, we must remain equivocal. That is why we must simply refer to intelligent cause.[41]

The power of this philosophical objection arises from the huge confusion generated by mixing the categories and terms of science and philosophy. In science we use the experience-based terms *natural* and *intelligent*. As in the case cited earlier—that of detecting intelligible signals from space—we use the term *intelligent cause*. When the discussion involves an intelligent cause that is outside or beyond the cosmos, however, we use a different term that is philosophically recognizable. We use the term *supernatural,* thus indicating that it is transcendent, i.e., beyond experience.

Science also includes the experience-based term, natural cause, when inferring the cause of ripple patterns on a beach. But when the discussion involving natural cause extends outside or beyond experience, into the philosophical, there is not a different philosophical term used. In fact a variant of the same word natural is used, *naturalism*. Often the term *natural* is used without clearly indicating a transition from scientific to philosophical discussion. Much confusion thus arises from this equivocation on the term natural. How this confusion arises can be seen by putting the two dichotomies side by side, where the term natural appears in both:

Science
natural/intelligent

Philosophy
natural/supernatural

A better arrangement of terminology could not be devised if you want to deceive somebody. All you have to do is begin a discussion talking science, using the term *natural* in an appropriate way, and then somewhere along the way simply ease into philosophy, again using the term *natural* in an appropriate way. Just fail to inform your listeners or readers that you have moved on to philosophy. By this method of sleight you might "persuade" your audience.

It is easy to see how this could happen without any intent to deceive. It was a tragedy bound to happen because of the linguistic terms used.

Consider, for example, the quotations below. The first is from British physicist Paul Davies, and the second by Leslie Orgel, a prominent figure in origin of life research:

> The origin of life remains one of the great scientific mysteries. . . . The problem is to understand how this threshold could have been crossed by ordinary physical and chemical processes without the help of some supernatural agency.[42]

> Any "living" system must come into existence either as a consequence of a long evolutionary process or a miracle.[43]

Both of these authors meant their words to be understood in the context of science, concerned to find a scientific answer to the mystery of life's origin. Yet both engaged in the practice of mixing categories, science and philosophy. In science the proper term for an alternative to physical and chemical processes (Davies) and evolutionary process (Orgel), is intelligent cause, not supernatural agency (Davies) or a miracle (Orgel).

Mixing categories is clearly inadvisable for meaningful communication. Such quotations present a false choice between science and philosophy to the reader. Whatever the intent of the authors in doing this, whether deliberate or not, the effect is to leave the reader with science (or is it naturalism?) as the only acceptable choice.

In summary, the philosophical objection to an intelligent cause for DNA assumes that an intelligent cause is supernatural. This is usually accompanied by mixing the categories and terms of science and philosophy. In science the proper experience-based alternative to a natural cause is an intelligent cause.

Methodological

A second objection to an intelligent cause for DNA is methodological. According to this objection we proceed in scientific inquiry by restricting ourselves to natural causes, whether one's philosophical view is naturalism[44] or theism, an approach some advocates have called *methodological naturalism*.[45] Therefore, intelligent cause is unacceptable in science; it is metaphysical.

The intent of this objection is laudable, which is to promote science and to exclude from science those philosophical and religious views that masquerade as science. Methodological naturalism, however, is not a true principle of science; it abandons the appropriate method of following experience in order to fit a preconceived image of science.

Methodological naturalism has a short history, dating from the insistence of scientific naturalists in the nineteenth century that science must include only natural causes. It may seem to some today that methodological naturalism had an innocent beginning. By ignoring the significance of the cultural shift from theism to naturalism, and the concomitant interest in origins, it is easy to imagine scientists following the proper method of inferring causes from experience over an extended period of about four hundred years and systematically finding natural causes in each case. So unerringly did the method of following experience lead to natural causes that it may have seemed to some that in the domain of science we *must* restrict ourselves to natural causes. Nonetheless methodological naturalism is flawed because it does not follow experience. The informational molecules exposed methodological naturalism as an arbitrary restriction on nature and an unwarranted demand on scientific methodology, both of which are contrary to the spirit of science.

Many outside the DNA disciplines still do not know the significance of these informational molecules, and that the abductive method implies an intelligent cause as their most probable source. Methodological naturalism, which determines in advance that the cause must be natural, cannot accept intelligent cause. Consistent application of methodological naturalism would insist that NASA scientists continue looking for natural causes for any intelligible signals received from space and that any structures with specified complexity found on any planet must likewise have had a natural cause.

If there is, as I now believe, no valid methodological basis for disputing an intelligent cause of DNA, then what conclusion do we draw about those who remain opposed? Metaphysical naturalists will remain opposed until they find a way to incorporate the result into their metaphysical viewpoint. In the meantime, however, they will dispute intelligent cause, but will be decreasingly able to use the old argument that their natural-cause-only view is "just science." It will become clear to a much larger audience that metaphysical naturalists have been for many years smuggling metaphysical naturalism into the culture under the name of science.

But what about metaphysical theists, particularly those who have maintained that they are only opposed to intelligent cause in science for methodological reasons? It is hoped that, as they learn the true status of methodological naturalism as an arbitrary restriction on nature and an improper demand upon methodology, they will make open acknowledgment of this and then help to acquaint a broader audience of this important result. The need for open acknowledgment is clear. Unless methodological naturalism can be justified on some new ground, it will be indistinguishable from metaphysical naturalism.

Psychological

A third objection to the intelligent design of DNA is psychological. Many Christians in the sciences, including many who subscribe to methodological naturalism, are psychologically conditioned against considering anything other than natural causes. In the past, through a god-of-the-gaps approach, i.e., calling upon God in an *ad hoc* manner to fill some gap in human knowledge, many Christians were put in the unpleasant situation of seeing God removed by degrees from science. This happened as science showed many examples of mysterious natural phenomena accounted for by natural causes. The lesson was painfully absorbed by the church and has now become a psychological reason why many Christians in the sciences and in the larger culture resist intelligent cause; they envision a repeat episode of this admittedly sad chapter in church history.

There is no ground to expect the DNA design inference to be overturned by some new scientific discovery of a natural cause for the informational sequences in DNA. If such a discovery of natural causes producing specified complexity is made, then much more than one more disappointment will be involved. The whole presumed knowledge of the past can be doubted. Our knowledge of antiquity, for example, based on the supposed decipherment of ancient languages, will be in jeopardy. For we only "know" about antiquity based on the soundness of the method of causal inference from experience to show us that an intelligent cause most probably produced the artifacts and strange writings found in those long-ago places. Even that birth certificate in the attic that "identifies" you as the legitimate family heir may not be trusted.

Summary and Conclusion

The abductive method of inferring causes from experience is a recognized scientific method. This method is open to natural and intelligent causes. The story of a detective sifting clues to solve the mystery of someone's death is a classic example of abductive reasoning. Even though intelligent cause and design continued in some branches of science, it disappeared in natural science after Darwin.

184

Breakthrough discoveries since 1950 in mathematics and biology have led to the recognition that at the heart of the life process is the DNA molecule, a molecule that is characterized not by order but by specified complexity, i.e., information. The structures of DNA and a written linguistic message are mathematically identical. This structural identity and the fact that intelligence is the only known cause of specified complexity, i.e., information, is the basis for a significant revival of the design argument in a new and more powerful form. Three primary objections, i.e., philosophical, methodological and psychological, to the new design argument were singled out and a response given.

I am well aware that the majority today are persuaded that a natural cause process accounted for life upon this planet, and that many theists hold that God designed the process. To them it seems such an obvious fact. Without direct evidence, however, all such scenarios are based on circumstantial evidence. Even though many cases are properly settled this way, it is well to recall what that venerable supersleuth Sherlock Holmes noted in another baffling mystery:

> "Circumstantial evidence is a very tricky thing," answered Holmes thoughtfully. "It may seem to point very straight to one thing, but if you shift your own point of view a little, you may find it pointing in an equally uncompromising manner to something entirely different. . . . There is nothing more deceptive than an obvious fact."[46]

Endnotes

[1]I would like to express my thanks for valuable discussion and editorial feedback to four readers: Mark Hartwig, Steve Meyer, Steve Olsen and Nancy Pearcey; and a special thanks to the ETS for stimulating this paper into being by extending the opportunity and privilege to give a plenary address to the 1995 annual convention.

[2]William Paley, *Natural Theology*, ed. Frederick Ferre (New York: Bobbs-Merrill, [1802] 1963).

[3]Isaac Newton, *Mathematical Principles of Natural Philosophy*, Great Books of the Western Word, Robert Maynard Hutchins, ed. vol. 34 (Chicago: Encyclopedia Britannica, 1687 [1952]).

[4]Richard Dawkins, *The Blind Watchmaker: Why the Evidence of Evolution Reveals a Universe without Design* (New York: W. W. Norton, 1986), 1.

[5]Paul Davies, "Physics and the Mind of God," The Templeton Prize Address, 1995, *First Things* (August/September 1995).

[6]Robert Wright, *The Grand Design* (New York: Times Books, 1988).

[7]Paul Davies, *God and the New Physics* (New York: Simon and Schuster, 1983).

[8]Freeman Dyson, *Disturbing the Universe* (New York: Harper and Row, 1979).

[9]John D. Barrow and Frank J. Tipler, *The Anthropic Cosmological Principle* (New York: Oxford University Press, 1988).

[10]George Greenstein, *The Symbiotic Universe* (New York: William Morrow, 1988).

[11]Heinz R. Pagels, *Perfect Symmetry* (New York: Simon and Schuster, 1985).

[12]Heinz R. Pagles, *The Cosmic Code* (New York: Bantam, 1983).

[13]N. Pearcey and C. Thaxton, *The Soul of Science* (Wheaton, IL: Crossway, 1994), ch. 1.

[14]David Hume, *An Enquiry Concerning Human Understanding*, R.M. Hutchins, ed. (Chicago: Great Books of the Western World, [1748], 1952), 462, 499.

[15]For a general description of abductive reasoning, see Edward C. Moore, "Introduction to Charles S. Peirce," *Writings of Charles S. Peirce: A Chronological Edition*, ed. Edward C. Moore, et al., vol 2 (Indianapolis, IN: Indiana University Press, 1984). For application and analysis of the use

of abductive inference in the stories of that inimitable detective Sherlock Holmes, see Gian P. Capretti, "Peirce, Holmes, Popper," in U. Eco and T. Sebeok, eds., *The Sign of Three* (Bloomington, IN: University of Indiana Press), 135-153. See also S.C. Meyer, "The Methodological Equivalence of Design and Descent," in *The Creation Hypothesis*, ed. J.P. Moreland (Downers Grove, IL: InterVarsity, 1994).

[16]NASA photo appearing in several publications. See Fred Hoyle, *The Intelligent Universe* (New York: Holt, Rinehart and Winston, 1983), 104.

[17]J.I. Hester, *Introduction to Archeology* (New York: Holt, Rinehart and Winston, 1976), 29.

[18]For additional insights into pitfalls and methods of recovering the past, see Peter Lipton, *Inference to the Best Explanation* (London: Routledge, 1991) and E. Sober, *Reconstructing the Past* (Cambridge, MA: MIT Press, 1988).

[19]*USA Today*, International Edition, November 1, 1995.

[20]A.N. Whitehead, *Science and the Modern World* (New York: MacMillan, Free Press, 1925), 12.

[21]Isaac Newton, "General Scholium," in *Mathematical Principles of Natural Philosophy* (Chicago: Great Books of the Western World, [1687] 1952), 360.

[22]*London Times*, September 19, 1970, p. 9. Cited in Alvar Ellegard, *Darwin and the General Reader* (Chicago: University of Chicago Press, [1958] 1990), 88.

[23]Carl Becker, *The Heavenly City of the Eighteenth Century Philosophers* (New Haven, CT: Yale University Press, 1932).

[24]Ibid.

[25]Robert Chambers, *Vestiges of the Natural History of Creation* (Leicester, England: Leicester University Press, [1844] 1969).

[26]Dov Ospovat, *The Development of Darwin's Theory* (Cambridge: Cambridge University Press, 1981), 7.

[27]For discussions of the development of Darwinian method, see Michael Ruse, *Darwinism Defended* (London: Addison-Wesley Publishing, 1982), chapter 2; M.T. Ghiselin, *The Triumph of the Darwinian Method* (Berkeley,

CA: University of California Press, 1969).

[28]Charles Darwin, *The Origin of Species* (New York: Washington Square Press, [1859] 1963).

[29]Various works of Ilya Prigogine amply illustrate order by natural causes. See, for example: Ilya Prigogine, *From Being to Becoming* (San Francisco: W.H. Freeman, 1984), I. Prigogine and I. Stengers, *Order out of Chaos* (New York: Bantam, 1980).

[30]Agnesa Babloyantz, *Molecules, Dynamica and Life: An Introduction to Self-Organization of Matter* (New York: Wiley Interscience, 1986). The book includes practical experiments that show how to produce self-ordered systems, such as the hexagonal patterns on oil, 150.

[31]Discussions of thermodynamics are filled with pitfalls for the uninitiated. For a discussion of open, closed and isolated systems, their definition and application to origin of life questions, see chapters 7-9 of *The Mystery of Life's Origin* by C. Thaxton, W. Bradley and R. Olsen (New York: Philosophical Library, 1984), repr. Lewis & Stanley Publishers, Dallas, TX, 1992.

[32]For a critique of modern origin of life theories and additional discussion of order, complexity and information, see *The Mystery of Life's Origin*. For a similar and less technical critique of origin of life theories, see Robert Shapiro, *Origins* (New York: Summit Books, 1986).

[33]For a short introduction to the DNA story and how it fits into modern biology, see chapter 10 in *The Soul of Science* by Nancy Pearcey and Charles Thaxton (Wheaton, IL: Crossway Books, 1994).

[34]J.D. Watson and F.H.C. Crick, "A Structure for Deoxyribose Nucleic Acid," *Nature* 171 (April 25, 1953): 737-738.

[35]Cited in Horace Freeland Judson's *The Eighth Day of Creation: Makers of the Revolution in Biology* (New York: Simon & Schuster, 1979), 178.

[36]Leslie Orgel, *The Origins of Life* (New York: John Wiley & Sons, 1973), 190.

[37]See especially chapters 8 and 9 of *The Mystery of Life's Origin*.

[38]Earlier presentations of the DNA argument from design can be found in the Epilogue of *The Mystery of Life's Origin*, ch. 5; "Information & the Origin of Life," by W. Bradley and C. Thaxton, in J.P. Moreland, ed., *The Creation Hypothesis* (Downers Grove, IL: InterVarsity, 1994); "A Word to the Teacher," by C. Thaxton, in *Of Pandas and People*, P. Davis and D. Kenyon (Dallas, TX: Haughton Publishers, 1988); ch. 10, "A Chemical Code," in *The Soul of Science*.

[39]Hubert P. Yockey, "Self Organization, Origin of Life Scenarios and Information Theory," *J. Theoret. Biol.* 91, 13 (1981): 16.

[40]Although I don't discuss here the question of whether science does of necessity exclude the supernatural, it has been explored elsewhere. For a reasoned case against this view, see, for example, ch. 1 in *The Creation Hypothesis*. The references therein will lead the interested reader to the opposing view.

[41]Attempting to further identify the intelligent cause takes one outside the scientific domain. It is the apologetic task to divulge the identity of the intelligent cause, which is known from an inference that is common to human experience. But clearly apologetics—whether theistic, naturalistic or pantheistic—is not science. I am focusing on the scientific case.

[42]Paul Davies, *God and the New Physics* (New York: Simon & Schuster, 1983), 68.

[43]Leslie Orgel, *The Origins of Life* (New York: John Wiley, 1973), 192.

[44]Theism affirms a fundamental distinction between the Creator and the creature, while naturalism denies this absolute distinction and defines all of reality in terms that theists see as some aspect of the created world. Western naturalism has typically defined the world in material terms, and Eastern naturalism has emphasized the spiri-

tual, e.g., pantheism. What identifies both of these great metaphysical traditions as naturalistic is that both deny an absolute Creator who is truly distinct from creation, even if, as with some Eastern naturalisms like Hinduism, there are creators.

[45]See, for example, the discussion of methodological naturalism by Paul de Vries, "Naturalism in the Natural Sciences: A Christian Perspective," in *Christian Scholar's Review* 15 (1986): 388-396.

[46]Arthur Conan Doyle, "The Bonscombe Valley Mystery," in *The Adventures Sherlock Holmes* (London: Penguin Books, [1892] 1981), 78.

Between Jerusalem and the Laboratory: A Theologian Looks at Science

Michael Bauman

> *"It is absolutely safe to say that, if you meet somebody who claims not to believe in evolution, that person is ignorant, stupid, or insane."*
> —*Richard Dawkins, Oxford zoologist*
> *in* The Blind Watchmaker

We live in but one world. Science and theology are united in that they both seek to understand that one world and to explain it. They do so according to their own respective method (or methods) of knowing. In that sense, both science and theology are a hermeneutic, or a way of interpreting, the world around us. Because we have but one world to interpret and not a scientific universe alongside a theological universe, only one full and correct answer exists for any well-formed question relating to it. A well-formed question is one that seeks and helps to make possible an answer that is both full (that is, comprehensive) and true (that is, accurate). The answer to a well-conceived question, whatever that answer might be, is correct because it comports fully with reality. Answers that do not comport fully with reality are at least partly inadequate, if not flatly wrong. An ill-formed question is one that makes comprehensive and accurate answers not only more difficult to find than they need to be, but might actually make them impossible, as do modern scientific questions, which seek only the material causes to physical phenomena. But as Aristotle observed long ago, the one who would succeed in any intellectual pursuit must ask the right preliminary questions. Questions arising from metaphysical materialism are "the right preliminary questions" only if matter is all that is, or only if matter is all that matters, two propositions that cannot be demonstrated—indeed, that are patently false.

The instances where scientists and theologians agree in their description of that one reality which we all inhabit are many and varied. But they are not my concern. Rather, I intend to focus attention on those places (they too are numerous) where scientists and theologians diverge. I do so in order to offer some guidance on adjudicating between the respective truth claims of science and theology and in order to reduce the scope of their future disagreement, as well as its attendant animosity. In the process, I intend to direct my criticisms primarily toward the scientists rather than the theologians. I do so precisely because I am not a scientist. That is, if scientists are to be undeceived about their own shortcomings or blindspots it probably will be because someone who did not share those blindspots was able to point them out. That is my intention: I want to suggest to the scientists that, at least to some outsiders, they sometimes appear narrowly informed, unteachable and as dogmatic as any ecclesiastical or political inquisition could ever hope to be. I leave it to others to identify for the theologians just what the theologians cannot see and where they fail. Because I do not wish to hold the reader in suspense, much less to be vague or disingenuous, I tell you now that I think much of the adjustment and retrenchment in the sometimes heated dialogue between scientists and

192

theologians needs to be done by the scientists, and that much of the error and unteachability in this dialogue seems to circle around the laboratory and not the seminary. The burden of this essay, therefore, is to explain why I think as I do. I offer but four observations, observations that are, at the same time, both caveats and pleas.

First, the history of both science and theology as intellectual disciplines tends to make me significantly more skeptical about the allegedly secure answers offered by the scientists than I am about those offered by the theologians. That is, science seems a far more fickle pursuit than theology, especially when viewed over time. While Christian orthodoxy seems to have remained stable over two millennia, and while the constant refinement of Christian tenets in the crucible of hard reality seems not to have required any fundamental reorientation in orthodoxy,[1] the record of science is far different. The constant testing of fundamental scientific beliefs has yielded a long series of significant reorientations, some so far-reaching as to topple many, sometimes most, of the supporting pillars of any and every previous (and ardently held) scientific worldview. The post-Einsteinian worldview is beginning to succeed the Einsteinian, which succeeded the Newtonian, which succeeded the Copernican, which succeeded the Ptolemaic, which succeeded an earlier paradigm. What shall succeed the post-Einsteinian (and what shall succeed *that*) we can only guess. If the history of science is a guide to its future, we can be confident something shall—and that, whatever it is, it shall depart quite noticeably from its antecedents both near and far. As Austin Farrer once wryly observed, cosmological theories have a short life nowadays.

But not so the Apostles' Creed, which, though it has grown over time, has never required anything resembling a fundamental overhaul, much less several. Liberal theologians of every age (aided by the not-inconsiderable efforts of non-Christian thinkers of all sorts) have tried to argue differently and have tried to put orthodoxy under siege. But their dissenting and often idiosyncratic schools of thought themselves have proved transitory and have passed into deserved obscurity. But not the creed. In other words, theological orthodoxy, unlike its several scientific counterparts, has undergone centuries of analysis and assault and survived largely and widely intact. Christian orthodoxy has successfully sustained meticulous scrutiny by both its friends and its enemies and yet has shown itself, and continues to show itself, sufficient to many of the most brilliant minds in history, even over a period of centuries, a claim no scientific explanation of reality can yet make. The scientists in every age, I imagine, suppose they can escape—indeed, suppose they have escaped—the fate of their predecessors. They fancy they shall avoid being greatly transcended, though none has yet managed the trick. The face of scientific orthodoxy seems to have a nose of wax.

The transitoriness of scientific speculation and the uniformity and staying power of theological orthodoxy often get hidden behind both the wide diversity of theological beliefs prevalent at any one moment in time, on the one hand, and the absence of many public indications of division within the scientific community on the other. Widespread theological disagreement seems obvious to the man on the street, who sees the Presbyterian church, the Baptist church and the Roman Catholic church all standing tall and serene on their respective street corners, their spires rising toward the heavens. What the man on the street does not see is the underlying unity of the Presbyterians, the Baptists and the Catholics (to name but a few). He does not readily recognize their common belief in—and devotion to—the same God, the same Christ, the same creed, the same salvation. Nor does the man on the street see the various schools of thought in science, which normally do not erect edifices of difference on tree-shaded side streets in every city and village in the free world. He does not see hundreds, indeed thousands, of buildings (or television programs, for that matter) dedicated to Newtonian or

Ptolemaic theories standing next to the edifices of post-Einsteinianism. Unlike their ecclesiastical counterparts, those Newtonian and Ptolemaic buildings were rarely ever built, and are not now being built, because the scientific worldviews they represent have been so fully overthrown that they are consigned almost entirely to the dustbin of history. This is not to say that no valuable or enduring elements from within these systems have survived the collapse of the system from which they emerged; it does mean that those systems have been greatly and widely transcended.

Here is my point: While a cross section of views at any one moment yields more agreement among the scientists of that age than among the theologians, a cross section taken over time yields the opposite result, and that result, I argue, is more significant because it reveals both the fundamental staying power of the theological interpretation of the world and the (to date) transitory nature of scientific speculation. Science does not speak with one voice, especially over time. That fact not withstanding, science still seems to me far less likely to take any cues[2] from theology about in which direction to proceed than theology is to take advice from science, which might help explain the transitoriness of the one and the stability of the other. So also might the fact that, unlike nature, God wills to be understood and actively reveals Himself to us.

We apparently are not near the end of scientific intellection, though we are closer now than when Aristotle or Galileo walked among us. We do not know where the next grand turning in the road of scientific learning will lead us or when it will come, any more than did Ptolemy, Newton or Einstein. We ought, as a result, to be far more hesitant than we have been to identify scientific results as final. If you contend that scientists do not treat scientific results as final, I simply point to the theory of evolution, which gets treated almost universally not as theory but as established and unassailable fact requiring, at most, not proof, only further nuance. The epigraph by Richard Dawkins, which heads this essay, is a telling case in point, and can be multiplied *many thousands of times*, both in print and in the classroom. It seems to me, Dawkins' arrogance aside, that we ought to be far more wary of Darwin and his hide-bound modern disciples than we now are, because even though these followers of Darwin now admit that Darwin was not entirely right, they too often refuse to admit that Darwin's religious critics are not entirely wrong. Or, to make the point from a different science, one of the positive effects of quantum theory on the dialogue between theology and science seems to be the increasing awareness we gain from it that virtually no physical or geometrical picture of scientific phenomena is wholly accurate, even though such notions or paradigms were (and still are) widely and enthusiastically set forth, whether as models or as heuristic devices. We need to be more measured in the confidence we place in the scientist and in our estimate of what exactly the scientist has actually accomplished.

Second, because scientists are human beings, and because human beings tend to resist the overthrow of their most cherished beliefs, scientific theories, once accepted, are often exceedingly difficult to supersede. The shameful treatment of Pierre Duhem at the hands of his institutional superiors is a well-known case in point. All too often, the new, even when it carries great weight of evidence, gets routinely derided as outlandish. That scientists are intellectually conservative, of course, is good. Their conservatism helps protect them from the multiple embarrassments of intellectual trendiness. But that scientists are unduly entrenched, when they are, is lamentable. That entrenchment reveals that scientists sometimes are, like the rest of us, resolutely unteachable. The Dawkins epigraph above is but one example of the entrenchment, perhaps even intellectual bigotry, about which I speak. Scientists who think in that fashion seem to me to be what one dictionary defined as "proof-proof": the state of mind of one upon whom contrary evidence and argument have no persuasive effect, regardless of their strength. I am not alone in this observation, of course. Many writers, Kuhn and Laudan among them, have shown how dogmatism—yes, dogmatism—characterizes the periods of what we might call *normal* science. Whether we want to admit it or not, there is a remarkably comprehensive scientific orthodoxy to which scientists must subscribe if they want to get a job, get a promotion, get a research grant, get tenured or get published. If they resist, they get forgotten.

Given how changeable previous scientific worldviews have been, one wonders how chimerical they would have proven without this dogmatism. I am not here debating the relative merits or weaknesses of dogmatism; I simply say that scientists are by no means free from it and should not be treated as if they were or permitted to speak and act as if dogmatism were a characteristic only, or even primarily, of theologians.

Third, scientists often fail to admit, sometimes even to recognize, that so many of the issues and findings of science are neither purely scientific nor genuinely empirical. Because all empirical endeavors build upon, and proceed according to, various presuppositions, and because those presuppositions and procedures are inescapably philosophical, no scientist and no scientific procedure is truly philosophy-free. Empiricism and the empiricalist procedures that arise from it are philosophy-laden worldviews and techniques, and not necessarily the best. If ideas have consequences, and if (as some philosophers strongly argue) empiricism and empiricalism are highly suspect—perhaps even greatly flawed—then scientists are likely to be misled if they apply these notions uncritically to their work. To put a point on it, if, as some scientists insist, real science is truly empirical and reduces only to empirical methods and to the conclusions reached by using them, then there is no real science, because the theory-independent observation, analysis and conclusions needed to establish such empirical premises are simply not possible. Because none of us is presupposition-free, and because (despite much contrary insistence) scientific theories often deal with the unobserved and the unobservable, the laboratory is no philosophy- or theology-free zone. Scientific methods and conclusions cannot be purely empirical because the unavoidable philosophical and theological underpinnings upon which those scientific methods rely are not the result of those allegedly empirical methods.

Put another way, the claim to objectivity and empiricality falls down on both sides—on the side of the scientist and on the side of science. When eating their curry, many people like to build for it a nest of rice. To employ a more American image, people like to mold a bowl in their mashed potatoes in order to hold their gravy. Science, it seems to me, has its nest, its bowl. Science always has its philosophical and theological underpinnings; physics always has its metaphysics—always.[3] To declare science a philosophy-free zone is to have a philosophy; to declare science a procedurally agnostic or atheistic endeavor is to have a theology; to claim that science ought to be value-free is to make a value statement. The question is never whether or not the scientist in a laboratory has a philosophy, a theology or an ethic when doing scientific work; the question is whether or not the philosophy, the theology and the ethic the scientist has are any good and are worth having. This problem they cannot escape.

Even in the pursuit of something as fundamental as self-definition, science alone is utterly insufficient. To the question "What is the proper definition of science?" one can give only a philosophical (and, by extension, theological) answer because the question itself presupposes and requires a vantage point from outside science. Because we cannot tell who are the scientists and who are not until we know what science itself is, one cannot answer this question, as scientists too often do, by resorting to the tautology that science is that which is done by the scientist. The question "What is science?" is a question about science, not a question of science. Scientists want, indeed claim, to be empirical. But please note: "empirical" is a philosophical category. Without the aid of the humanities, science cannot even identify itself, much less justify—or even invent—its procedures.

To make the point in a different direction, science is not theology-free, and that is so precisely because science intentionally operates according to a procedural agnosticism, if not procedural atheism. That is, science operates as if God cannot be known or else as if He were altogether irrelevant, if not entirely absent. By its means and its conclusions, science implicitly, perhaps even explicitly, denies that Christ is Lord of the universe, an inescapably theological denial. What I, as a theologian, want to tell my scientific colleagues is that, as Lord of the universe and all that is within it, Christ is not something *in addition* to science, He is Someone in relation to it. To operate as if He were utterly irrelevant to the laboratory is to answer, probably without careful analysis and theological acumen, the question raised long ago in the gospels: "What think ye of Christ?" Because Christ is foundational to the universe, he is foundational to science. As Thomas Torrance once explained to me,

> . . . the countries of the Far East and of the Southern Hemisphere want our science and technology, but they have no doctrine of creation. They do not realize that science and technology rest upon, indeed arise from, Christian foundations. This is true both historically and epistemologically. We must show them that it is the Creator God himself who stands behind everything, and that he provides the rational ground upon which the various sciences rest, as well as the world those sciences unlock and help to tame. Theology and technology come as a pair. We must be quite firm about both this and their function in serving and respecting the integrity of nature.[4]

Like it or not, the systematic and procedural denial, not to say the intended destruction, of metaphysics and of theology is the death of scientific truth, if for no other reason than that it posits a dual or dichotomized universe, which we noted at the outset was untrue. Answers to questions predicated upon that same bifurcated basis, while they are perhaps true as far as they go, do not go all the way and are not the whole truth.

Perhaps an illustration will serve. No physicist today can reckon with miracles and interventions from outside the material order or with interventions that break that order open. No theory they devise, no answer they propose, permits such ideas or recognizes such data, even though such data and ideas might be absolutely and comprehensively true. That analytical inability reveals the limitations, indeed the willful blindness, of modern physics. Modern physics does not reveal the limitations of God and his actions, much less God's nonexistence or irrelevance, assumptions implicit in scientific method as now understood and practiced. God, if we need to be reminded, works in perfect freedom and not according to the Kant-Laplace theory of determinedness or to any of its current or future descendants.

Let me put it more graphically: Any intellectual endeavor in which theology is segregated from the other disciplines and relegated to an intellectual ghetto is an instance of Jim Crow come again to the college campus because it explicitly asserts that the best intellectual paradigm is not well-informed academic integration but some framework of "separate but equal," which, as we learned in the old South, meant separate but unequal, not because of actual inferiority, but because of bigotry. By acting as if God Himself were irrelevant to the universe He has made and to our understanding of it, scientists, in effect, practice "disciplinism," a widespread form of intellectual bigotry whereby the research and discoveries of other scholars are systematically disregarded simply because those scholars are members of another discipline. The Queen of the Sciences has been banished to the back of the bus by her own bigoted descendants. The fool has said in his heart that there is no God, and the scientist permits himself to operate as if the fool were right.

Science is not an autonomous set of empirical disciplines. Nothing about science properly, or actually, prevents philosophical or theological concepts from entering into it. Science, like all intellectual disciplines, ought not to conduct its business in an imaginary, air-tight compartment, isolated from all other strivings of the human mind after knowledge. Because too many scientists have cut themselves off from those other strivings, they condemn themselves to discovering all on their own many things already widely known by others. For example, even though such ideas appeared new and revolutionary to some of the unphilosophical practitioners of science, most of Mach's notions were already standard fare in the writings of a number of earlier philosophers. The high price some scientists pay for their intellectual isolationism and prejudice is that they must repeatedly reinvent the intellectual wheel.

But there is more to theology in science than procedural agnosticism and atheism. Our ape ancestors are treated with immense respect, even toadying homage, as the secular Adam and Eve. No attacks upon their status, much less their existence, are tolerated. Read Dawkins' epigraph again. Not to do obeisance to the fossil remains of ancient animals ranks as scientific sacrilege, as scientific heresy. Religion, albeit pagan, has come to the laboratory, and the allegedly secular scientist has become its new high priest.

Furthermore, many of those very scientists who insist on divorcing religion from science seem sometimes especially eager to use their science as a basis for theological (or at least extra-scientific) pronouncements. The literature of science is replete with anti-theistic language and conclusions: The universe was not designed; the universe has no purpose; human beings result from random and mindless natural processes—or so we are repeatedly told.

Put another way, to the adoration of God and of virtue, some moderns have added the adoration of science (or at least what goes by that name). But you cannot deify the scientific method without at the same time devaluing or debasing both theology (the human understanding and application of revelation) and philosophy (the human understanding and application of reason). Many scientists, therefore, without meaning to do so, undermine our only sources of morality and freedom: God and reason. They do so by believing, writing and teaching that only those things that are testable under controlled laboratory conditions qualify as hard knowledge; all else is merely opinion. But even a moment's reflection reveals that if every question of morality, of politics, of philosophy and of theology is a matter of mere untestable opinion, they can be settled only by force, not by reason. In that way (and in others) scientists sometimes lead us to tyranny. Fascism and pseudo-liberalism are the not-too-distant offspring of modern man's widespread belief that science alone is trustworthy and that whatever lies beyond its pale is little more and little else than irrational prejudice, unsubstantiatable conjecture and transitory emotion incapable of reasoned support. This vision of life most modern persons learn in the science classroom. Too often scientists teach and write as if the only real options available to us are science or mysticism, empiricism or bias, fact or feeling.

Simply because no test tube yields a "should" or an "ought," "should" and "ought" are not thereby banished or made suspect; science is. Moral questions—questions about right and wrong or good and bad—cannot be answered (or even raised) by the scientific methods now prevalent in either the natural or the social sciences. That does not mean, however, that they cannot be answered, have not been answered or have no answers. It means only that with regard to the diagnostic and fundamental questions of life, science is impotent, though dangerous. The one who has not learned to ask, much less to answer, the fundamental questions of life is indeed no man at all, but still a child, still benighted. To answer such questions, even to raise them, science is powerless. Consequently, while technical schools and scientific laboratories are important and laudable things, to advertise them as colleges or universities or to say that those who have passed through them are truly educated men and women is to lie.

To put the point differently, God is the Lord of the entire world of knowledge, including science and technology. Science and technology that are atheistic in both conception and conduct, that are consciously cut loose from all formal considerations about God and morality, are not your dream come true; they are your worst nightmare. To utilize science and technology wisely or else to become their victims—that is the choice before us. But the wisdom that saves us from our science and technology is no commodity derived from either of them or from both. To paraphrase something C.S. Lewis said in another context, science ceases to be a demon only when it ceases to be a god. It can never cease until it figures out a way to let God be God, even in the laboratory.

Fourth, we ought to be more skeptical than we are both of scientific taxonomy and of the translation of the world outside our heads into numbers. That is, scientists do not simply deal with the world as they find it; they manipulate that world into words of their own choosing, into categories of their own making, into experiments of their own devising and into numbers. Forcing a creature into one or more categories based upon our intellectual manipulations and speculations regarding its body pattern and parts, or upon our understanding of its physical makeup and upon our conjectures regarding its biological descent, is at least partly arbitrary, partly subjective. Such categories, though helpful and serviceable, are manmade. They unintentionally and sometimes unwittingly collapse the distinction between what we discover and what we invent. While the beings that populate such categories most emphatically do exist, the families, orders, classes and phyla into which we have pigeon-holed them do not. Such pigeon-holings are a taxonomist's useful fiction, but *do not exist outside the taxonomist's mind*. That is, while those taxonomical categories are constructs based upon careful observation, they are constructs nevertheless. Of course, I am not saying anything so silly as that there exist no genuine and recognizable differences between a dog and a man or that "dog" and "man" are useless fictions devoid of all external reference or reality. But let us not too quickly or uncritically identify "useful" as "true" or as "real" categories that in many cases and ways are quite different.

Yet not only are we required to accept the taxonomist's scheme of classification as both real and true, we are required to accept that the occupants of these various man-made categories are linked by a long series of nonliving intermediate creatures (also duly classified and arranged), most of whom are not found to exist anywhere in the fossil record, a radically incomplete record we interpret according to the taxonomical grid provided for us. (The circularity of this procedure seems to go unnoticed and unremarked.) Furthermore, we are also required to believe that all the seemingly discontinuous and taxonomically divisible groups now alive are the descendants of a common ancestor, another phantom of which (or of whom) we have no direct evidence. Please note that "ancestor" and "descendant" are part of a taxonomical scheme and are no less so than is "phantom," a word from which my scientist readers would naturally recoil. Their own language, the scientists must remember, is the source of great recoil as well. It rarely seems to occur to some scientists that the rapid evolutionary branchings posited in some theories are but a euphemism for mystical scientific leaps, though they are called by other names, such as Stephen Jay Gould's "punctuated equilibrium." Of such leaps I am more than a little skeptical.

Further, not only is taxonomical classification significantly theory-laden, it is context-dependent and subtly subjective. That which we classify as the observed in one case fails to be so classified in another, even though the thing itself is the same. That is, what is foreground and what is background vary according to the judgment of the observer, an observer who is never context-free or presuppositionless. Thus, scientists are driven back, whether they acknowledge it or not, upon the problem "What is context and what is content?", the answer to which seems to vary from situation to situation depending upon the experimenter and the experiment, even though the aggregation of things involved might be basically the same. Nor are the experiments themselves pristinely empirical and objective, for experiments are highly stylized sets of phenomena, sets from which as many variables as possible have been artificially eliminated by the will and work of the experimenter, however well or however poorly. Of course, I am not saying that the data yielded by such experimentation are therefore untrue, only that they are not pristine. In other words, some scientists need frequently to be reminded of the significantly non-literal and pragmatic nature of their experiments, of their theories and of the language in which those experiments and theories are conceived and articulated.

Like taxonomy, quantification might itself be a movement away from the world around us, not into it. The translation of things into numbers is, after all, a translation. Neither the words nor the numbers in scientific theories are complete and exact representations of the constitution and behavior of the universe, much less are they the things themselves which they are intended to describe in words or embody in numbers and formulae. Newton had his numbers; Einstein had his; post-Einsteinians have theirs. Newton's and Einstein's formulae worked (so to speak) and were the basis for considerable correct prediction regarding natural phenomena. Nevertheless, on many important points, Newton and Einstein were also quite wrong, something from which their seemingly correct numbers did not and could not save them. I am not reluctant to think that the same fate awaits many of their scientific descendants.

The classification of physical phenomena as suitable and useable scientific data, the arrangement of that data into groups, the translation of that data into numbers, the manipulation of those numbers via computation and the transformation of the results of that computation into more data and new conclusions are all guided by philosophical deliberations that are prior to and apart from science's alleged empirical nature and militate against it—all of which ought to cause us to hold science's supposedly assured results with less assurance. Judging from the philosophical and theological naivete of most of the scientists with whom I have ever spoken, those intellectual deliberations might not have been deliberations at all, but merely the unexamined and unacknowledged *a priori* assumptions of a mind utterly untrained in a number of difficult but acutely relevant fields throughout the humanities.

The related assertion that science is measurement is, of course, a philosophical assertion, an assertion that is flatly unprovable. Indeed, as even a moment's reflection will demonstrate, because it is not itself measurable, this assertion is unscientific on its own terms. It is, in fact, autophagic—it eats itself up. Nor can we prove this assertion by invoking the principle of prediction and thereby assert that a scientific hypothesis is true if it can be shown accurately and successfully to predict the action of physical phenomena. The principle of prediction, while clearly important and serviceable, is at least as closely related to pragmatism as to truth. That is, to be able to predict more accurately than all other theories means only that one's theory is pragmatically preferable, not that it is necessarily true. We must remember that false, or partly false, theories have demonstrated impressive powers of prediction in the past. The ancient Babylonian astronomers, for example, by no means shabby forecasters, were working from premises and principles quite off the mark. In other words, while prediction seems to be a necessary attribute of a true scientific theory, it must not be considered a sufficient attribute. Prediction is not proof, no matter how impressive it seems. Too many scientists nevertheless still think, write, argue and teach as if accurate prediction demonstrated truth. How many times this has been done, is being done, and shall continue to be done, only God knows. But it seems not at all likely to stop. Or, to make the case in a different direction, if prediction were really the reliable indicator of truth that some think it to be, then physics itself, which has an abysmal record of prediction with regard to some individual entities, would be radically undermined. Furthermore, as clear thinking philosophers and theologians understand, pragmatic preference is an utterly insufficient basis for determining the virtue of an action. If pragmatic preference is an exploded mode of justification in ethics, I am inclined to regard it as such in scientific epistemology. Its epistemological failures are not magically eradicated simply because we now concern ourselves with a laboratory.

That is how the laboratory looks from the seminary, or at least to this member of it. Having watched many of them in action, I think the scientists would be better served (and would serve better) if they were more humble and more eclectic in pursuit of their worthy enterprise. I should hope that when they do their work the scientists would listen at least as much to those outside the laboratory as they would like those outside the laboratory to listen to them. This, after all, is the golden rule of scholarship.

Finally, though it is clearly beyond both my intention and my competence to dictate to the scientists exactly how their jobs ought to be conducted and in what specific direction they ought to proceed, let me offer but one outsider's opinion, an opinion motivated by sincere goodwill for my laboratory colleagues. I believe that what we need now is not something akin to an aimless collection of more data, but research (of every sort) directed by principles, illumined by ideas. Those guiding principles and those illuminating ideas must, by their very nature, come to science from outside science, at least until we figure out how science ought to be restructured and redefined in order to avoid its current myopia. Science, to be kept serviceable and humane, must be kept humble and teachable. And it must acknowledge its debts, debts it always has.

To the question "Is science enough?" the answer is emphatically "No."

Endnotes

[1]Creeds are not imposed by simple ecclesiastical fiat. Instead, like scientific definitions in other branches of knowledge, creeds typically undergo what might roughly be described as a five-stage development: observation, reflection, articulation, testing and confirmation or rejection. In the first stage, Christian thinkers examine carefully the text of Scripture (that is, the content of revelation) and the course of their own and others' experience of living in agreement with Scripture, at least as they understand it. Second, they reflect deeply and carefully upon what they have observed in order to grasp its true significance. Because they must not be content with an inarticulate devotion, to this perceived significance and to their conclusions concerning it they naturally try to give thoughtful and precise expression. Their newly formulated ideas are then submitted to testing in the twin crucibles of life and thought to see if those ideas can withstand the rough-and-tumble of genuine human experience and the rigors of systematic intellectual scrutiny. If they cannot they are rejected, or else modified and tried again. In this informal but effective way, the Church has invested decades, even centuries, in capturing in precise creedal form the tremendous truths revealed in the historical events connected with Jesus of Nazareth. Of course, this is not to say that creeds have nothing

to do with the pronouncements of bishops and councils; they often do. But creeds typically find their roots elsewhere, in revelation and in the life and thought of the church. This is especially true of the Apostles' Creed, which though at some points is still controverted, has been tested by long experience and careful, repeated reflection upon that experience in the light of Scripture and reason. Furthermore, because the Apostles' Creed has grown out of centuries of biblical exegesis, human experience and reflection, it continues to be both relevant and reliable. It continues to ring true because, like all good theology, it is deeply rooted in divine revelation on the one hand and human reason and reality on the other.

[2]What might be the precise nature and content of such cues I cannot now say. How philosophy and theology ought ideally to be introduced into the sciences is a question the answering of which might require a radically new way of doing science. That I myself am currently unable to supply this new paradigm is neither an embarrassment to me nor a refutation of my claim that it might be needed. I offer only an analogy, drawn from criminology. When a detective attempts to solve a crime, he not only searches for clues, he invents hypotheses. In this search and invention, the detective has this great advantage: He knows he is deciphering not some random occurrence, but tracking the work of a mind. Knowing this, the detective suitably modifies the character of his hypotheses and alters both the nature and focus of his search for clues, as well as his definition of what might or might not be relevant data. Human criminals, for example, unlike mindless and lifeless matter, have discernible motives and sometimes concoct false alibis in order to cover their tracks. In short, they leave clues of a very distinctive sort. The scientist, by the same token, if he were to entertain the God factor in his laboratory and decide to trace the workings of Infinite Mind rather than of mindless matter, might need to alter what he considers the boundaries of acceptable hypothesis, what he admits as

relevant data, how he forms and executes his experiments, how he draws and articulates his conclusions and what he imagines constitutes a convincing proof or refutation.

[3]I am not saying that all physicists must or do have the same metaphysic, only that while they are doing their work they cannot avoid having one and applying it.

[4]Michael Bauman, *Roundtable: Conversations with European Theologians* (Grand Rapids, MI: Baker, 1990), 115.

Science, Apologetics and Orthodoxy: A Case Study and a Plea for Caution

David W. Hall

One of the most contentious arenas for apologetics in this century has been the creation-evolution debate. Of late, some of the hostility seems to be diminishing as it becomes fashionable to argue that there should be little debate because the ancients were amazingly anticipatory of modern notions. This harmonic convergence, however, appears to be simple revisionism. A central argument of this essay is that neither science nor apologetics is strengthened by ill-founded revisions of earlier Christian thought.

Rather than deal exclusively with the historical dimensions, I desire to use this as a case study of the interaction of science and apologetic method. One might even view this study as an application of the scientific method (hypothesis, experimentation, conclusion) to these theories: "Pre-Darwinian theologians admitted the possibility of a long period for creation. The best apologetic method conforms itself to the science of the day." What follows is a testing of these hypotheses to see if they are capable of falsification.

It is frequently claimed, for example, that evangelicals need not hold out for a short sequence of creation insofar as earlier fathers and earlier biblical interpreters did not. Professor John A. McIntyre has warned against a "Christian amnesia," which allegedly forgets the earlier commentators on creation:

> [Some] Christians have introduced a modern, naive
> 24-hour interpretation for days in Genesis, disagree-
> ing with the classical, sophisticated analysis of these
> days by Augustine, Aquinas, and Calvin. . . . How can
> Christian scholars today ignore so completely the
> great Christian scholars of the past?[1]

Is it correct that Augustine, Aquinas, Calvin and the current of orthodox expounders of creation held to a view
which has immense "semantic elasticity"[2]? To isolate the
matter, if those who lived before Darwin—thus uninflu-
enced by that type of evolutionary thought—believed in
long periods of continuous creation or progressive creation,
or if they believed in a developmental gradualism that did
not demand a special creation, then indeed, perhaps later
Christians too are justified in jettisoning *creatio simul et ex
nihilo*. As one examines these questions, openness and humility are fitting. In our search of ancient interpretations
of the creation narratives, we desire to avoid haughty or
provincial approaches which insist that one's own tradition
or generation is superior to all past generations and interpretations. We do not wish to arrogantly disqualify earlier
Christians from the discussion—simply because of their
moment in history. In its pioneering effort, the Templeton
Center for Humility Theology (Bryn Mawr, PA) exempli-
fies an "open minded" examination—"always ready to rethink what is known and to revise the assumptions and
preconceptions behind our knowledge." We seek to follow
their path as a historical question arises which must be answered humbly, even if it calls into question now-dominant
theories: Did earlier Christians hold to instantaneous creation *ex nihilo*, or did they allow for lengthy evolutionary
gradualism?

The modern hypotheses for creation by developmental
and gradual means over a long period of time seem foreign
to earlier evangelicals. Even if an idiosyncratic or ambiguous reference may be found (often capable of alternative ex-

planation) in some writers, an altogether compelling case to view ancient evangelicals as compatible with a framework hypothesis still must be made.[3] If one wishes to make the case against short periods of creation, he will likely have to move closer to the present than the Reformation. Yet this mistake is becoming fairly widespread.

Older antagonists such as Andrew Dickson White claimed that Augustine (a major focus of this essay) "revolted against the conception of an actual creation of the universe by the hands and fingers of a Supreme Being."[4] White also put into Augustine's mouth a "belief in the pre-existence of matter"; stated that "Calvin opposed the idea of an instantaneous creation" and that those who hold such view "basely insult the Creator, [and] expect a judge who will annihilate them"[5]; and even attributed to Augustine the lead in the purported medieval revolt away from literalism—and this due to Augustine's reliance on Scripture as more authoritative than human ingenuity.[6]

More recently, Hugh Ross has conceded:

> Many of the early church fathers and other biblical scholars interpreted the creation days of Genesis 1 as long periods of time. The list includes . . . Irenaeus . . . Origen . . . Basil . . . Augustine, and later Aquinas to name a few.[7]

Ross includes an argument for long days of creation[8] and blames fundamentalism for the genesis of creationism. However, the best that Ross, White and others can do in their presentation of Augustine's and Calvin's views is to demonstrate that symbolic language is appreciated in their respective commentaries.[9] It is a reach, nevertheless, to infer a repudiation of traditional (pre-Darwinian) creationism from these authors' use of a symbolic hermeneutic.[10]

Furthermore, despite Henry Morris's interpretation that Augustine's doctrine of "seed principles" sounds like a "modern theistic evolutionist,"[11] it would take far more to transform Augustine into a theistic evolutionist than these claims—if the rest of his writing is taken into account. Morris even concedes that Augustine grants continuous creation in *De Trinitate*.[12] Did Augustine stand out from his day and hold to views of creation that are more akin to twentieth-century views? Can one really agree with Henry Morris that "The end result of the teachings of Augustine, Aquinas, and other well-intentioned theologians was an undermining of biblical authority"?[13] It seems that Augustine can speak for himself and should be consulted prior to accepting revisionary studies. Is either science or apologetics enhanced by reimagining earlier theologians to be so tony as to fit in with late twentieth-century views of continuous creation, developing over billions of years?

I intend to challenge the claim that Augustine, Aquinas, Calvin and others erected theories compatible with a 16-18 billion-year-old cosmos—an apologetic revision of epic proportions. The strategic revision is clarified by contrasting two eras: (1) pre-Darwinian theology and (2) post-Darwinian theology.[14] The bulk of this essay examines the frequent assertion that the orthodox strain of beliefs on creation has always allowed wide latitude in this *loci*, rendering the ancients virtually indistinguishable from moderns.

It was, after all, the same Andrew White as above who—despite his wish to the contrary—admitted that Calvin had a "strict" interpretation of Genesis and that "down to a period almost within living memory [this was written in 1896], it was held, virtually 'always, everywhere, and by all,' that the universe, as we now see it, was created literally and directly by the voice or hands of the Almighty, or by both—out of nothing—in an instant or in six days. . . ."[15] Even opponents find it difficult to mangle this testimony, although with the effect of cumulative misquotations that is becoming more frequent.

214

Pre-Darwin

A representative survey of pre-Darwinian theologians will disprove that the ancients uniformly endorsed long periods of creation, non-momentary creation or original cosmological development—purported citations notwithstanding. Many of the claims alleged to support a dubious point—when set in their proper context—allow an alternative interpretation and do not necessarily buttress the more modern schemes. Such citations are often based on inaccuracy of quotation, are contradictory to the larger context or are idiosyncratic (not necessarily typical of mainstream orthodoxy).

Ambrose of Milan (339-397) was one of the first theologians to explicate a mature view of creation. In his *Hexameron*, he admitted that even in his day some believed that matter "is considered to have given the power of creation to all things."[16] His view, however, was: "The language is simple: 'God created heaven and earth.' He created what was not, not what was."[17] Regarding the creation of the cosmos by divine Word, he added later:

> When the word "light" is used, it is not intended to mean merely the preparation for performance; rather, it is the splendor of the operation itself in action. . . . He did not speak in order that action should follow; rather, that action was completed with the Word [followed by a reference to Psalm 148:5].[18]

While there is no suggestion that the days were long, Ambrose affirmed that on the fifth day, "At this command the waters immediately poured forth their offspring. The rivers were in labor. The lakes produced their quota of life. The sea itself began to bear all manner of reptiles and to send forth according to its kind whatever was there created. . . . Dolphins frolicked in the waves. Shell-fish clung to the rocks. Oysters adhered to the depths and the sea-urchins waxed strong."[19] He apparently believed that multiple species were created immediately and instantaneously, rather than by gradual development: "The whale, as well as the frog, came into existence at the same time by the same creative power. Without effort does God produce the greatest things. He is not averse to creating the least."[20]

Elsewhere, Ambrose affirmed, "God created day and night at the same time. Since that time, day and night continue their daily succession and renewal."[21] In his fullest discussion of the lengths of the creation days, Ambrose noted the following:

> The beginning of the day rests on God's word: "Be light made, and light was made." The end of day is the evening. Now, the succeeding day follows after the termination of night. The thought of God is clear. First He called light "day" and next He called darkness "night." In notable fashion has Scripture spoken of a "day," not the "first day." Because a second, then a third day, and finally the remaining days were to follow, a "first day" could have been mentioned, following in this way the natural order. But Scripture established a law that twenty-four hours, including both day and night, should be given the name of day only, as if one were to say the length of one day is twenty-four hours in extent.[22]

The earliest, full treatise on creation ends with these sentiments:

> But now we seem to have reached the end of our discourse, since the sixth day is completed and the sum total of the work of the world has been concluded. . . . [W]e should now make our contribution of silence, since God has rested from the work of the world. . . . He the Creator rested.[23]

With such clarity, a fair question is: Will Augustine (354-430) later differentiate his position from Ambrose's? Does Augustine distance himself from the *Hexameron* to advocate an immense period of creation? At least on the surface, Augustine did not seem aware of being contrary to Ambrose.

Augustine's view of creation is not always opaque. In his *Enchiridion*, he stated that the Christian believes

> that the cause of all created things, whether in heaven or on earth, whether visible or invisible, is nothing other than the goodness of the Creator, who is the one true God. . . . By this Trinity, supremely and equally and immutably good, were all things created. (ch. 3)

A similar affirmation is given in *The City of God*, while arguing for the consubstantiality of the Son: ". . . the only-begotten Son who is the wisdom by which all things were created" (bk. 11, ch. 24). Frequently in *The City of God*, Augustine affirms: "There is no creator higher than God" (11.21); "nothing can exist apart from creation by God" (11.23); "[man's] natural being is created from nothing" (12.6); "But only a nature created out of nothing could have been distorted by a fault" (14.13; cf. also 14.11). Augustine had no hesitancy employing the *ex nihilo* terminology, and even accepts a chronology that seldom accompanies an evolutionary view: "From Adam to the flood there were 2,262 years according to the calculation data in our versions of the Scripture" (15.20). He concluded with a summary: "But to return to the three answers which, as I suggested above, should be given when we asked concerning any creature—Who made it? How? and Why?—the answers are: 'God'; 'by the word'; and 'because it is good'" (11.23).

In *Faith and the Creed*, Augustine stated:

If they admit that the world was made by an omnipotent God they must admit that he made what he has made out of nothing. If he were omnipotent there could be nothing of which he was not the Creator. Even if he did make something out of something else, as he made man out of clay, he did not make it out of something which he had not himself made. For he made the earth out of nothing, and clay comes from the earth. . . . [W]e must by no means believe that the matter out of which the world was made, however formless or invisible, could have existed as it was by itself, as if it were co-eternal and coeval with God.[24]

Contrary to the claims by moderns searching for support, Augustine's statements in *The Confessions* do not lend support to viewing him as a precursor of evolutionary theory. At various places he affirmed: "[T]his earth was invisible and without order . . . before you formed this unformed matter and fashioned it into kinds, there was no separate being, no color, no shape, no body, no spirit" (12.3);[25] "Lord, you made the world out of formless matter . . . 'Let it be made,' and so it was made" (12.8); "all these visible things were made and set in order during those various days . . ." (12.17). At a trenchant summation in *The Confessions*, Augustine said, "True it is that you, from whom are all things have made not only created and formed being, but also whatsoever is capable of being created and formed" (12.19). Later he argued: "Why should we not understand, with Truth teaching us, that also formless matter, which Scripture calls earth invisible and unformed . . . was made by God out of nothing, and therefore is not coeternal with him . . . ?" (12.22). A long age of development or progressive creation does not seem compatible with these sentiments. He went so far as to pray for "patience" when those who oppose Moses' intent do so "because they are proud and have not known Moses' meaning, but love their own, not because it is true, but because it is

218

their own" (12.25). He accused those who would distort the meaning of Moses of "rash judgment; not insight but pride."

Augustine repeatedly affirmed that God made heaven and earth in the beginning (13.2): "Out of nothing have they been made by you, not out of yourself, not out of anything not your own, or which previously existed, but out of concreated matter, that is, out of matter simultaneously created by you, since without any intervening time you gave form to its formlessness. . . . [Y]ou made the matter entirely out of nothing" (13.33).

Despite the claim that Augustine manifested a "striking anticipation of some modern evolutionary doctrines,"[26] such claim is at best a classic case of conforming the ancient to the modern—whether the revisionary shoe fits or not. Augustine should also be remembered for asserting that God "would not be omnipotent, if he were unable to create anything good, unless he were assisted by that matter which he had not created" (7.5). The following should be factored into revisionary claims about Augustine's view of creation:

> What was your engine for doing this mighty work? You did not work as does the human artist, who transforms one body into another. . . . You made the artist's body; you, the soul that gives orders to his members; you, the matter out of which he fashions things. . . . All these praise you, the creator of all things. . . . You did not hold in your hand anything out of which to make heaven and earth. . . . You spoke, therefore, and these things were made, and in your Word you made them. (11.5)

This is a robust view of creation embracing special creation *ex nihilo*, *simul* and *verbe*. Gradualism—absent some superimposed presupposition—is not obvious in these early writings which are, of late, so misrepresented.

In *The Literal Meaning of Genesis*, Augustine—the alleged adherent to the framework hypothesis—commented:

> Hence it seems that this work of God was done in the space of a day, at the end of which evening came on, which is the beginning of night. Moreover, when the night was spent, a full day was completed, and the morning belonged to a second day, in which God then performed another work.[27]

Augustine's sensitivity to symbolism ought not be transformed into a cosmology which fits with a 16-billion-year-old cosmos, apart from numerous, explicit and consistent iterations.

It is true that Augustine's discussion of certain topics is somewhat bizarre and difficult to interpret.[28] For example, he averred that the Sabbath had been annulled,[29] that the seventh day "kept recurring to make up months and years and ages"[30] (4.14) and that the sixth day symbolized completeness because it is the first number which is the sum of its parts. Despite these eccentricities, he theorized:

> The more likely explanation, therefore, is this: these seven days of our time, although like the seven days of creation in name and in numbering, follow one another in succession and mark off the division of time, but those first six days occurred in a form unfamiliar to us. . . ."[31] (4.14)

However, lest one think that Augustine was arguing for an expanded period of creation so as to permit lengthy development, he also argued that the entire creation happened in only one day:

> Perhaps we should say that God created only one day, so that by its recurrence many periods called days would pass by. . . . All creation, then, was finished by

the sixfold recurrence of this day, whose evening and morning we may interpret as explained above.[32] (4.20, 26).

Augustine believed:

> Thus, in all the days of creation there is one day, and it is not to be taken in the sense of our day, which we reckon by the course of the sun; but it must have another meaning, applicable to the three days mentioned before the creation of the heavenly bodies. This special meaning of "day" must not be maintained just for the first three days. . . . But we must keep the same meaning even to the sixth and seventh days.[33] (4.26)

He continued to explain: "That day in the account of creation, or those days that are numbered according to its recurrence, are beyond the experience and knowledge of us mortal earthbound men"[34] (4.27). Still, he did not want to be confused with figurative or allegorical interpretations,[35] (4.28) and he believed that "the whole of creation was finished in six days"[36] (4.14). He suggested that as angels beheld the creation, there were no intervals of time, i.e., that time stood still[37] (4.29-30; cf. also 2.8); however, there was order of sequence.

Augustine argued that the firmament, the waters, plants, trees, heavenly bodies and all living creatures were "made simultaneously"[38] (4.33). So far was he from advocating a gradual evolution that he said:

> "Perhaps we ought not to think of the creatures at the moment they were produced as subject to the processes of nature which we now observe in them, but rather as under the wonderful and unutterable power of the Wisdom of God. . . . For this power of Divine Wisdom does not reach by stages or arrive by steps. It

was just as easy, then, for God to create everything as it is for Wisdom to exercise this mighty power. . . . Creation, therefore, *did not take place slowly in order that a slow development might be implanted in those things that are slow by nature; nor were the ages established at the plodding pace at which they now pass.*[39] (4.33)

That Augustine is incompatible with modern notions is seen from his comment:

[B]ut there was no passage of time when they [creatures] received these laws at creation. Otherwise, if we think that, when they were first created by the Word of God, there were the processes of nature with the normal duration of days that we know, those creatures that shoot forth roots and clothe the earth would need not one day but many to germinate beneath the ground, and then a certain number of days, according to their natures, to come forth from the ground; and the creation of vegetation, which Scripture places on one day, namely the third, would have been a gradual process.[40] (4.33)

Augustine believed that there was no "before" or "after" in the moment of creation: "It follows, therefore, that he, who created all things together, simultaneously created these six days, or seven, or rather the one day six or seven times repeated"[41] (4.33).

One can conclude the following about Augustine's views: (1) they were directed toward a certain set of ideas of the time; (2) his argumentation should be set in that context and not snatched from that context to argue for later ideas; (3) his views of creation seem rather unique and idiosyncratic in the history of theology; i.e., few, if any, theologians approached the Genesis narratives as creatively as did Augustine (for example, his concern for the angelic observation of creation is rather unparalleled); (4) he did not wish to be interpreted as using the allegorical method; his intent was to be as literal as possible; (5) he recognized that the day of creation was a non-normal day; (6) he maintained that it was not a solar day, insofar as at least three "days" occurred prior to the creation of the sun; (7) he did not believe that creation took a long period of development, but to the contrary; (8) Augustine believed that all of creation occurred simultaneously, at one instant; (9) He also believed that Jesus' saying in John 5 ("My Father is still working") applied only to governance, not "of creating any new nature."[42] Thus, it is difficult to sustain the argument that Augustine believed in continuous creation. Augustine believed (10) that Adam was "made from the slime of the earth and the woman from the side of her husband"[43] (6.5). Ernan McMullin confirms that following the Alexandrine fathers who believed that creation was in a single moment, Augustine clearly did not believe that creation "days" were indefinitely long periods of time:

> In fact, he insisted that the creative action whereby all things came to be was instantaneous; the six "days" refer (he suggests) to stages in the angelic knowledge of creation. In properly temporal terms the "days" reduce to an indivisible instant, so that all the kinds of things mentioned in Genesis were really made simultaneously.[44]

Nor did Augustine "hold that one species could arise out of another."[45]

At best, when debaters try to convert Augustine into a theistic evolutionist who held to long unspecified days and continuous creation, they can be understood as presuppositionally selective in their choice of quotations; for even their choicest of citations do not prove their point, nor do other statements within the corpus prove compatible with such anachronisms. Even if the benefit of the doubt is given to interpretations which conform Augustine to the modern, other pre-Darwinian supporters of such interpretations are few and far between—certainly not the analogy of faith.

Augustine, Anselm, Lombard and Aquinas are frequently alleged to have supported long days. John Collins confirms: "Augustine and Anselm do not actually discuss the length of the creation days. . . . Certainly Augustine and Anselm cannot be called as witnesses in favor of a day-age theory."[46] Augustine having been discussed above, Anselm rarely drawn upon for this issue and Lombard noted below,[47] suffice it to say that neither did Aquinas consistently nor explicitly hold to "long days."[48] Aquinas (1224-1274) believed: "The words *one day* are used when day is first instituted, to denote that one day is made up of twenty-four hours."[49] Moreover, he commented elsewhere: "But it [the cosmos] was not made from something; otherwise the matter of the world would have preceded the world. . . . Therefore, it must be said that the world was made from nothing."[50]

Later, one of the greatest medieval theologians, Peter Lombard, continued the analogy of faith on the subject of creation. Lombard, along with other contemporaries, recognized creation *ex nihilo*, Adam and Eve's special creation, and that "the Catholic faith believes that there was one principle, one cause of all things, namely God."[51] Moreover, Lombard affirmed the "essentially hexameral plan" of creation, taking a clear position that God

> creates the angels and the unformed matter *simul* and *ex nihilo*. Then, in the work of six days, he produces individual creatures out of the unformed matter. . . . The days referred to in Genesis are to be understood literally as lasting twenty-four hours.[52]

If one retains a proper understanding of the philosophical audiences and contexts of the great theologians prior to the Reformation, a majority of orthodox commentators did not explicitly hold to long days, gradual development or an old earth as is frequently claimed.[53]

John Calvin (1509-1564) had a quite consistent view of creation, speaking of it as a "mirror" through which the invisible God makes himself visible. He was quick to affirm: "God, by speaking, was Creator of the universe."[54] Moreover, Calvin agreed: "Indeed, the testimony of Moses in the history of creation is very clear," that God created out of "formless matter."[55]

Rather than speaking of continuous creation, Calvin noted, "we are drawn away from all fictions to the one God who distributed his work into six days that we might not find it irksome to occupy our whole life in contemplating it."[56] He repeatedly and consistently referred to Moses as "a sure witness and herald of the one God, the Creator."[57] Calvin also wrote: "[C]reation is not inpouring, but the beginning of essence out of nothing."[58]

In his major discussion of creation, Calvin began by stating agreement with earlier orthodox treatments of this subject by Basil and Ambrose (see above). Summarizing the "first history of the creation of the universe, as it has been set forth briefly by Moses," Calvin noted:

> From this history we shall learn that God by the power of his Word and Spirit created heaven and earth out of nothing; that thereupon he brought forth living beings and inanimate things of every kind, that in a wonderful series he distinguished an innumerable variety of things, that he endowed each kind with its own nature, assigned functions, appointed places and stations.[59]

The aim of his discussion was practical knowledge, i.e., to have the believer not merely know the truths about creation, but also to be led to praise of the Creator. God is so powerful that, far from six days being too short a span of time to create all the beauty around us, Calvin averred:

For it is not without significance that he divided the making of the universe into six days, even though it would have been no more difficult for him to have completed in one moment the whole work together in all its details than to arrive at its completion gradually by a progression of this sort.[60]

In fine, *The Institutes* do not proffer a doctrine of progressive or theistic evolution, nor creation from already existing matter.

Calvin's view may be confirmed from a perusal of his *Commentaries* on key verses. Commenting on Genesis 1:1, the Genevan Reformer stated:

When God in the beginning created the heaven and the earth, the earth was empty and waste. He moreover teaches by the word "created," that what before did not exist was not made. . . . Therefore his meaning is, that the world was made out of nothing. Hence the folly of those is refuted who imagine that unformed matter existed from eternity; and who gather nothing else from the narration of Moses than that the world was furnished with new ornaments, and received a form of which it was before destitute.[61]

Commenting on the fifth day of creation, Calvin observed that even God's shaping of new life from that which does exist is praiseworthy:

Therefore, there is in this respect a miracle as great as if God had begun to create out of nothing those things which he commanded to proceed from the earth. And he does not take his material from the earth, because he needed it, but that he might the better combine the separate parts of the world with the universe itself.[62]

Calvin did not prohibit God from creating out of existing elements; rather he was constrained to praise God for any and every mode of creation. However, praise for creation out of something, in no way was intended to denigrate creation *ex nihilo*.

Calvin commented on Hebrews 11:3:

> For they who have faith do not entertain a slight opinion as to God being the Creator of the world, but they have a deep conviction fixed in their minds and behold the true God. And further, they understand the power of his word, not only as manifested instantaneously in creating the world, but also as put forth continually in its preservation.[63]

Earlier on this passage, he had noted that "even infidels acknowledge" creation.[64] On Isaiah 40:22 Calvin observed:

> Formerly he spoke of the creation of the world, but now he comes to the continual government of it; for God did not only for a single moment exert his power for creating the world, but he manifests his power not less efficaciously in preserving it. And this is worthy of observation; for our minds would be little impressed by knowing that God is the creator of the world, if his hand were not continually stretched out for upholding it in existence.

Once again, in context, it is seen that Calvin—far from minimizing momentary creation—extolled it; but also urged upon the sanctified mind the importance of continually knowing God and his governance.

Interestingly, had Calvin wanted to lobby for "long days," two ideal verses presented themselves: Psalm 90:4 and Second Peter 3:8. Oddly, while commenting on both of them, Calvin refrained from injecting the idea that the first days of creation could be as long as millennia. The exegesis which is becoming so common was avoided by earlier exegetes. These verses were not interpreted to satisfy certain scientific theories; rather they were interpreted simply to mean that God is above time. All in all, Calvin presents a rather consistent view on this subject, and it is antithetical to the modern attempts to recraft it after their own image.[65]

Martin Luther's view is largely uncontested, so explicit is it.[66] Numerous other citations could be assembled, but Luther is rarely misappropriated. It deserves to be stated, however, that the frequent omission of reference to Luther (and others) illustrates the selectivity of sources drawn upon. A search for the mainstream of orthodox interpretation on this subject would not omit Luther, even if he mitigated the propositions maintained.

These claims that ancient Christians believed in anything less than a strong view of special creation are akin to other revisionist efforts. Upon scrutiny, the claim is found to be indefensible, relatively recent and more a function of accommodating ideology than historical accuracy. If the scientific method (hypothesis, experimentation, conclusion) is applied to the hypothesis: "Pre-Darwinian theologians admitted the possibility of a long period for creation," then such hypothesis is falsified by these experiments. Prior to Darwin, evangelicals did not recognize creation as occurring apart from the direct involvement of God intervening in space and time to initiate the cosmos. Robert C. Bishop concurs, "Neither the original audience of that book [Genesis] nor anyone else until about two hundred years ago would have understood a 'geological era' to be a meaningful concept."[67] There is scant evidence, if any, that prior to the nineteenth century any view of creation that accorded with macro-evolution was anything but aberrant.

The point deserves stating: Apologists ought be leery of giving up parts of historic orthodoxy if for no other reason than current theories. A vigilant apologetic, one based on sound principles, will not be so culture-accommodating. It will be less trusting of the human mind unaided by revelation, and more suspect of the noetic effects of sin. It will also be an apologetic which guards against strategic concessions, especially those which claim to reinterpret history. This earlier apologetic was less accommodationistic than the post-Darwinian one.[68] Perhaps we should let the scientist Isaac Newton have the final word on whether or not the days were fictitious. His view in 1681 may be gleaned: "methinks one of the Ten Commandments given by God in Mount Sinai, pressed by divers of the prophets, observed by our Savior, his Apostles, and first Christians for 300 years ... should not be grounded on a fiction."[69]

Post-Darwin

Most modern American evangelicals have tremendous respect and admiration for nineteenth-century stalwarts such as Charles Hodge and Benjamin B. Warfield. Yet indebted as one may be, it is nonetheless curious to review one glaring weak link: they seemed oblivious to the danger of apologetic revision in the area of evolution. As intentionally orthodox as these were, still, they seem to have adopted a secular scientific methodology rather uncritically. It appears that these angels were unaware of the inherent dangers of accommodation at this juncture. As Theodore Bozeman perceptively wrote at the conclusion of his book:

> It may be questioned whether religious leaders at any previous point in the nation's past had achieved a more unabashed union of gospel and culture than this. Doubtless if the Old School could have foreseen Darwin or the triumph of a physics of forces undermining the older empiricism they would not have been so eager either to canonize Bacon or to embrace scientific endeavor as a natural patron of belief.[70]

Indeed, Bozeman corroborates:

> It is revealing that [other] prominent Old Schoolers
> . . . were now willing to suggest that if an 'indisput-
> able' result of thorough induction manifestly con-
> tradicted an existing doctrine of the church, the
> theologian *must reconsider* his interpretation of God's
> word, and see if he has not misunderstood it. In
> view of the firm biblical literalism and the unbend-
> ing confessionalism to which the Old School was
> committed, this was a substantial concession.[71]

Science could at least *theoretically* have preeminence over
Scripture—at least as an intermediate hermeneutic.

Hodge and other evangelicals had a categorically different attitude toward science than did another evangelical
apologist, Abraham Kuyper.[72] In fact, Kuyper rebuked
Hodge for conceding on this apologetic point.

Abraham Kuyper: An Apologetic Contrast and Earlier Critic

Jonathan Wells observes that as early as 1863 Hodge was
indeed accused of "[r]emaining open to the possibility that
Scripture would have to be reinterpreted in light of scientific
evidence."[73] Further, the *New York Observer* claimed that
Hodge let "science lead the way and the Bible followed."[74]
On several occasions Hodge had to defend himself from his
contemporaries that he was "not guilty of subordinating
Scripture to science." Thus, in at least this one instance,
other contemporaries suspected that Hodge could be "persuaded by scientific evidence to modify his interpretation of
Scripture" and that he served to "reconcile Scripture with established scientific facts."[75] That Hodge was contouring the
Bible to the findings of science is seen from his comment in
an 1856 review: "If science should succeed in demonstrating
that the earth is millions of years old, then we will with the

utmost alacrity believe that the days of creation were periods of indefinite duration."[76]

Although Hodge was at times able to resist the strong pull of certain scientific theories, still he exhibited a lofty "[c]onfidence in the harmony of religion and science . . . [which led] to some extent [to] the independence of science and religion."[77] Wells perceptively remarks: "Although Hodge died without conceding that evolution could be reconciled with the Bible, his theology contained the seeds for such a reconciliation."[78]

Another more potent criticism is contained in the criticism of Abraham Kuyper, a later contemporary of Hodge, who was greatly respected by the Princeton theologians. Kuyper implicitly and explicitly accused Hodge of conceding too much to the realm of autonomous fact. Kuyper at one point said, "There is, to be sure, a theological illusion abroad . . . which conveys the impression that, with the Holy Scripture in hand, one can independently construct his theology from this principium."[79] Kuyper goes on to say that Calvin is even "at times thought of as being affected by the same illusion."[80] In this criticism, Kuyper was likely thinking of Hodge and others who championed scientific orthodoxy based on their presupposition of the finality of facticity, although a proper hermeneutic of Calvin repudiates this.

Kuyper criticized Hodge by name in another section. He faulted Hodge for his "combination of facts and truths" which overthrows his own system. Kuyper said that Hodge demanded that the "theologian be the one to authenticate these truths."[81] Further, Kuyper accused Hodge of succumbing "to the temptation of placing Theology formally in line with the other sciences."[82] Continuing his critique, the Dutch theologian said: "The authentication of his facts brought him logically back again under the power of naturalistic science. And though as a man of faith he bravely resisted this, his demonstration lacked logical necessity . . . the entire subsequent development of theological study has actually substituted an utterly different object, has cut the historic tie that binds it to original theology, and has accomplished little else than the union of the sub-divisions of psychology and of historic ethnology into a new department of science, which does not lead to the knowledge of God, but aims at the knowledge of *religion* as a phenomenon in the life of humanity."[83]

Kuyper protested "every appearance of neutrality, which is after all bound to be dishonest at heart."[84] In contrast to Hodge, Kuyper maintained that there could be no neutrality toward the scientific datum—an early form of a presuppositional apologetic. Ahead of his time, Kuyper was keen to note that even the knowing observer was not isolated from "the stream of history in which he moves," nor is this observer "able to make an all-sided and complete exhibition of the object of his investigation."[85]

Whatever the root cause, Kuyper's apologetic approach to science was starkly different from that of Hodge. Kuyper consistently stressed the inescapability of the religious presupposition: "There is, therefore, no perception or observation possible, unless there is a receptivity for the object in our human consciousness, which enables our consciousness to grasp it after its nature and form."[86] Thus he would not allow evidence alone to speak by itself.

Kuyper spelled out the inherently presuppositional nature of science: "All prosecution of science which starts out from naturalistic premises denies the subjective fact of palingenesis, as well as the objective fact of a special revelation, which immediately corresponds to this."[87] Kuyper warned that not only is science affected by sin, but further science will be reduced if it does not acknowledge the effect of sin on its own varied behavior. He warned that sin "exercises a mighty dominion upon the whole content of our consciousness . . .— what used to be called one's life-and-world-view, by which the fundamental lines lie marked out in our consciousness."[88] Affirming the noetic effects of sin, he admonished: "If, then, we make a mistake, or a single inaccurate move, how can it fail but communicate itself disastrously to our entire scientific study?"[89] He further warned "that every scientific reproduction of the knowledge of God must fail, as long as this sense remains weakened and this impulse falsified in its direction. . . . [I]t will not do to omit the fact of sin from your theory of knowledge."[90] Kuyper said, "sin modifies so largely all those data with which you have to deal in the intellectual domain and in the building-up of your science. Ignorance wrought by sin is the most difficult obstacle in the way of all true science."[91] So persuasive was the spread of sin that Kuyper must maintain, "it cannot be denied that a false representation of the real has made its way into almost every department of life. . . ."[92] His was a superior apologetic in this instance; it estimated the observer's role as well as sheer evidence.

A few years later in a 1915 work taken from the *Princeton Theological Review* entitled "Calvin's Doctrine of Creation," B.B. Warfield is even found defending one of the claims of modern science. One must marvel at Warfield's hermeneutical gymnastics as he tried to make Calvin into a proto-evolutionist. Warfield was even at the point of saying: "Calvin doubtless had no theory of evolution; but he teaches a doctrine of evolution. He had no objection and so teaching it, cut to preserve the creative act."[93] Warfield even speculated that had certain preconditions come about "Calvin would have been a precursor of the modern evolutionary theorist."[94] In a footnote rebutting Herman Bavinck, Warfield concluded: "Calvin accordingly very naturally thought along the lines of a theistic evolutionism."[95] If one consults Calvin's *Institutes* or other Calvinalia, the possibility that Calvin might have been an evolutionist is quite a remote notion.

It is a distinct irony that such stalwarts and defenders of orthodoxy as Hodge and Warfield, were unwittingly part of the problem instead of part of the solution. Perhaps this study will illuminate some of the warning signs of revisionism. We might do well to be a little more leery of an epistemology which seeks conformity to modernity. A naivete regarding scientific totalitarianism is beneficial neither for the progress of science or apologetics.

The point is that often as believers grapple with the epistemology of modernism they tend more toward true accommodation than true apologetics. In order to avoid such in the future, if this episode above has enduring pedagogical value for the future, one must have a better apologetic methodology, one that is more resistant to the winds of modernity—and its stepchild, revisionism.

Perhaps it has been underestimated: hand-to-hand combat apologetics is insufficient. Indeed, a purely evidentialistic approach will never bring about conclusive proof. One weakness of this method is the naive acceptance of current cosmological theories. The preference for the inflationary version of the Big Bang theory, may still concede too much priority to current-but-ever-changing theory. Would that the apologists' rigorous evidentialism not be forgotten when they examine these latest cosmologies, lest they fall into an uneasy alliance with contemporaneity. Evidentialists would do well to recall that these latest cosmologies may one day be disproven as well. The adopted evidentialistic posture guarantees that outmoded (evidentialistic) theories be discarded upon discovery of evidential novelty. Yet along with that is also the canonization of the latest in evidential findings. Sadly, the evidentialist approach proves to be a two-edged sword. While it cuts the prior errors of cosmology, the blade swings back and eviscerates other accounts, as Scripture is regrettably submitted to the newer evidences of the latest fads in cosmology, which themselves may be based on high proportions of theory and little observation.

A Plea for a More Cautious Reconstruction and a Humbler Apologetic

The recent dating of the universe at 7.3 billion years[96] means that some foundational premise of this cosmology is faulty. With recent estimates trending toward a younger cosmos, theories are not given up easily. At the latest date-setting, one commented that astronomers could be fooled "into believing that the universe got to its present size in less time than it really took. The effect is akin to measuring the average speed of a race-walker without realizing that she sprinted when no one was looking."[97] Would the evidentialist at some point serve the cause better by admitting that the evidence does not exist apart from a theory? Apparently, the theory is foundational.

In light of this evidentialistic flaw, two erroneous claims should now be recognized as specious: (1) Ancient evangelicals did *not* hold views compatible with theistic evolution or modern mutants of it; and (2) Some post-Darwinian evangelicals—even though stalwarts in many other areas—conceded at some points; but they should not necessarily be imitated. Thus, no norm from either period compels concession to modern claims if respect for our earlier siblings is a criteria.

The proposed apologetic also yields two other areas of benefit: (1) In evidentialism, the noetic effects of sin are understated but should not be minimized. Remembering the biblical teaching on the fallenness of the will and the darkness of the heart (Ephesians 4:17-19 and 5:8), one should suspect that the majority of non-Christians will not easily affirm revealed truths based on mere evidences. Theoretically, and in practice, the set of excuses to deny biblically interpreted truths can be infinite; thus sheltering the unbeliever from ever conclusively and logically being convinced. One should not underestimate the fallen creativity that is capable of spawning a seemingly infinite number of substitutions for God (Romans 1:21-25), rather than simply accepting and submitting to the only living God.

(2) It is unwise to concede to unbelieving notions—which is not the role of apologetics. This study has sought to show how it is also unfruitful. The earlier apologists did not concede at these points. We have no obligation from a

fair reading of history to concede to revisionist views of creation. Good science and good theology should be compatible. However, inaccurate history, theological revisionism and inferior apologetics seldom advance the discussions. Both science and apologetics will be strengthened by more cautious and respectful treatments of the history of ideas and evidence.

Endnotes

[1] John A. McIntyre, *The Misuse of Science* (unpublished manuscript, 1993), 24.

[2] This phrase is taken from an excellent summary, "How Old is the Earth: Anthropomorphic Days in Genesis 1:1-2:3" by C. John Collins, *Presbuterion* 20.2.110 (Fall 1994). In that essay, Collins also suggests that to label as the "path to compromise" the thought of the likes of Charles Hodge, William Shedd, E.J. Young and Francis Schaeffer is to cast reproach on them. However, it is also possible to retain high regard for such in general, while disagreeing with some particulars in their thinking. Our respect for fathers in the faith does not mandate that they be held as infallible (as Collins notes), nor that their conclusions be granted immunity from revision. Rather, as this essay intends, high respect for their work can best be maintained by honest criticisms of their weak points.

[3] Collins, cited above, agrees that the framework hypothesis as set forth by M.G. Kline is ruled out on exegetical grounds (p. 116, n. 29). Moreover, he confirms that much of the argumentation for long days based on idiomatic considerations in Genesis 2:4 "give[s] us no information on the range of meanings of *yom* outside this bound form" and that "the day-age theorists have not been able to say by what criteria we may discern an extended sense of *yom* as 'age,' or what contextual clues seem to tip us off. This seems to be a fatal weakness" (p. 110).

[4] Andrew Dickson White, *A History of the Warfare of Science with Theology* (New York: D. Appleton and Co., 1896), 49.

[5]Ibid., 73.

[6]Ibid., 72.

[7]Hugh Ross, *The Fingerprint of God*, 2nd ed. (Orange, CA: Promise Publishers, 1991), 141. For support, particularly of Augustine's view, Ross cites the following: *The Literal Meaning of Genesis*, bks. 4 and 5; *The Confessions*, 13.48-52 (a mistake); *The City of God*, 11.7-8, 30-31.

[8]Ibid., 146-158. Cf. also Hugh Ross, *Creation and Time* (Colorado Springs, CO: NavPress, 1994), 45-71.

[9]We do not find it necessary to assert that biblical narratives on creation are intended to be literal in every aspect. Non-literal or symbolic hermeneutical conclusions are different from the positive assertion that earlier exegetes maintained notions compatible with quite modern theories.

[10]Collins is helpful to note the distinction between allegory and anthropomorphism (p. 120, n. 48). While it might be sustained that ancient evangelicals used an anthropomorphic interpretation in numerous places, that is not necessarily the same as pleading that they lobbied for long days in this instance.

[11]Henry Morris, *The Long War Against God* (Grand Rapids, MI: Baker, 1989), 203.

[12]A search of *De Trinitate* (esp. 3.9, 16) did not turn up any such notions. In *The Literal Meaning of Genesis*, however, Augustine makes it clear that the "rest" of God demonstrates that God completed the work of creation after the sixth day. Cf. 4.11-12 and 5:3.

[13]Morris, 205.

[14]In another essay, I have examined leaders from reformed evangelicalism in the nineteenth century, Cf. my "Angels Unaware: The Ascendancy of Science over Orthodoxy in Nineteenth Century Reformed Orthodoxy," *Proceedings of the Wheaton Theology Conference*, Timothy Phillips, ed. (Wheaton, IL: National Association of Evangelicals, 1994).

[15]Andrew White, 60.

[16]*The Fathers of the Church: St. Ambrose, Hexameron, Paradise, Cain and Abel*, John J. Savage, trans. (New York: Fathers of the Church, Inc., 1961), 42:3. Ambrose also believed in the Mosaic authorship of Genesis (p. 5) and that the work of creation should not be confused with the eternality of God (4).

[17]*Hexameron*, 34.

[18]*Hexameron*, 38-39.

[19]*Hexameron*, 160.

[20]*Hexameron*, 163.

[21]*Hexameron*, 72.

[22]*Hexameron*, 42-43.

[23]*Hexameron*, 282-283.

[24]*Augustine: Earlier Writings*, John H.S. Burleight, ed. (Philadelphia: Westminster Press, 1953), 354.

[25]Citations taken from John K. Ryan, ed. *The Confessions of St. Augustine* (New York: Doubleday, 1959).

[26]*Confessions*, 415.

[27]"The Literal Meaning of Genesis" in *Ancient Christian Writers: The Works of the Fathers in Translation*, Johannes Quasten, Walter J. Burghardt and Thomas Comerford Lawler, eds. (Ramsey, NJ: Paulist Press, 1982), 1:29.

[28]Even Aquinas admitted that "Augustine differs from other expositors" and that Augustine interpreted: "angelic knowledge is appropriately called day." St. Thomas Aquinas, *Summa Theologica* (London: Burns Oates & Washbourne, 1921), 1.74.2.

[29]St. Augustine, *The Literal Meaning of Genesis*, John Hammond Taylor, trans. (New York: Newman Press, 1962), 1:119.

[30]Ibid., 125.

[31]Ibid., 125.

[32]Ibid., 128, 133.

[33]Ibid., 134.

[34]Ibid., 135.

[35]Ibid., 135.

[36]Ibid., 125.

[37]Ibid., 136-137.

[38]Ibid., 141.

[39]Ibid., 141. Italics added.

[40]Ibid., 142.

[41]Ibid., 142.

[42]Ibid., 117.

[43]Ibid., 183.

[44]Ernan McMullin, *Evolution and Creation* (Notre Dame, IN: University of Notre Dame Press, 1985), 11-12.

[45]Ibid., 15.

[46]Collins, 113-114.

[47]Shedd's citation of Lombard (*Dogmatic Theology*, 475) likely should be surrendered in light of the recent study and conclusions of Marcia Colish, *Peter Lombard* (Leyden, Netherlands: E.J. Brill, 1994), 1.330-331.

[48]Collins admits that Hugh Ross's claim that Aquinas held to long days is mistaken, even though in other ways Aquinas did follow Augustine (125-126).

[49]*Summa Theologica*, 1.74.3.

[50]*Summa Theologica*, 1.46.2.

[51]Colish, 330-331.

[52]Ibid., 337, 340-341. Marcia Colish, a leading historian of medieval theology, summarizes: "According to Peter, God and God alone is the cause of creation *ex nihilo*. He rejects the idea of exemplary causes, however understood, along with preexistent matter. Further, he sees God as such as doing the whole work of creation. . . . God cannot be equated with the forces of nature he creates. . . . In all these respects, God transcends the world he creates" (Ibid.).

[53]In an appendix, David Kelsey collects a number of earlier opinions on the subject. Cf. his "The Doctrine of Creation from Nothing," Ernan McMullin ed., *Evolution and Creation* (Notre Dame, IN: University of Notre Dame Press, 1985), 192-195. He cites, among others, Anselm as affirming creation *ex nihilo*; the Fourth Lateran Council (1215): "Firmly we . . . confess . . . the true God . . . who by his own omnipotent power at once from the beginning of

time created each creature from nothing . . ."; The Council of Florence (1441): "God . . . is the creator of all things visible and invisible, who, when he wished, out of his goodness created all creatures, spiritual as well as corporal; good, indeed . . . since they were from nothing . . ."

[54]John Calvin, *The Institutes of the Christian Religion*, J.T. McNeill, ed. (Philadelphia: Westminster Press, 1960), 1.13.7.

[55]*The Institutes*, 1.13.14.

[56]*The Institutes*, 1.14.2.

[57]Ibid.

[58]*The Institutes*, 1.15.5.

[59]*The Institutes*, 1.14.20.

[60]*The Institutes*, 1.14.22.

[61]John Calvin, *Commentary on Genesis* (Grand Rapids, MI: Baker, 1979), 1:70.

[62]Ibid., 90.

[63]John Calvin, *Commentary on the Epistle to the Hebrews* (Grand Rapids, MI: Baker, 1979), 264-265.

[64]Ibid.

[65]His disciple, Theodore Beza, also affirmed that Hebrews 11:3 taught creation *ex nihilo*. Moreover, Beza explained: "Mundum conditum ex nihilo: nemo potest compraehendere, quod ex eo quod non est fiat id quod est." ("The world is formed ex nihilo. We are not able to comprehend how from this which is not made, is that which is [made].") Cf. Theodore de Beze, *Cours Sur les Epitres aux Romains et aux Hebreaux (1564-1566)* in *Travaux d'Humanism et Renaissance* (Geneva: Library Droz, 1988), 226:311. Further, in his *Confession de Foi du Chretien* (1558), Beza affirmed that God the Father "has created all out of nothing" (2.2) and "We believe that he has not only created the visible world, the heaven and the earth and all that they contain, but also invisible spirits." (2.3; Cf. the English translation, *The Christian Faith* by James Clark (East Sussex, England: Christian Focus Ministries Trust, 1992), 3.

[66]Cf. e.g., Martin Luther, *Luther's Works* (St. Louis, MO:

Concordia, 1972), 17:29, 118.

[67]Robert C. Bishop, "Science and Theology: A Methodological Comparison" in *Journal of Interdisciplinary Studies* vol 5, no. 1/2 (1993): 155.

[68]John Collins, who has presented one of the more researched and balanced studies of these issues, argues that William Shedd was more tolerant in this area. However, in keeping with my thesis, it must be noted that Shedd's claims were made nearly thirty years after Darwin and modern geological dating; thus indirectly supporting my central claim. While still holding high regard for Shedd in many *loci*, it appears that he fell in with Hodge, Warfield and Dabney in committing this apologetic mistake. Collins' reference to John Macpherson's 1882 work is answered similarly.

Collins raises challenging testimony to my thesis by his reference to William Ames (p. 114, n. 21). Collins suggests that Ames was certainly "not under pressure from modernism to allow for" six days, with "intervening spaces" between the days. However, an amplified translation of Ames's *Medulla Theologica* 1.8.28 from the Latin edition (1634) is: "Creation [*creatio*] of these parts [*harum partium*, various parts of the creation; cf. 1.8.27] of the world, however [*autem* signifies the connection to the previous paragraph], was not done simultaneously and in one moment [*contra* Augustine], but was accomplished through parts, each in its turn, succeeding in six days, with [normal] intervention [between each day]." Mr. Robert Bailey, a Latin instructor from Yazoo City, MS has kindly provided an accurate translation from the original: "However, the creation of these parts of the world did not occur at the same time and in one moment, but it was accomplished through parts, succeeding themselves in the space of six intervening days." Macpherson's commentary on *The Westminster Confession of Faith* (1882), refracts Ames to support "that the active creative periods were six natural days, with indefinite intervals between them." However, it seems that this addition of "indefinite" is Macpherson's redaction, not so much a direct citation from Ames. Moreover, when section 28 is compared with the previous paragraph, it seems clear that the reference is not to creation *en toto*, but to the creation of various parts (*partes, partium*) of the cosmos. Thus, what Ames asserted was that—contrary to Augustine—the entire cosmos was not created *simul & uno momento* (simultaneously and in one moment); rather, the various *parts* were created "each in turn, succeeding in six days, with [normal] intervention [between each day]." If Ames is understood as opposing the Augustine/Alexandrine view that all six days of creation occurred in a singular instant, then Ames's claim is little more than a reaffirmation of Ambrose's (traditional) view. Further, insofar as Ames was not commonly understood as holding to long periods of creation, nor was that the majority view of the other testimony above, more than Macpherson's redaction is needed to prove that Ames had such a modern view.

Collins's appendix is honest, but not exhaustive. The references to Josephus and Irenaeus (as claimed by Hugh Ross) only show that they believed in a young earth. His Appendix contains no reference to Basil (also claimed by Hugh Ross), Ambrose or Luther. Anselm, Aquinas and Calvin are represented fairly.

[69]H.S. Thayer, ed. *Newton's Philosophy of Nature: Selections from his Writings* (New York: Hafner Publishing Company, 1953), 64-65.

[70]Theodore Bozeman, *Protestants in an Age of Science* (Chapel Hill, NC: University of North Carolina Press, 1977), 174.

[71]Bozeman, 118.

[72]Cf. my "Angels Unaware: The Ascendancy of Science over Orthodoxy in Nineteenth Century Reformed Orthodoxy" in Timothy Phillips, cited above.

[73]Jonathan Wells, "Charles Hodge on the Bible and Science," *Journal of Presbyterian History* (Fall 1988): 66:3.161.

[74]Ibid., 160.

[75]Ibid., 161.

[76]Ibid., 160.

[77]Ibid., 158.

[78]Ibid., 163.

[79]Abraham Kuyper, *Principles of Sacred Theology* (Grand Rapids, MI: Baker, 1980), 574.

[80]Ibid., 575.

[81]Ibid., 318.

[82]Ibid.

[83]Ibid., 319.

[84]Ibid., 50.

[85]Ibid., 49-50.

[86]Ibid., 71.

[87]Ibid., 224.

[88]Ibid., 109.

[89]Ibid., 110.

[90]Ibid., 113.

[91]Ibid., 114.

[92]Ibid.

[93]Mark Noll, ed., *The Princeton Theology, 1812-1921* (Phillipsburg, NJ: Presbyterian and Reformed Publishing Co., 1983), 298.

[94]Ibid.

[95]Ibid.

[96]*Newsweek*, 7 November 1994, 55.

[97]Ibid.

Scientific Problems for Scientism

Robert C. Newman

*O*ne of the major opponents of biblical Christianity in the West since the rise of modern science has been scientism, the claim that—to use the words of Carl Sagan—"the cosmos is all that is, or ever was, or ever will be."[1]

This view has been given various names, depending on the nuance in mind. As an absolutizing of science to be the only means to true knowledge, it is called "scientism."[2] As the claim that matter-energy is the ultimate reality, it is called "materialism."[3] As the belief that everything can be explained by the operation of purely natural forces without miracles at all, it is called "naturalism."[4] As the view that all the complex organization in our universe has developed by unguided processes working within natural laws, it is called "evolutionism."[5] Though there is some divergence among these views, for simplicity we will lump them together and call them scientism.

Scientism has had significant influence beyond the circle of its own proponents. It changed the definition of what constitutes true scholarship.[6] In every academic field it led to the rise of models that banished the supernatural from its own territory. Some examples are:

1. Liberal biblical criticism, e.g., the JEDP theory—that the first five books of the Old Testament were not written by Moses, an eyewitness of miracles narrated in them, but by anonymous authors and editors living cen-

turies later and reworking myths and legendary material;[7]

2. Darwinian evolution, the claim that all the diversity of life on earth can be explained by the operation of random variation and survival of the fittest;[8]

3. Marxism, the ideology that human political history is preeminently a function of economics—in particular, the struggle of various social classes for domination;[9]

4. Freudianism, the claim that human behavior is a result of non-logical, non-moral forces acting upon or within the human psyche.[10]

These models, in turn, have provided ammunition for groups with very different worldviews than scientism, who have typically employed it to attack biblical Christianity. Muslims, for instance, use liberal biblical criticism to discredit the Bible and keep their people from seriously considering its message.[11] Liberal Christendom has adopted most of the results of scientism and turned many away from the faith, all the while trying to retain some place for spirituality and religion.[12] Liberation theology has borrowed its insights from Marxism.[13] The New Age movement has taken over evolution and given it a pantheistic or polytheistic flavor.[14] Even within evangelical Christendom, there has been some heavy influence from non-biblical psychologizing.[15]

Here we propose to look at five areas in which scientism has made large and influential claims, and to show that such claims face serious scientific problems—not just theological objections as would convince only committed Christians. In this way, I trust, we may be strengthened ourselves and become more effective in helping those around us who may be attracted by scientism or by its ideas which have penetrated into other circles. The five areas we shall consider are: (1) prediction; (2) continuity; (3) mindlessness; (4) eternality; and (5) locality.

Prediction

The French mathematician Pierre Simon de Laplace (1749-1827) was one of the early proponents of the idea that the universe is a vast machine which can be explained totally by the operation of natural laws. His popular work *Exposition of the System of the World* (1796) proposed that the sun and earth had arisen from a large gas cloud. Shortly thereafter, Laplace was reportedly introduced to Napoleon, who asked him what place this left for God. "Sire," he replied, "I have no need for that hypothesis."[16]

Laplace and others claimed that since the world operated totally on the basis of natural laws, it would in principle be possible (once these laws were discovered) to calculate the entire future merely by knowing the position and velocity of all the particles in the universe at one time. Let us call this the Laplacean program for prediction. To the extent that this project was substantially fulfilled, it would be a powerful apologetic for the worldview of scientism. In fact, the mere attraction of the idea itself, given the astonishing advances science was making, convinced many that scientism was true even without this test.

The Laplacean program, however, has always been in trouble computationally. Consider, first of all, the question of how big a computer would be needed to make this calculation. Even assuming that nothing but particles and forces exist, one would need to be able to calculate the movement of each particle in the universe under the influence of every force acting on it. There appear to be at least 10^{80} elementary particles that would need to be tracked by the computer.[17] Each of these particles exerts at least one kind of force on all the other particles within the range of that force, and the range for two of these forces—the electromagnetic and gravitational—is effectively infinite.[18] The number of calculations involved for each time-step is thus astronomically larger than even the number of atoms and electrons in the universe!

A far more economical strategy would be to build a universe just like ours and watch what it does.[19] But to do this, we need to know exactly what our universe has in the way of particles and forces. Then we need to get this information set up in the form of a parallel universe. Then we need to place all the particles in their proper locations with the right velocities. Then we need to figure out how to make this universe run much faster than ours does so it can get ahead of ours and be of some use for predicting the future. The project looks like something God might do, but nothing we will ever be capable of replicating.

Two basic discoveries of this century—quantum phenomena in the 1920s and chaotic behavior more recently—only serve to bury this project even deeper under its own arrogance.

The strange world of the very small with its quantum phenomena has frightened both Christians and non-Christians with some of its implications.[20] The problem with which we are here concerned, however, involves our inability to locate the position and velocity of the small elementary particles exactly. This is more than just a matter of limited precision in measurement, which afflicts all human activity. The fact is that the nature of light and matter is such that to measure position more and more accurately, we have to use light of shorter and shorter wavelength and so larger and larger energies. Eventually we cross a threshold where the energy of the light we are using disrupts the very thing we are trying to measure. To measure a particle's position very accurately, we lose information on its velocity; to measure velocity, we lose information on position. The result is that we cannot even set up our parallel universe exactly in the first place, and (even if we could) we would have to be satisfied with statistical predictions of what will occur rather than specific details.

Much has been made in the past few years of so-called chaotic phenomena.[21] Nature often does not behave as simply as we would like. Though scientists have tended to think that small errors in measurement will only produce small effects in prediction, it is now clear that this is not the case in many situations. For instance, in the complex world of weather—the interaction between our air (with its dust and water vapor) and the sun, land and oceans—a small change will not always remain small, but may grow so large that prediction is impossible. This situation is called the "butterfly effect," because it appears that the disturbance produced in the air by the flight of a single butterfly might sometimes make a big difference in the weather a continent away and a week later!

Thus the Laplacean program is dead. Even if the universe were a closed system of cause and effect, it would not be possible to prove this by making predictions of what must happen. The Christian worldview, by contrast, features the intervention of a prayer-answering God, a common experience among believers and one that has often functioned to bring unbelievers to salvation. More publicly testable is the phenomenon of fulfilled prophecy, which has rightly been an important part of Christian evidences for most of church history.[22]

Continuity

Scientism has shown a distinct antagonism toward (and fear of) discontinuities in nature—apparent gaps, breaks and singularities. Doubtless this is because such phenomena smack of divine intervention and have regularly been used by Christians as evidence of such. This antagonism shows up quite strongly in both cosmology and biology, though we will save our comments about cosmology for the section "Eternality," below.

One of the major attractions of Darwin's evolutionary proposal (for himself and many of his followers) was that it pictured all change as virtually continuous, being produced by the natural selection of innumerable small variations. The discontinuities between present varieties of living things were seen as the result of slow, relatively continuous processes acting over long periods of time. The violent reaction of biologists in the 1940s to Goldschmidt's "hopeful monster" hypothesis (with its large mutational jumps) illustrates the powerful emotions raised by even a naturalistic attack on continuity.[23] But neither the fossil record nor the testable abilities of the Darwinian mechanism really suggest that this assumption of continuity fits reality.

Though it is "the trade secret of paleontology," it is true that there are no transitional sequences of fossils between upper levels of the biological classification scheme.[24] Darwin felt the force of this objection, one of the strongest presented in his own time. He proposed that the fossil record was woefully incomplete, but that—should it be possible to fill it in sometime in the future—these transitions would surely show up.

The 135 years of collecting since Darwin wrote his *Origin of Species* have turned up an enormous number of fossils from all over the earth—we now have something like 200 million fossils catalogued in museums.[25] Still no transitional fossils! Already by the 1930s, this lack of transitions was troubling enough to require evolutionists to postulate that all significant evolution takes place in small, isolated groups of plants or animals, so that we would hardly be likely to find the transition fossils. We will say a bit more about this under our discussion on mechanism later. It is enough to note here that the major events of evolution are missing from the record. Certainly the fossil record is no argument for continuity!

Another fossil problem is the shape of the fossil record. Textbooks commonly picture the fossils as showing a "tree of life," beginning with a single trunk early in earth's history (representing the primitive single-celled organisms), followed by the major branches into plants and animals. On each of these branches in turn, we have smaller branches and then twigs going off to form the living things which exist today. Ignoring the fact that most of the branching junctions on this tree are hypothetical, the tree has the wrong shape. If Darwinian evolution is true, it should begin with one species and gradually mutate into more species. Then the species should become divergent enough to form genera, the genera eventually forming families, and so on upwards in the biological classification scheme to phyla, the major body plans among the plants and animals. Instead, the fossil record is upside-down! Virtually all the animal phyla appear to have formed in a very brief period called the "Cambrian explosion" right near the beginning of multi-celled life, and none (or one) have formed since.[26] This certainly looks like a discontinuity!

The Darwinian mechanism—mutation and natural selection—is very attractive not only because it avoids discontinuity but because at first sight it seems to be obviously true. If variation occurs in all populations of plants and animals (and it does), and if those variations which help an organism better to survive in a given environment are more likely to be passed on to the next generation than their competitors (they are), then how could we avoid getting better and better plants and animals in the course of time? This appears to be true, and suggests that Darwin's discovery of natural selection really has located a mechanism by which organisms adapt to changing environments.

But Darwinists typically jump from here (microevolution) right to so-called amoeba-to-man evolution (macroevolution) without taking seriously the question of whether a mechanism for small-scale change will really produce large-scale changes. Since extrapolation from one size-scale to another in other sciences often breaks down (e.g., weather to climate or Newtonian physics to relativity), we need to look at the data to see whether or not it does here also, rather than just plugging in our worldview to solve the question.

When we look at the data, we find trouble. Even if mutation and selection can change (a few) dark and (many) light-colored moths into (a few) light and (many) dark ones, it doesn't follow that it can produce moths in the first place. Attempts to simulate mutation and natural selection on a computer do not work.[27] Apparently random processes cannot be expected to produce high levels of organization even in the time and space provided by our whole universe.[28] This is a problem not only for producing the first living things from non-living,[29] but also for all the really substantial changes thereafter. These latter changes require fully functional pathways from one working system to another, like converting a Volkswagen into a Cadillac without taking it off the road. How do we get legs to change to wings with all the intermediates not only fully functional, but good competitors with everything else in their ecological niche? How can scales convert to feathers? Or a two-chambered heart to a three- and then a four-chambered one? Similar problems exist for explaining the simplest functional forms of various biochemical systems necessary to photosynthesis, locomotion, vision and respiration.[30] A great deal of hand-waving takes the place of evidence or even specific proposals for pathways here.

Creationists are regularly sneered at for their "God of the gaps" explanation, which was frequently plugged into places later explained by natural law. The same procedure, however, is regularly used by scientism in the form of a "natural law of the gaps." Just as Bible-believers have sometimes inserted miracles anywhere in science there appears to be a gap, proponents of scientism will in the same places (1) suggest an unknown natural law, (2) propose that there is no gap but only missing data or (3) invoke the semi-miraculous powers of mutation and natural selection to bridge the chasm. But science has not succeeded in filling in these gaps. On the contrary, it appears that several of them are gaps in reality.

Mindlessness

For scientism, the only kind of minds that exist in the

universe are those which have developed in the course of its history by mutation and natural selection. Some think this has happened only once—here on earth—but the more popular view is that life and intelligence may be rather common out there.[31] In either case, the beginning of the universe as we know it, and of life, are mindless. Both Darwin[32] and recently Dawkins[33] try to explain reality without recourse to a mind behind the universe. Darwin's work, in fact, has been widely hailed as destroying Paley's argument that design implies a designing mind behind it.[34]

But the existence of design in inanimate nature is devastating to this program, and so is the question of where the complex organization came from that characterizes even the simplest living things.

In non-living things—like the basic forces of the universe, the nature of the chemical elements and compounds, the frequency of various environments in the universe—there is no mutation and natural selection to produce the observed order. How is it, then, that our universe is not only fit for life (if it weren't, we wouldn't be here), but that this fit involves a level of "fine-tuning" that takes one's breath away?

For example, the precise fit between the four basic physical forces in our universe is staggering. The strongest force known is the strong nuclear interaction, 100 times stronger than the electromagnetic force. Electromagnetism, in turn, is a thousand times stronger than the weak nuclear force, and the weak force 10 million billion billion billion (10^{34}) times stronger than gravity. These forces span a range in strength of nearly forty powers of ten, yet small changes in the strength of any one of them would render the universe uninhabitable.

If the strong force were only five percent weaker, stars wouldn't burn; if it were five percent stronger, stars would explode. If electromagnetism were a few percent stronger or weaker, the electrons around an atom would be held too strongly or too weakly; in either case, there would be insufficient chemical bonding for life molecules. If the weak force were a few percent stronger or weaker, there would be no elements heavier than hydrogen and helium outside stars, thus no planets to live on and no chemicals to support life. If gravity were slightly weaker, stars would never get hot enough to turn on their nuclear furnaces and no heavy elements would be formed; if slightly stronger, the stars would be too hot, burn up too quickly and provide no stable environment for life. A precise balance between gravity and the expansion speed of the universe is necessary for it to form galaxies and stars. The positive and negative charges of the electromagnetic force must cancel out almost exactly so that gravity can dominate at astronomical distances and provide habitable planets around efficient stars.[35]

The uniqueness of many chemical elements and the compounds they form is also striking, but too involved for discussion here.[36]

Though science (and science fiction) writers regularly picture a universe with lots of earth-like planets and intelligent beings living on them, the right conditions for life now look like they may be unique to earth in the entire universe.[37] Certainly we live in a universe that would look designed to an unbiased observer.

Proponents of scientism speak rather glibly about a naturalistic origin of life through a series of chemical reactions in the atmosphere, oceans and tidal ponds of the early earth. But when actual details and scenarios are examined (as Robert Shapiro does in his book *Origins*) and when actual numbers are supplied for the probabilities, the whole idea moves from the plausible to the ludicrous.[38] The time and opportunity are not there—not on earth, not on a thousand earths, not in a thousand universes. As William Dembski has said, "the probabilistic resources" of the universe are insufficient for something like this to have taken place.[39]

But a mind can construct a level of order that would never happen by chance. That is why an archaeologist can look at a chipped stone and immediately discern that it is an arrowhead, the work of a mind and not of the random chipping and cracking that nature produces. Yet the amount of information contained in the exact placement of the chips that make the stone an arrowhead is minuscule compared with the information stored in the simplest DNA molecule. Thus, the claim that the universe was initially mindless is merely the proposal of a worldview and not the conclusion of a scientific research program. The enormous amount of information stored in DNA points rather in the opposite direction.

Eternality

In scientism, the universe must somehow be eternal. Proponents of scientism generally realize that there is no rational alternative within their system to postulating that the universe (in some sense) has always existed. Recall Sagan's remark that "the cosmos . . . is all that ever was." The recent triumph of the Big Bang cosmology in its no-bounce form badly undercuts this claim.[40]

In the last century, atheists typically opted for the visible universe being eternal and basically static. They were aware that no known laws would allow the stars to burn forever, but no one knew how to make them burn as long as they obviously had. They knew that gravity was only attractive, so that a static universe would have to have some force holding the stars apart or it would eventually collapse. Yet the problem of a universe with a beginning was not squarely faced.

As we learned more about atoms and their nuclei in this century, it was realized that mature stars burn by converting hydrogen into helium. Life spans were calculated for the various star-sizes, and it became apparent that the visible universe had not been around forever, but only for some billions or tens of billions of years. A long time, no doubt, but pretty short when compared to infinity.

About the same time, it gradually became apparent that the universe was expanding—distances between ourselves and all galaxies but the local ones were increasing. Einstein could already have predicted this in 1915 from his general theory of relativity, but the atmosphere of scientism at the time was so much against this that he added a "fudge factor" to make the universe static. It wasn't until Slipher and Hubble measured the recession rates of various galaxies that the fact had to be faced. We live in a universe in which the galaxies are moving apart.

But if the universe is getting bigger, it must once have been smaller. Extrapolating this trend backward into the past would point to a universe that was very small and very hot at a beginning some billions of years ago. The Catholic astronomer George Lemaitre made such a proposal in the late twenties (the earliest version of the Big Bang theory), and the history of cosmology since then has been a frantic attempt to avoid this beginning in spite of mounting evidence in its favor.

George Gamow, for instance, sought to change the beginning into a bounce. In his view, the universe from eternity past had existed as a mass of thin hydrogen gas which was collapsing under its own gravity until just a few billion years ago, when it became sufficiently dense and hot to rebound. Other cosmologists decided this single-bounce universe was too contrived and opted for an oscillating universe which bounced every hundred billion years or so. Both models restored the idea of an eternal universe and were the popular versions of the Big Bang theory until quite recently.

Meanwhile Fred Hoyle, Thomas Gold and Herman Bondi tried another tack to rescue the universe from a beginning. They proposed an infinite, eternal universe with stars running down and galaxies moving apart, but each place always looked about the same because new matter was continually popping into existence to fill up the gaps and provide new star-fuel. They called this the "steady-state" universe.

New discoveries in astronomy put pressure on the steady-state theory first. The model predicted that objects such as galaxies and quasars should be uniformly distributed throughout space (so long as the volume being considered was big enough to average out random fluctuations). But in the 60s and 70s it became apparent that there were far more objects long ago (at great distances) than there are now. Then the radio radiation predicted by the Big Bang theory was discovered, and for most astronomers, this put the last nail in the steady-state's coffin. The universe was hotter and denser in the past than it is now.

Since the early 70s, the competition has been between various forms of the Big Bang theory. Did the universe begin at the Big Bang? Or was the Big Bang just a bounce from a previous contracting phase of its history? One problem was that a universe which collapsed to the densities and temperatures that characterize the Big Bang would not bounce but become a black hole. And if the theory of general relativity is true, then space and time (as well as matter and energy) came into existence at the Big Bang. Thus the Big Bang itself appears to be a creation event.

Stephen Hawking attempts to avoid a creator at this point by postulating that the universe popped into existence without a cause![41] This suggestion is so at odds with the basic methods of science that some scientists more sensitive to embarrassment would be ashamed to hold such a theory and simultaneously sneer at Christians for their supernaturalism. We at least propose an adequate cause for the universe. Thus the apparent non-eternality of our universe is a serious scientific problem for scientism.

Locality

In a universe with matter-energy as the ultimate reality, one would naturally expect the interactions between particles to be local, one bumping against the other. This is how the ancient Greek atomists viewed it. When Newton proposed that forces operated at a distance by means of fields, the materialists of his time were very skeptical; it seemed to them to smack of spiritism.[42] Even after physicists got used to Newton's idea of fields, the basic view was that two particles interacted by direct (local) contact of each with the field produced by the other. The rise of quantum mechanics has put serious pressure on this idea, and it now appears that there is something like instantaneous interaction between widely separated locations.

Some of the strangeness of quantum phenomena in this regard can be seen in the famous two-slit experiment and its relation to the controversy over whether light is particle or wave.[43] In an otherwise darkened room, light is sent out from a very small source at one end of the room and detected by a photographic plate on the wall at the other end. With no intervening screens, the plate will just fog up rather uniformly, which either waves or particles might do. If a screen with a single narrow slit is set up a few feet in front of the wall, the plate when developed will show one strongly exposed line which is an image of the slit, but with a pattern of dimmer lines around it, a phenomenon called "diffraction." These extra lines are not something particles would make, but this is how waves operate. When the screen is made with two parallel slits in it, the pattern changes to a whole series of nearly equally bright lines (called an "interference pattern") rather than just two images of the slits. Again, what we would expect from waves. So light appears to be a wave, from this perspective.

Now comes quantum mechanics. If we turn down the intensity of the light to a very low level, it will not only take a long time for this two-slit interference pattern to form, but if we look at the plate we will see that the pattern forms by an increasing number of dots on the plate which gradually form this pattern, rather than by the whole interference pattern just getting clearer as more light arrives. Apparently, the photographic plate is absorbing the light at a particular spot each time (rather than all over at once), as though the light was arriving in particles instead of waves. But particles would not form interference patterns, and waves would not be absorbed at single points. What is happening? Are we dealing with some kind of dispersed, non-local particles?

We are not finished yet. If one turns down the intensity of the light so much that only one "light-particle" would be in flight from the source to the plate at any time, we still get our interference pattern! But if we block up one of the slits or even try to measure which slit the particle went through, the pattern will not form. The same results are obtained if we run the experiment using electrons rather than light. Somehow the particle "knows" about the other slit, whether you think it only goes through one of them or both at once. There is something decidedly non-local about matter and light.

This non-locality can extend to great distances, as we see more clearly in Einstein's attempts to circumvent the uncertainty principle. Einstein proposed measuring two identical particles which had just separated from one another in a decay event. Since they are identical, they will be moving at equal speeds in opposite directions. So if we measure the speed of one and the position of the other, we indirectly learn the speed and position of both, violating quantum uncertainty. And if we measure the two when they are far enough apart, neither will know what kind of measurement we did on the other, since information cannot be conveyed faster than the speed of light. But a version of this experiment has recently been done, and Einstein was wrong. Somehow the one particle did "know" what was done to the other, even though there was not time for light to travel from one to the other![44]

Theoretical physicist John Bell has also shown that, if the quantum facts are correct—no matter what sort of theory we use to explain them—reality must be non-local in the sense that mutual influences can take place at rates exceeding the speed of light.[45] Here again, we arrive at a scientific result that is counter-intuitive to scientism, but consistent with a God who is everywhere present and does need not to wait for light to bring information from some distant source.

Conclusions

In this paper we have looked at five areas where the view of reality proposed by scientism is challenged by actual scientific observation. We called these areas prediction, continuity, mindlessness, eternality and locality.

First, we saw that the predictive program of Laplace which, if successful, would have effectively demonstrated the truth of scientism, has collapsed. The structure of nature is such that there appears to be no way from within the universe to make accurate predictions beyond rather trivial ones that are either broad-stroke, short-term or local.

Second, we saw that the attempt of scientism to explain reality without recourse to discontinuity in nature faces serious empirical challenge. We looked in some detail at gaps in the fossil record and at the inadequacy of the Darwinian mechanism, both of which point to real discontinuity in the history of life. We might also have mentioned the origin of the universe and the origin of life as further examples. All these are consistent with a theism in which God sometimes reveals himself by intervention in nature.

Third, we saw that Darwin's and Dawkins' proposal of no mind behind the universe is no better than its ability to explain such apparent design as is known to exist. Though this proposal is widely hailed as successful in biological evolution—which we dispute in our discussion under "continuity," above—it founders in explaining evidence of design in inanimate nature, both the structure of the universe as a whole and the specific "fine-tuning" of our own environment here on earth. Rather, these features are just the sort of thing we would expect from a Designer like the God of the Bible.

Fourth, we saw that the necessity for scientism to have a eternal universe has stumbled over the evidence that the cosmos began at the Big Bang some billions of years ago. Those who espouse a materialist worldview must now retreat to a universe popping into existence without cause, thus abandoning one of the primary axioms of science. Or they must propose that our universe is just part of a much larger universe of which we can never have any evidence, thus abandoning their claimed empirical superiority over Christianity. The believer's faith in the unseen is at least based on objective evidence of divine revelation.

Lastly, we saw that the program of scientism to have a universe of merely local causation—where particles and fields only interact by contact—seems to be doomed by developments in quantum research. The apparently instantaneous interaction at a distance observed in Aspect's experiment seems more consistent with an omnipresent, omniscient God than with a universe of mindless particles and fields.

This should encourage us as Christians not to fear the forces of secularism that seem so powerful and daunting in the media and education today. The God of the Bible really exists. He has not left Himself without testimony. We can trust Him to keep His promises. He will not abandon us to our enemies. May we seek to study and proclaim the truth, both as it is revealed in God's Word—the Bible—and in God's world, the universe.

Endnotes

[1]Carl Sagan, *Cosmos* (New York: Random House, 1980), 4.

[2]"Scientism," *Webster's Third New International Dictionary of the English Language Unabridged* (Springfield, MA: G. and C. Merriam Co., 1966), def. 2, 2033; *Webster's Ninth New Collegiate Dictionary* (Springfield, MA: Merriam-Webster, 1983), def. 2, 1051 gives a more pejorative meaning: "an exaggerated trust in the efficacy of the

methods of natural science applied to all areas of investigation."

[3]"Materialism," in *Webster's Third Unabridged*, def. 1a, p. 1392; *Webster's Ninth Collegiate*, def. 1a, 753, gives: "a theory that physical matter is the only or fundamental reality and that all being and processes and phenomena can be explained as manifestations or results of matter."

[4]"Naturalism," *Webster's Third Unabridged*, def. 2, 1507; *Webster's Ninth Collegiate*, def. 2, 780, gives: "a theory denying that an event or object has a supernatural significance; specif. the doctrine that scientific laws are adequate to account for all phenomena."

[5]"Evolutionism," *Webster's Third Unabridged*, def. 2, 789, is somewhat broader than what I have in mind here: "adherence to or belief in evolution, esp. of living things." I am concerned with the specifically naturalistic version of this as promoted by Richard Dawkins, *The Blind Watchmaker* (New York: Norton, 1986) and critiqued by Phillip E. Johnson in his paper "The Religion of the Blind Watchmaker," *Perspectives on Science and Christian Faith* 45 (March 1993): 46-48.

[6]Note *Webster's Third Unabridged* under "scientism," def. 2, 2033: "a thesis that the methods of the natural sciences should be used in all areas of investigation, including philosophy, the humanities, and the social sciences: a belief that only such methods can fruitfully be used in the pursuit of knowledge." A helpful recent response to this claim is Roy A. Clouser's *The Myth of Religious Neutrality: An Essay on the Hidden Role of Religious Belief in Theories* (Notre Dame, IN: University of Notre Dame Press, 1991).

[7]For the classic presentation of the JEDP theory, see Julius Wellhausen, *Prolegomena to the History of Ancient Israel* (1878; English reprint, Cleveland, OH: Meridian, 1957) and S.R. Driver, *An Introduction to the Literature of the Old Testament* (1897; reprint, Cleveland, OH: Meridian, 1956). Otto Eissfeldt, *The Old Testament: An Introduction* (Oxford: Blackwell, 1965) gives a rather detailed tour of the

whole liberal scheme of biblical criticism, with material on the JEDP theory in 155-241. Evangelical responses are given (in general) by R.K. Harrison, *Introduction to the Old Testament* (Grand Rapids, MI: Eerdmans, 1969) and specifically for JEDP by William Henry Green, *The Higher Criticism of the Pentateuch* (1895; reprint, Grand Rapids, MI: Baker, 1978); Oswald T. Allis, *The Five Books of Moses* (Phillipsburg, NJ: Presbyterian and Reformed, 1964); and Allan A. MacRae, *JEDP: Lectures on the Higher Criticism of the Pentateuch* (Hatfield, PA: IBRI, 1994).

[8]Charles Darwin, *The Origin of Species* (1859; frequently reprinted, e.g., New York: Collier, 1962); Richard Dawkins, *The Blind Watchmaker* (New York: Norton, 1986).

[9]Karl Marx and Frederick Engels, *The Communist Manifesto* (New York: International Publishers, 1948). For evangelical responses, see Francis Nigel Lee, *Communism Versus Creation* (Nutley, NJ: Craig Press, 1969); Lloyd Billingsley, *The Generation That Knew Not Josef* (Portland, OR: Multnomah, 1983).

[10]Robert D. Nye, *Three Psychologies: Perspectives from Freud, Skinner, and Rogers*, 2nd ed. (Monterey, CA: Brooks/Cole, 1981), 2-3.

[11]E.g., Maurice Bucaille, *The Bible, the Qur'an, and Science* (Indianapolis, IN: American Trust Publications, 1979). For an evangelical response, see William Campbell, *The Qur'an and the Bible in the Light of History and Science* (Upper Darby, PA: Middle East Resources, 1992).

[12]Hugh Ross Mackintosh, *Types of Modern Theology: Schleiermacher to Barth* (London: Nisbet, 1937); William Hordern, *A Layman's Guide to Modern Theology* (New York: Macmillan, 1955), ch. 4. For evangelical responses, see J. Gresham Machen, *Christianity and Liberalism* (New York: Macmillan, 1923; reprint, Grand Rapids, MI: Eerdmans, 1946); Carl F.H. Henry, ed., *Christian Faith and Modern Theology* (New York: Channel, 1964).

[13]Gustavo Gutierrez, *A Theology of Liberation* (Maryknoll,

NY: Orbis, 1973); J. Andrew Kirk, *Liberation Theology* (Atlanta, GA: John Knox, 1979). For a recent evangelical response, see Humberto Belli and Ronald H. Nash, *Beyond Liberation Theology* (Grand Rapids, MI: Baker, 1992).

[14]E.g., see Marilyn Ferguson, *The Aquarian Conspiracy: Personal and Social Transformation in Our Time* (Los Angeles: Tarcher/St. Martins, 1987), 157-167; Benjamin Creme, *Maitreya's Mission* (Amsterdam: Share International, 1986), 151-197. For evangelical responses, see Douglas R. Groothuis, *Confronting the New Age* (Downer's Grove, IL: InterVarsity, 1988); Vishal Mangalwadi, *When the New Age Gets Old* (Downer's Grove, IL: InterVarsity, 1992).

[15]William Kirk Kilpatrick, *Psychological Seduction* (Nashville, TN: Nelson, 1983); Martin and Deidre Bobgan, *Psychoheresy* (Santa Barbara, CA: Eastgate, 1987); Gary R. Collins, *Can You Trust Psychology?* (Downer's Grove, IL: InterVarsity, 1988).

[16]The Napoleon/Laplace story is mentioned in several places, e.g., James Hastings, ed., *Encyclopedia of Religion and Ethics* (1909), 2:178a.

[17]See D.W. Sciama, *Modern Cosmology* (Cambridge: 1971), 124-125; P.C.W. Davies, *Accidental Universe* (Cambridge: Cambridge, 1982), 59, 76-77.

[18]The range of a force is the distance within which the force has a significant effect. For the strong nuclear force, this distance is roughly the diameter of an neutron or proton (10^{-13} cm). For the weak nuclear force it is about one hundred times smaller. For the electromagnetic and gravitational forces, the strength decreases with the square of the distance from the source instead of having a rather sharp cutoff as the other two forces do. Thus their range is sometimes spoken of as infinite, though obviously their significant effect becomes negligible at finite distances. In any case, the range of the electromagnetic and gravitational forces is much longer than those of the two nuclear forces.

[19]This would replace the many parts in the computer to represent each particle with just one—the particle itself.

[20]P.C.W. Davies and J.R. Brown, eds., *The Ghost in the Atom: A Discussion of the Mysteries of Quantum Physics* (Cambridge: Cambridge, 1986); Nick Herbert, *Quantum Reality: Beyond the New Physics* (Garden City, NY: Anchor/Doubleday, 1985); Hugh Ross, *The Creator and the Cosmos* (Colorado Springs, CO: NavPress, 1993), ch. 12.

[21]James Gleick, *Chaos: Making a New Science* (New York: Viking, 1987).

[22]A survey of biblical prophecies, both those already fulfilled and others still future is given by J. Barton Payne, *Encyclopedia of Biblical Prophecy: The Complete Guide to Scriptural Predictions and Their Fulfillment* (New York: Harper and Row, 1973). Books specifically dealing with fulfilled prophecy as evidence for the truth of Christianity are Robert C. Newman, ed., *Evidence of Prophecy* (Hatfield, PA: IBRI, 1990) and John Warwick Montgomery, ed., *Evidence for Faith* (Dallas, TX: Probe/Word, 1991), part 4.

[23]Phillip E. Johnson, *Darwin on Trial*, 2nd ed. (Downers' Grove, IL: InterVarsity, 1993), 37-41.

[24]The phrase is Stephen Jay Gould's in *Natural History* 86, no. 5 (1977): 14. See also Charles Darwin, *Origin of Species*, ch. 10; George Gaylord Simpson, *The Major Features of Evolution* (New York: Simon and Schuster, 1953), 360; Steven M. Stanley, *Macroevolution: Patterns and Process* (New York: Freeman, 1979), 82.

[25]D. Raup, "Conflicts Between Darwin and Paleontology," *Field Museum Bulletin*, January 1979, 22.

[26]Stephen Jay Gould, in "The Power of This View of Life," *Natural History*, June 1994,: 8, says: "All but one phylum arose in a single geological whoosh, within some five million years or so, at the dawn of Cambrian times, 530 million years ago. . . ." See also Jeffrey S. Levinton, "The Big Bang of Animal Evolution," *Scientific American*, November 1992, 84-91; Richard A. Kerr, "Evolution's Big Bang Gets Even Bigger," *Science*, September 3, 1993, 1274-75.

[27]Murray Eden, "Inadequacies of Neo-Darwinian Evolution as a Scientific Theory," in Paul S. Moorhead and Mar-

tin M. Kaplan, eds., *Mathematical Challenges to the Neo-Darwinian Interpretation of Evolution* (Philadelphia: Wistar Institute, 1967; reprint, New York: Alan R. Liss, 1985); Mark A. Ludwig, *Computer Viruses, Artificial Life and Evolution* (Tucson, AZ: American Eagle, 1993).

[28]William A. Dembski, "On the Very Possibility of Intelligent Design," in J. P. Moreland, ed., *The Creation Hypothesis: Scientific Evidence for an Intelligent Designer* (Downer's Grove, IL: InterVarsity, 1994), 113-138, followed up by the actual evidence in the succeeding chapters. More detail is given in William A. Dembski, "The Incompleteness of Scientific Naturalism," in John Buell and Virginia Hearn, eds., *Darwinism: Science or Philosophy?* (Richardson, TX: Foundation for Thought and Ethics, 1994), 79-94.

[29]Fred Hoyle compares this to the likelihood of a tornado assembling an airplane from parts in a junkyard! "Hoyle on Evolution," *Nature*, November 12, 1981, 105. See my discussion in Robert C. Newman, "Self-Reproducing Automata and the Origin of Life," *Perspectives on Science and Christian Faith* 40 (1988): 24-31 and responses in *PSCF* 41 (1989): 26-28 and *PSCF* 42 (1990): 113-14. See also Ludwig in note 27 above.

[30]Michael J. Behe, "Molecular Machines: Experimental Support for the Design Hypothesis," paper presented at the national meeting of the American Scientific Affiliation, Seattle, 1993; see also Michael J. Behe, "Experimental Support for Regarding Functional Classes of Proteins to Be Highly Isolated from Each Other," in Buell and Hearn, *Darwinism: Science or Philosophy?*, 60-71.

[31]Carl Sagan, *The Cosmic Connection: An Extraterrestrial Perspective* (New York: Dell, 1973); Edward Regis, Jr., ed., *The Extraterrestrials: Science and Alien Intelligence* (Cambridge, Cambridge: 1985); G. Siegfried Kutter, *The Universe and Life: Origins and Evolution* (Boston: Jones and Bartlett, 1987); Thomas Michael Corwin and Dale Wachowiak, *The Universe: From Chaos to Consciousness* (Orlando, FL: Harcourt Brace Jovanovich, 1989). Some evan-

gelical perspective is provided in the August 1977 issue of the *SCP Journal* and in Hugh Ross' *The Creator and the Cosmos* (Colorado Springs, CO: NavPress, 1993).

[32]See Johnson, *Darwin on Trial*, 2nd ed., 33, and Dawkins, *The Blind Watchmaker*, 249.

[33]Dawkins, *The Blind Watchmaker*.

[34]Dawkins, *The Blind Watchmaker*, 4-6, 37; John D. Barrow and Frank J. Tipler, *The Anthropic Cosmological Principle* (New York: Oxford, 1986), 76-87.

[35]Hugh Ross, *The Fingerprint of God*, 2nd ed. (Orange, CA: Promise, 1991), ch. 12; Ross, *The Creator and Cosmos* (Colorado Springs, CO: NavPress, 1993), ch. 14; see also P.C. Davies, *The Accidental Universe* (Cambridge, Cambridge: 1982) and Barrow and Tipler, *Anthropic Cosmological Principle*.

[36]See Barrow and Tipler, *Anthropic Cosmological Principle*, ch. 8. Much of this material was originally collected in Lawrence J. Henderson, *The Fitness of the Environment* (Cambridge, MA: Harvard, 1913; reprint, Magnolia, MS: Peter Smith, 1970).

[37]Hugh Ross has compiled this material in his *Creator and the Cosmos*, ch. 15. More detail and documentation is provided in his *Fingerprint of God*, ch. 14.

[38]Robert Shapiro, *Origins: A Skeptic's Guide to the Creation of Life on Earth* (New York: Summit Books, 1986). See also Charles B. Thaxton, Walter L. Bradley and Roger L. Olsen, *The Mystery of Life's Origin: Reassessing Current Theories* (New York: Philosophical Library, 1984; Dallas, TX: Lewis and Stanley, 1992).

[39]See note 28.

[40]Robert C. Newman, "The Evidence of Cosmology," in John Warwick Montgomery, ed., *Evidence for Faith* (Dallas, TX: Probe/Word, 1991), 71-91; Ross, *Fingerprint of God*, chs. 6-10; and Ross, *Creator and the Cosmos*, chs. 3-11.

[41]Stephen W. Hawking, *A Brief History of Time: From the Big Bang to Black Holes* (Toronto: Bantam, 1988), ch. 8.

[42]A. Rupert Hall, *From Galileo to Newton 1630-1720*

(London: Collins, 1963), 312; Nancy R. Pearcey and Charles B. Thaxton, *The Soul of Science: Christian Faith and Natural Philosophy* (Wheaton, IL: Crossway, 1994), 73, 89-90.

[43]J.C. Polkinghorne, *The Quantum World* (Princeton, NJ: Princeton, 1984), 34ff; Davies and Brown, *Ghost in the Atom*, 7-13.

[44]Davies and Brown, *Ghost in the Atom*, 13-17. I have simplified the discussion considerably.

[45]Nick Herbert, *Quantum Reality*, 50-52.

Part IV

Defending the Faith Theologically

Christian Apologetics in a Non-Christian World

Thomas C. Oden

I feel deeply honored to be asked to speak to this distinguished evangelical colloquy on how the faith once delivered to the saints is to be rightly guarded, reasonably championed and wisely advocated in our special historic situation. I find it useful to divide this broad assignment into several decisive apologetic issues:

1. Is the willingness to suffer for truth intrinsic to the Christian understanding of truth?
2. How is the concept of the "non-Christian world" best understood evangelically?
3. What is happening in the confessing evangelical movements within the North American mainline?
4. Is the history of exegesis recoverable after a century of reductionist historicism?
5. At what point will evangelicals learn to kick the "post" out of an ultramodernity camouflaging as "postmodern"?
6. Whither postmodern paleo-orthodoxy: Where is the Holy Spirit leading evangelical apologetics?
7. Will the church endure? Reappraising the question of indefectibility

We are attempting to answer these questions within the framework of the *consensus fidelium*, celebrating two mil-

271

lennia of Christian exegesis, amid a great cloud of witnesses:

1. Is the Willingness to Suffer for Truth Intrinsic to the Christian Understanding of Truth?

Is the willingness to put one's body on the line for the truth an indispensable premise of the very concept of truth in evangelical testimony? To speak of truth without willingness to suffer for the truth is backhandedly to debase the truth.

No Christian teacher is worth listening to who is not willing to suffer if need be for the truth that is being taught.[1] The readiness to suffer for the sake of the truth is intrinsic to the whole fabric of Christian living, and hence teaching, and thus is not an optional part of the equation of the equipping of the public teacher of Christianity.[2]

Paul's teaching was personally validated by his willingness to be "suffering even to the point of being chained like a criminal. But God's word is not chained" (2 Timothy 2:9). Some hearers will find in the truth of the one who was "nailed to the cross" merely a "stone of stumbling" and "folly" (1 Corinthians 1:23; cf. Romans 8:17-18). Jesus did not hesitate to make it clear that his disciples must be prepared to "be handed over for punishment and execution; and men of all nations will hate you for your allegiance to me."[3]

The truth, Christianly understood, is an event in history, a birth, death and resurrection, God's own personal coming to us in mercy and grace, a Word spoken through a personal life lived, a personal event in which we are called personally to participate. To tell the truth rightly is to follow the One who is truth.

The "right method" for guarding Christian truth was set forth in Luther's three concise instructions: *oratio, meditatio, tentatio*—first by prayer, then by textual meditation, but decisively by suffering temptation and the experience of testing through affliction. Listen to him poignantly acknowledge how much he owed to his enemies: "Through the raging of the devil they have so buffeted, distressed, and terrified me that they have made me a fairly good theologian, which I would not have become without them."[4]

These plenary sessions have been asking:

2. How Is the Concept of the "Non-Christian World" Best Understood Evangelically?

My first impulse is to invert the question by unpacking its premise: In what sense is the world in which we are privileged to attest grace rightly described as a "non-Christian world"? "Non-Christian world" cannot mean that the world which is God's gift now exists without God. It cannot mean that the work of the Spirit is totally eclipsed or dysfunctional within the estranged world, just because it has been willfully spurned. It cannot mean that the world lacks the accompaniment of the crucified and risen Son or the governance of the all-wise God.

It can only mean the world that has defiantly decided to proceed as if the Incarnate Lord had not come in our midst and has no abiding relevance for the world. It can only mean, for Christian apologetic reasoning, that unbelievers have falsely posited a world that lacks the justifying grace of the Son and from which the sanctifying fruits of the Spirit are absent. It can only point to a world which lives in despair, not realizing its reception of redeeming love by the incarnate living God. It lives already under the judgment of the Holy One whose judgment will be made complete on the last day.

Meanwhile the actual fallen world, the ongoing cosmos that runs on twenty-four hour standard time, is still in the process of being reconciled and its sin overcome by the crucified and risen Redeemer. "Actual fallen world" refers to a penultimate world situation which has not yet come to itself in repentance and faith, an actual world that still despairs over its failure to be itself before God.

Apologetics within that sort of posited world must be careful not to take that world in its fallenness more seriously than it takes that world's decisive redemption. Apologetics within that sort of world which is hypothesized as if it were still unmet by the living God, as if it were still awaiting the Christ, must be careful not to be swallowed up by the power of the unredeemed imagination as to its own finality.

To *reify* is to treat an abstraction as if substantially existing, to attribute reality to something. The reification of the concept "non-Christian world" invites the critical qualifier that the world is and remains God's, who so loved the world that He gave His only Son that all who believe on Him might have eternal life. This world is already recipient of God's saving redemption in Jesus Christ, a gift given for all and appropriable by all who repent and believe. Christian apologetics in the heat of its temporal struggle amid the fallen world is forever tempted to overestimate the fleeting temporary power of the fallen world.

Christian apologetics has the privilege of speaking to the fallen world not merely in reference to fallen humanity's assumptions about itself, but more so in reference to God's own assumption of humanity through the Son. This communication always takes place within a particular *Zeitgeist*. But the *Zeitgeist* cannot itself dictate the terms of salvation or redefine the vocabulary of the apostolic testimony so that one concedes to the *Zeitgeist* the absolute truth of all its premises, many of which are false, and only then begins to seek despairingly to find some tiny opening for the light of Christian truth. That is not contextualization but abandonment of mission.

Christian apologetics, just as Christian caregiving, has the task of reaching out for the fallen and hungry precisely where they are fallen and hungry, yet without encouraging the demonic pretense that this fallenness is the last word.

Due to its specific commission to communicate with the fallen world in its own language, Christian apologetics is continually tempted to magnify the very power and vitality of the fallen world which almighty God is acting to redeem. With the best of intentions such efforts may tend to forget the incomparable power of the One who has acted decisively to save the world from its fallenness. By excessive attentiveness to the transient power of the fallen world, the fatigued apologist may be suckered into becoming inattentive to the majesty of that One from whom all things come and into whom all things return, in whom there is no shadow of change or turning. So the praise of God is inadvertently diminished in the interest of taking seriously the fallen world. Under the noble motivation of taking the world seriously, grace is trivialized.

Faith encounters that conjectured world with the real world as God's gift, which when fallen, has been redeemed. The apostolic testimony within that real world does better to offer its own gifts to the world than to borrow hungrily from the world's skewed self-understandings. This requires apologetics to attend to its own texts and share its own distinctive gifts. Faith need not be thrown off track by the presumed vitality of a dying world, the imagined power of an evanescent world.

Another aspect of my assignment in concluding this series of plenary sessions is to try to survey and describe the apologetic situation of the theological scene in North America. So I want to focus now upon a special part of that arena:

3. What Is Happening in the Confessing Evangelical Movements within the North American Mainline?

I speak as an evangelical apologist within North American mainline Protestantism. By mainline Protestantism I mean those communions whose leadership has for several decades been deeply entangled in cultural accommodations, doctrinal softening, hypertoleration on matters of doctrine and in many cases, political messianisms, utopian social experimentalism, protomarxian economic conjectures, absolute egalitarian sentimentalism, bureaucratic ecumenism, regulatory politics and the idealized fantasies of controlled economies.

I speak particularly and penitently of my own United Methodist Church, but the same observations apply to the Presbyterian Church USA, United Church of Canada, United Church of Christ, Disciples of Christ, Episcopalians and to some lesser degree the Evangelical Lutheran Church of America.

In each of these communions there has been a three-decade radical hemorrhaging of vitality, membership and witness. But more promising in the longer view, within each there is an active movement of the Holy Spirit and a growing renewal of classic Christian teaching—a confessing movement, such as the Confessing Movement within the United Methodist Church, Disciples for Renewal, Pro Ecclesia, Christians for Biblical Renewal, Presbyterians for Renewal and the reform movement within the United Church of Canada.

These Scripture-centered accountability movements are at this juncture of history relatively small but gaining rapid momentum. Their journals are thriving. The expectation is increasing that they may soon affect major theological and polity reforms within the oldline. Every event which attempts to reimagine God in reductionist terms as a bland reflection of modernity's excesses only serves as an encouragement to these resistance movements and stimulates their determination to confess anew the Sonship and Lordship of Jesus Christ.

Hence these times call not merely for generating moral outrage and repeating negative grievances, but for asking how the Spirit is calling the faithful within academic and church communities to work constructively together toward practically reclaiming stolen church bureaucracies and renegade ecclesial establishments.

The promising future of mainline Protestant evangelicals has potentially grace-laden repercussions for the future of both Catholic and Orthodox traditions the world over—and a deepened, chastened, penitent new conversation between evangelicals who are inside the mainline churches and those evangelicals in the dissenting traditions is being prepared by the Holy Spirit. Most promising is the potential dialogue between Reformed evangelicals and evangelicals of the Anglican-Wesleyan tradition.

Can evangelicals and doctrinal traditionalists and classicists within the mainline churches come together cooperatively to form a plausible accord which effectively resists the apostacizing temptations so endemic within the mainline? Can they unite with a trustable and viable agenda for reclaiming the church and rescuing it from its slippery doctrinal slopes? Can a trajectory be set that will neither slide toward heterodoxy and imprudence nor become inwardly turned toward resentment and reactionary defensiveness? Can those who hold steadfastly to classic Christian teaching find a hopeful voice to challenge the long-dominant hegemony of doctrinal latitudinarians, hypertolerationists, egalitarian activists, neopagan activists and pantheists? Can loyal stay-inners cope with ongoing temptations to walk away and abandon the struggle? These questions are being contested at a thousand different levels.

A massive moral crisis is now facing the deteriorating liberal mainline church leadership, its academic institutions, bureaucracies and local churches. It is time to reconceive a common vision sharable by evangelicals, moderates and traditionalists for repossession of those church institutions that have been either abandoned, neglected or, in some cases, ideologically hijacked. It is time to set feasible goals for the rehabilitation of a tradition-deprived church. How do we go about reclaiming our identity, our institutions, our academies, our mission?

I know that many of you are not in the mainline. You feel yourselves spared these dilemmas. You have no obligation to fight these battles. But analogous battles are being fought in all Christian ministries.

I have no interest here in boasting of the achievements of the mainline, particularly at this juncture of history, which so radically calls us all to repentance. I do not speak in a triumphalist tone in the presence of those of evangelical traditions who do not cotton to the mainline establishment or identify in any way with liberal church institutions. I only wish to communicate what a great work God the Holy Spirit is doing among evangelicals within these churches, and hope it will hearten you wherever you serve.

4. Is the History of Exegesis Recoverable after a Century of Reductionist Historicism?

The Holy Spirit has a history. When this history is systematically forgotten, it is incumbent upon evangelical guardianship to recover it by new rigorous historical effort. This is why the apologetic task for biblical studies in our time must focus in a deliberate way upon the early history of exegesis. We have a right to learn from the reasonings and arguments that have sustained Christian textual interpretations and spiritual formation through many previous modernities, especially in their earliest prototypical forms. The canonical text has a history of interpretation which has been systematically ignored in the last century of historicist investigation.

Evangelical scholarship is already sorely tempted to become co-opted by reductionist nineteenth-century historicist models of interpretation which approach the text by disavowing that it could be the revealed Word of God. To overcome this amnesia, evangelicals need to take the lead in biblical scholarship in recovering the history of exegesis.

This is why most of the rest of my life will be primarily devoted to editing a twenty-seven volume *Ancient Christian Commentary on Scripture*. Its goals are: the renewal of Christian preaching based on classical Christian exegesis; the intensified study of Scripture by laypersons who wish to think with the early church about the canonical text; and the stimulation of Christian historical, biblical, theological and pastoral scholars toward further inquiry into the exegesis of the ancient Christian writers.

This verse-by-verse commentary will consist of carefully chosen selections in dynamic equivalent English translation from the ancient Christian writers of the first eight centuries. Texts are now being selected by an international team of experts out of the ancient Christian tradition from Clement of Rome to John of Damascus, ranging through the early centuries of Christian exegesis (100-750 A.D.). We are making accessible the most penetrating patristic passages on Scripture, pericope by pericope. Our selections will feature both the varieties of classic Christian exegetical argumentation and their overarching cohesion grounded in ecumenical consensual exegetical reasoning. In this way Protestant, Catholic and Orthodox audiences will be served and renewed by this commentary.

This work stands in the early medieval *catena* tradition of patristic exegesis and will benefit by utilizing and adapting that tradition in appropriate ways. This after-modern effort has antecedents in Eastern Orthodox and in seventeenth-century Lutheran and Reformed heirs of the tradition of the *glossa ordinaria*. It will offer, for the first time in this century, the earliest Christian comments and reflections on all Old and New Testament texts to a modern pastoral and lay audience.

Translations will be made afresh where needed; insofar as current English translations are adequate, they will be used, and where adequate but archaic they will be de-archaized.

On each page the Scripture text will be presented in the center surrounded by well-referenced direct quotations of comments of key consensual early Christian exegetes. The most succinct way to visualize this is to picture the printed text of the Talmud, a collection of rabbinic arguments and comments of the same period as the patristic writers, surrounding and explicating the texts of the sacred tradition.

Modern preaching has remained largely bereft of easily accessible patristic exegetical resources. This series will provide the pastor, lay reader, exegete and student with convenient means to see what Athanasius or John Chrysostom or Leo the Great said about a particular text for preaching, for study or for meditation.

How were these early exegetes viewed in the early evangelical revivalist tradition? The Fathers are

> the most authentic commentators on Scripture, as being both nearest the fountain, and eminently endued with the Spirit by whom all Scripture was given. . . . I speak chiefly of those who wrote before the Council of Nice. But who would not likewise desire to have some acquaintance with those that followed them? with St. Chrysostom, Basil, Jerome, Austin [Augustine]; and above all, the man of a broken heart, Ephraim Syrus?[5]

The exegesis of the church fathers is especially helpful in "the *explication* of a doctrine that is not sufficiently explained, or for *confirmation* of a doctrine generally received."[6]

5. *On Kicking the "Post" Out of Ultramodernity*

This leads us to ask: When nostalgic ultramodernity poses as trendy postmodern, what apologetic responses are fitting for evangelicals? At what point will evangelicals learn to kick the "post" out of a fatigued ultramodernity camouflaging as postmodern?

The term "postmodern" is still being used by ultramoderns as if the assumptions of modernity were going to continue forever. Postmodernity in their sense only refers to an intensification of the despairing messianisms of modernity.

Modernity is the period, the ideology, and the malaise of the time from 1789 to 1989, from the Bastille to the Berlin Wall. The gawky, ungainly term "postmodern" points ironically to the course of actual hazardous history following the death of modernity. The period after modernity is a required course for evangelicals who attest the risen Lord amid a dying culture.

The evangelical take on postmodernity was well established long before 1980, well before anyone had heard of Derrida or Foucault. In 1979 the text of *Agenda for Theology* clearly documented an emergent, hopeful pre-'80s evangelical postmodern community of discourse. As early as the '60s some of us were trying to speak to the "new breed of spirit questers" in the postmodern situation, amid "the maturing twentieth century."[7]

Already by the late '70s, before the postmodern fad of the '80s, I was attempting to differentiate sharply between modernity, later-stage modernity ("third quarter of the twentieth century") and postmodernity ("preparing to enter the third millennium"), as I looked toward the emergence of a

> postmodern orthodoxy, having been immersed in the deteriorations of later stage modernity, now reawakened to the power and beauty of classical Christianity, seeking to incorporate the achievements of modernity into an ethos and intellectus that transcends modernity under the guidance of ancient ecumenical Christianity.

That was the "agenda for theology," as I saw it in 1979 and remains so for many more today than in 1979.

> This is what I mean by postmodern orthodoxy. Its spirit is embodied in the student who has been through the rigors of university education, often through the hazards of the drug scene, through the

281

ups and downs of political engagement, through the head shrinks and group thinks of popular therapies, and through a dozen sexual messianisms, only to become weary of the pretentious motions of frenetic change. Finally they have come on Christ's living presence in the world in an actual community of Christians and now have set out to understand what has happened to them in the light of the classical texts of scripture and tradition.[8]

The agenda for theology in the last quarter of the twentieth century, following the steady deterioration of a hundred years and the disaster of the last two decades, is to begin to prepare the postmodern Christian community for its third millennium by returning again to the careful study and respectfully following of the central tradition of classical Christianity.[9]

Then belatedly after 1980 came Foucault, Derrida and Rorty with a weaker, thinner, chic definition of postmodernity, which caught the imagination of ultramodern academics in literary and hermeneutic theory. It was only then that the popular press caught sight of the concept of postmodernity according to this later despairing ultramodern definition. Since the media elites have controlled this definition since the early 1980s, it has intruded itself belatedly upon theological dialogue as if normative. I appeal to you to return to the pre-'80s definition of postmodernity which is evangelically more hopeful, culturally more realistic and providentially more circumspect.

When evangelicals today hear reckless talk of postmodernity by avant garde academics, there is no longer any reason to break out in a sweat. The cure is easy: Just quietly strike out the "post" and mentally insert "ultra." That is what I call kicking the "post" out of ultramodernity.

Where postmodern has become a euphemism for ultramodern, paleo-Christians do not mind making a little jest over the difference. Where the value assumptions of modernity are nostalgically idealized and where ancient wisdoms are compulsively disparaged, you have only a thinly veneered ultramodernity, even where it calls itself postmodernity. It is like a moth winging frantically and circling ever closer to the flame of instant fad death.

The ploy is to make modern value assumptions appear eternal by co-opting them in what is called postmodernity. This postmodern toupee may look fetching and neat but underneath there is sparse growth with no regenerativity. The deconstructionist mask may look brave, but it doesn't fit; the knees are quaking and there is a tick in the smile. The nameplate may say postmodern but the intellectus was patented in the Enlightenment. The subterfuge is based on the deceit of trying to make the key values of corrupted modernity appear permanent by endowing them with the fake label postmodern. It is a cover-up that the liberal investigative journalists have not even begun to grasp and are too intimidated to investigate.

6. Whither Postmodern Paleo-orthodoxy: Where Is the Holy Spirit Leading Evangelical Apologetics?

Postmodernity in its paleo-orthodox definition is simply that period that follows the time span from 1789 to 1989 which characteristically embraced an enlightenment worldview that cast an ideological spell over our times, now in grave moral spinout.

The spinout phase of late modernity is epitomized by the reductive naturalism of Freud which is no longer marketable as an effective therapy, the idealistic historical utopianism of Marx which is now internally collapsing from St. Petersburg to Havana, the narcissistic assertiveness of Nietzsche which is drastically cutting life expectancy on urban streets, and the modern chauvinism typified by Feuerbach, Dewey and Bultmann that imagines the ethos of late modernity to be the unquestioned cultural norm that presumes to judge all premodern texts and ideas. Under the tutelage of these once brave modern ideologies so touted by the liberal media elites, sex has been reduced to orgasm, persons to bodies, psychology to stimuli, economics to planning mechanisms and politics to machinery. These malfunctioning ideologies are today everywhere in crisis, even while still being fawned over by isolated church bureaucratic elitists.

These tired, fading modern illusions are woven together in a ideological temperament that still sentimentally shapes the oldline liberal Protestant ethos, especially its politicized bureaucracies and academies, who remain largely unprepared to grasp either their own vulnerability or their divine calling and possibility within this decisive historical opportunity.

The Marxist-Leninism of the Soviet era is now gone; the Freudian idealization of sexual liberation has found it easier to make babies than parent them morally; the children of the post-psychoanalytic culture are at peril; the truculence of Nietzschean nihilism has spread to the bloody banks of Bosnian and Cambodian and Rwandan and Ukrainian rivers with a trail of genocide along the way; the modern chauvinism of once-confident Bultmannians is now moribund since the modernity they expected never arrived.

These once-assured ideologies are now unmasked as having a dated vision of the human possibility; for none have succeeded in engendering a transmissible intergenerational culture. Since each of these ideological programs has colluded to support the other, they are now falling synchronously down like tottering dominoes: the command economies; the backfiring therapeutic experiments; the patient-abusing therapists; the mythic fantasies of demythology; the interpersonal fragments of drug experimentation;

the exploding splinters of narcissism and their wholly owned ecclesial subsidiaries, theological hirelings and flunkies. If the Freudian project, the Bultmannian project, the Marxist project and the Nietzschean project are all functionally morose, then later-stage modernity is dead in any regenerative sense. That is what is meant by the phrase "terminal modernity." In a despairing search for a social utopia, we have blundered our way into the black hole of a social counter-utopia.

Renewing classic Christians are now being awakened and energized by this dawning realization: The Holy Spirit is determined to continue making alive the Body of Christ. It is only on the falsely hypothesized premise of the default of the Holy Spirit that the called-out people might seem at times to be coming to nothing. The demise of the Church is the least likely premise in the Christian understanding of history.

Those who willingly enslave themselves to passing idolatries should not be surprised when their gods are found to have clay feet. When beloved modern systems die, the idolaters understandably grieve and feel angry and frustrated. Meanwhile the grace-enabled community can celebrate the passage through and beyond modernity, and celebrate the intricate providences of history in which each dying historical formation is giving birth to new forms and refreshing occasions for living responsively in relation to grace.

What is happening today is a profound rediscovery of the texts, apologetic methods and pastoral wisdom of the long-neglected patristic exegetical tradition. For many evangelicals this means especially the Eastern Church fathers of the first five Christian centuries, which never suffered as deeply as did Western medieval Catholicism from the distortions of speculative scholasticism.

What is happening amid this historical situation is a joyous return to the sacred texts of Christian Scripture and the consensual exegetical guides of the formative period of

285

scriptural interpretation. Postmodern paleo-orthodox disciples are those who, having entered in good faith into the disciplines of modernity and having become disillusioned with the illusions of modernity, are again studying the word of God made known in history as attested by prophetic and apostolic witnesses whose testimonies have become perennial texts for this worldwide, multicultural, multigenerational remembering and celebrating and reconciling community of pardon.

7. Will the Church Endure? Reappraising the Question of Indefectibility

The decisive theological issue is the durability and indefectibility of the true church amid proximate temporary apostasy. This is the doctrinal issue that most deeply affects our moral courage and ability to relate to this cultural opportunity within what is sometimes mistaken to be a post-Christian world: the indefectibility of the Church that lives by the power of the Spirit. This is a theme well articulated by Augustine, Thomas Aquinas, Calvin and Cranmer, and now is a fitting time for orthodox Christians to rediscover it. Classic Christian apologetics is once again being called to reclaim the apostolic teaching of the perpetuity, imperishability and indefectibility of the Church. The one holy apostolic Church the world over is promised imperishable continuance, even if particular associations and groupings of apostate Christian ministries may languish, falter or atrophy.

Although the Church in some dissolute times and places appears virtually extinct, becoming "so obscured and defaced that the Church seems almost quite razed out . . . yet, in the meantime, the Lord has in this world, even in this darkness, his true worshippers."9 The foundation is standing sure and "the Lord knows those who are his" (2 Timothy 2:19). And there are "seven thousand who have not bowed the knee to Baal" (Romans 11:4). We are being offered a new opportunity to relearn of this remnant by observing the tenacious church in China following the Cultural Revolution, the heroic church in Cuba amid the disintegration of Fidelismo and the church in the former Soviet Union.

The Church's future is finally left not to human will or chance, but to the work of the Spirit and divine grace. Many branches of the seasonally changing vine may drop off in the varied storms and seasons of cultural histories. Once-vital ideas and institutions may become dysfunctional and atrophy. But the Church as Body of Christ will be preserved till the end of time. It is a Lutheran, Calvinist, Anglican, Wesleyan and Baptist tenet that the destiny of the believing Church is eternally secure. Faith remains the crucial condition of participating in this secure promise, but is not to be asserted so as to deny the power of the Holy Spirit to prevail over disbelief in God's own time.

Though individual believers may come to shipwreck, and even centuries of deteriorating traditions may lose their bearings during particular periods of confusion and crisis, the Church as Body of Christ is being guided by the Holy Spirit and sustained by grace until the end (John 16:1, 13). God will not be left without witnesses in the world (Acts 14:17). "One holy Christian church will be and remain forever."[10] According to my own church's traditional *Order for Receiving Persons into the Church*:

> The Church is of God, and will be preserved to the end of time, for the promotion of his worship and the due administration of his Word and Sacraments, the maintenance of Christian fellowship and discipline, the edification of believers, and the conversion of the world. All, of every age and station, stand in need of the means of grace which it alone supplies

I learned this passage by heart in the earliest days of my ministry.

287

Meanwhile the Church that sails on the turbulent seas of history continues to be vulnerable to those hazards that accompany historical existence generally. The Holy Spirit does not abandon the ever-formative Christian tradition amid these earthly struggles. God supplies that grace of perseverance by which the Church is enabled to remain Christ's living Body even while being challenged by infirmities, forgetfulness, apostasy, persecution and schism. The believing community is being preserved to "proclaim the Lord's death until he comes" (1 Corinthians 11:26). Against the Church "the gates of hell shall not prevail," Jesus declared, according to Matthew's gospel (16:18, KJV; cf. Luke 1:33; 1 Timothy 3:15). This means that the Church will never decline into total forgetfulness, since it is guided by the Spirit who promises always to accompany the faithful (John 14:16; Matthew 23:20), even when short-term ecclesial accountancy procedures do not add up, and management techniques show poor yields. The Church insofar as guided by the Spirit does not ever fall entirely away from the fundamental truth of faith or into irretrievable error. She is preserved by grace, not by human craft or numbers or political skill (Matthew 7:25).

Despite temporary real and devastating apostasies, it is unthinkable that God would allow the Church finally to become absolutely and continuously apostate or to lose all touch with the righteousness which Christ has once for all bestowed upon her. "For you have been born again, not of perishable seed, but of imperishable, through the living and enduring word of God. For 'All men are like grass,' but 'the word of the Lord stands forever.' And this is the word that was preached to you."[11] The promise of indefectibility is not toward a particular congregation or disciplinary approach or polity or denomination or generation or a passing period of history, but rather to the whole Church to preserve her from fundamental error in the long course of history—to the end.[12]

Insofar as the faithful are sustained by pure Word and

Sacrament, adhering to the "faith once delivered," their eucharistic sacrifice, Christ's own self-giving to redeem sin, is received by God as faultless.[13] The *Second Helvetic Confession* saliently captured this affirmation for Reformed believers, that the church "does not err, so long as it relies upon the rock Christ, and upon the foundation of the prophets and apostles." Insofar as "she lets herself be taught by the Holy Spirit through the Word of God," Calvin argued that "the church cannot err in things necessary for salvation."[14] Though particular assemblies may lapse, relapse or collapse, the elect people of God will not fall away from salvation due to the Spirit's guidance.

All those called and elected will not be allowed to err at the same time. This is not a conclusion of an optimistic anthropology but a doctrine grounded in the work of the Spirit. While grace does not coerce belief, neither does it ever bat zero in any given ecclesial season. It is unthinkable that God would create the Church at great cost only to let it fall finally into permanent or irremediable error. Thus indefectibility is more a teaching of the power of the Holy Spirit than of the self-sufficiency of human imagination or the strategic wisdom of the Church as a sociological entity.

Jesus promised disciples of all times that the Holy Spirit will "teach you all things and will remind you of everything I have said to you" (John 14:26). Always some seed of faith remains buried in the ashes even of the most divided and corrupt ecclesial remnant. Sometimes such seeds may seem to survive marginally as endangered species, as scattered all too thinly throughout a particular weed-infested culture, as relics of former vitalities of previous covenant communities. Yet wherever Word and Sacrament are being faithfully transmitted and delivered, they are never without effect, for "my word" shall "not return to me empty, but will accomplish what I desire" (Isaiah 55:11), says the Lord.

Classical Protestantism affirms that "the church does not err" in the sense that the whole Church does not at any given time err, and it does not err in the foundation, even if in temporary and non-essential ways it may.[15] Classic Protestants argue that the Church is ultimately sure or certain or indefectible (*asphales*) insofar as it clings to the revealed Word. Yet this does not diminish the recognition that still amid the history of sin the visible Church is ever prone to forgetfulness and fallibility. Nonetheless, that community which is being called into being by the Holy Spirit will not be found falling irretrievably into apostasy so as to make it impossible for all subsequent generations to hear the gospel. Yet this does not imply that the church is secure from making mistakes or errors of judgment. The relative fallibility of the Church in time is itself a stable Protestant dogma.

Since fallible persons are the recipients of God's saving grace (for the healthy do not need a physician, Mark 2:17), as long as the Church exists within the conditions of the history of sin, the Church will be prone to being distorted and vulnerable to those who wish to use it for their own purposes. Until the consummation of salvation history when the incurably wicked will be cut off from the living vine, the community of called out people will be blemished and distorted.

To flee from the scene of human corruption would be to flee from the Church's own arena of mission and servant ministry. But in so far as it is truly the Body of Christ living in faith, hope and love under the life-giving power of the Spirit, the Church can never become absolutely or finally or fatally corrupted (Matthew 16:18).

Among diseases of the history of sin that continue to plague the church and resist its full growth are: the partisan spirit that would divide it; the heretical spirit that would lead it to distort or forget apostolic teaching; the antinomian spirit that turns Christian liberty into libertinism; the legalistic spirit that would turn grace into law; and the naturalistic spirit that would treat grace as a determinant of nature. Despite these infirmities and challenges, which are permitted by a kind Providence to strengthen the church and enable it to grow stronger, the body lives on, the vine sends forth new shoots, the Spirit enlivens and heals and the Head continues to guide and order the whole organism (John 15:1-5; Colossians 1:18).

The continuing renewal of ecclesial life never comes by avoiding sinners, for their redemption is the reason why the Church exists. Clean-hands purists of all periods tend to flee the task of serving sinners, unlike Jesus, who mixed with them, ate and drank with those most despicable and rejected and profoundly identified with all sinners on the cross. The Body of Christ continues to struggle against tendencies toward a Montanism that would exclude sinners based on their lack of Spirit, a Donatism which would exclude sinners based upon inauthentic ministry or regionalism and a purist Novatian rigorism which would exclude sinners based upon their moral deficiencies.

The ecumenical councils and major consensual teachers attest ultimate indefectibility of the Church as a gift of grace.[16] The patristic exegetes pointed to the councils as evidence of the assent of the whole Church. It is this universal consent that is said to be reliable and finally indefectible.

While the Holy Spirit is the actuating principle of this indefectibility, the consent of the general laity is given as an evidence of proximate unity and the central criterion of ecumenicity. The Holy Spirit does not introduce new or post-apostolic doctrine through the conciliar process, but rather acts to illuminate and guard from error the original apostolic witness. This occurs not as if mechanically actuated by the Spirit, but working in a normal human manner through debate, inquiry, parliamentary deliberation, voting and the apparatus of policy formation.

The history of the church is not one of uninterrupted progress or *ekstasis*, without challenge or chastisement. Pascal in *Pensées* pictured Christianity as a thousand times having appeared to be "on the point of universal destruction, and every time that it has been in this condition, God has raised it up by some extraordinary stroke of his power." Each seeming defeat readies the community for a deeper level of understanding. Each apparent victory readies the community for a deeper level of conflict.

The residual vitality of the church, even in periods in which it seems to have been totally undone, is an amazing story recounted in actual human history, featuring startling recoveries after long periods of malaise and apparent death. The worst periods of martyrdom are characteristically accompanied by the profoundest movements of the witness of the Spirit. The deepest sloughs of demoralization and libertinism are followed repeatedly by such correctives as those of Benedict of Nursia, Bernard of Clairvaux, Francis of Assisi, Luther, Calvin, Teresa of Avila, Edwards, Wesley and Teresa of Lisieux. To know, the promise has held, even against great odds that the gates of hell have not prevailed against the *ekklesia*.

Endnotes

[1] 1 Peter 4:13-5:9; *The Martyrdom of Polycarp, Ante-Nicene Fathers* (hereafter ANF), 1:37-44.

[2] Philippians 3:10; Cyprian, *On the Lapsed*, ANF, 5:437-47; Kierkegaard, *Attack on "Christendom."*

[3] Matthew 24:9; Irenaeus, *Ag. Her.* 4.33.9, ANF, 1:508.

[4] Luther, *What Luther Says*, 3:11358-11360; cf. preface to Wittenberg ed., *Luther's Works* 34:283-88.

[5] John Wesley, *Address to the Clergy, Works*, i.2, 10.484; cf. *Journals of John Wesley* (hereafter JJW), 3:390.

[6] Wesley, *A Roman Catechism, with a Reply*, Preface, *Works*, 10:87, italics added; cf. JJW 1:367.

[7] Thomas C. Oden, *Structure of Awareness* (1968), 15, 275.

[8] Thomas C. Oden, *Agenda for Theology* (1979), 5, 31.

[9] *Second Helvetic Confession*; 1 Kings 19:18; Revelation 7:4, 9.

[10] *Augsburg Confession*, art.7.

[11] 1 Peter 1:24-25; cf. Calvin, *Commentaries*, 22:57-60.

[12] Matthew 28:20; cf. *Longer Catechism of the Eastern Orthodox Church*.

[13] Ambrose, *Six Days of Creation*, 4.2, 7; John Chrysostom, *On Eutropius; Confession of Dositheus*, 10-12.

[14] Calvin, *Institutes*, 4.8.13.

[15] Ursinus, *Commentary on the Heidelberg Catechism*.

[16] *Council of Nicea, Basil, Letter* 114; Gregory Nazianzen, *On the Great Athanasius, Orat. 21; Cyril, Letter* 39.

Modernity, Pluralism and Apologetics: Implications for Missions

Harold A. Netland

We had just moved from the lovely city of Kyoto, Japan to the sprawling megalopolis of Tokyo. I was completing language study in our first term of missionary service. My wife, Ruth, was expecting our first child. On one of her regular visits to the maternity clinic Ruth happened to meet an American woman who was married to a Japanese and living in Tokyo. Since we did not often encounter Americans in that part of Tokyo, Ruth invited the woman to our home. Expecting a casual visit full of small talk about things "back home," Ruth was shocked by what followed. After exchanging pleasantries the guest launched into an impressive and moving testimony of how she had "found peace and true meaning to life" in Nichiren Buddhism. The woman, it turned out, was an American convert to Soka Gakkai Buddhism and was a regional director of Soka Gakkai in Tokyo. In recounting the incident to me later, Ruth said that it was one of the most impressive testimonies she had heard— change a few key terms here and there and it could have been a beautiful Christian testimony.

This incident illustrates some of the new challenges facing Christian missions as we move into the twenty-first century. No longer is it a matter of the "Christian West" taking the gospel to the pagan East. The East has come West. And the West itself—a largely post-Christian, pagan culture—presents a formidable mission field. Furthermore, this encounter illustrates graphically the bankruptcy of a missiological approach limited simply to "sharing our story" and which refuses to support personal testimony with appeal to other corroborating factors. Evangelism based simply upon appeal to personal experience, to the pragmatic benefits of conversion or to authority by itself would be incapable of demonstrating why the woman ought to abandon Buddhism and embrace Christian faith.

At the heart of contemporary challenges to Christian faith—not just in the West but globally—is the set of assumptions and values associated with pluralism and the culture of modernity. Fundamental epistemological issues take on fresh and enormously complex forms in our multicultural and multireligious world. But these issues are inescapable. Accordingly, missions theory and praxis must take much more seriously than it has in the past the place of responsible apologetics in Christian witness.[1] And, given the increasingly diverse nature of Western societies, theologians and apologists in the West should become more sensitive to the range of intercultural and interreligious issues that have traditionally been delegated to missiology.

An integral component of effective evangelism and discipleship in contexts impacted by religious pluralism must be a vigorous Christian apologetic which is capable of engaging the intellectual forces of modernity in informed debate, is sensitive to the values and mores of the target culture and is conducted in conscious reliance upon the power and guidance of the Holy Spirit. What is needed, in other words, is a Spirit-controlled apologetic that aggressively challenges the plausibility structures[2] of modernity, that insists upon Christian belief as universally valid public truth and that restores confidence in the normativity of the gospel of Jesus Christ. Men and women today must be brought to the realization that Christian faith is not merely one of many equally legitimate alternative options, but that there is a significant sense in which they ought to accept Jesus Christ instead of opposing alternatives.

Some clarification on the place of apologetics in Christian mission is in order. We must recognize first that apologetics in and of itself will not result in the salvation of anyone. Nobody is argued into the kingdom. Apologetics— just as evangelism—is ineffective apart from the power and work of the Holy Spirit. For ultimately it is the Holy Spirit who brings about conviction of sin (John 16:8-11) and who liberates the spiritually blind from the grasp of the Adversary and gives new birth in Christ (John 3:5; 1 Corinthians 2:14-16; Titus 3:5). But, of course, this does not make apologetics unnecessary any more than it renders evangelism optional. Both evangelism and apologetics must be carried out with much prayer and conscious dependence upon the power of God. In our witness to an unbelieving world, primacy must always be given the simple, direct, Spirit-anointed proclamation of the gospel (Romans 1:16; Hebrews 4:12). But where appropriate, such witness should also be supplemented by informed and sensitive response to criticism and questions and demonstration of why one should accept the claims of Christian faith (1 Peter 3:15).

It is helpful here to make a basic distinction between what might be called theoretical apologetics and applied or context-specific apologetics. Theoretical apologetics, or apologetics as "problem solving," is concerned solely with the objective justification of the Christian faith, irrespective of any human response. Its purpose is to answer satisfactorily certain fundamental questions about the acceptability of Christian truth claims. Among these questions are the following: Does God exist? Can we know anything about God? Did Jesus rise from the dead, and if so what is the significance of this? Are the basic tenets of orthodox Christianity compatible with the fundamental teachings of Theravada Buddhism? If not, which perspective is to be accepted as true, and on what basis? And so on.

Theoretical apologetics is thus a highly rigorous and specialized endeavor, incorporating a variety of disciplines, although epistemological issues are central and inescapable.

Applied apologetics, or apologetics as persuasion, by contrast, is very much concerned with human response to the proclamation and defense of the gospel. It is the utilization of appropriate justification procedures and relevant data in the actual presentation and defense of the gospel to a particular target audience. Thus its purpose is to elicit a favorable response from the audience—it actively seeks to persuade. The methodology and level of sophistication of applied apologetics will vary greatly, depending upon one's audience. What is appropriate and effective in Kyoto may not be acceptable in Mexico City or Cairo. Considerable creativity and variety in approach are essential. Not only is there diversity among cultures, but even within a given culture there is remarkable diversity among individuals in terms of their interests, backgrounds and levels of education. Flexibility in approach and sensitivity to one's audience are essential on the level of applied apologetics. However, it is crucial to see that the answers to questions raised on the level of applied apologetics are logically dependent upon answers to corresponding questions in theoretical apologetics. Thus effective applied apologetics presupposes at least some familiarity with basic issues in theoretical apologetics.

Pluralism and the Culture of Modernity

Even a casual glance at the theological and missiological literature of the past half century indicates that the cluster of issues associated with religious pluralism are among the most controversial and pressing questions facing the church today. Gerald Anderson has observed that "No issue in missiology is more important, more difficult, more controversial, or more divisive for the days ahead than the theology of religions. . . . This is the theological issue for missions in the 1990s and into the twenty-first century."[3] Pluralism strikes at the very heart of orthodox Christian faith, for it rejects the notion that God has definitively revealed Himself in the Bible and that salvation is available only through the Person and work of Jesus Christ, the unique incarnation of God.

Yet our world has always been characterized by religious diversity. Indeed, the Mediterranean world of the New Testament was itself highly pluralistic. However, what makes pluralism such an explosive and urgent problem today is the pervasive impact of the culture of modernity. The values and assumptions of modernity support an environment in which the claims of orthodox Christianity appear increasingly implausible.

But what is modernity? Although there is an enormous body of literature dealing with the concepts of modernity and postmodernity—much of it attempting to clarify the distinction between the two notions—there is no clear consensus on the meanings of the terms.[4] By modernity, I mean the increasingly global culture which is rooted in (1) the process of modernization and (2) the intellectual heritage of the West during the past 300 years, which includes, but is not limited to, the eighteenth-century Enlightenment and its legacy. In very simple terms we might think of modernity as the culture (the worldview, set of values, ways of thinking and acting) produced by the process of modernization.[5] Today modernization is a global phenomenon, and the transformations it introduces are revolutionizing cultures worldwide. This understanding of modernity incorporates insights from two major models—the "history of ideas" approach which focuses primarily upon the intellectual history of the past 300 years or so and the "sociology of knowledge" approach which looks to the social dynamics which influence the ways in which people think and live. It seems to me that both models are necessary and provide insights into our contemporary situation.

When understood in these terms, the distinction between "modernity" and "postmodernity" becomes somewhat superfluous. For to be genuinely postmodern would require one to be beyond or outside of the modernization process and its influences—something that is virtually impossible today apart from total isolation from the world community. Furthermore, the frequently encountered sharp distinction between "modernity" and "postmodernity" tends to ascribe too much ideological uniformity to the past 250 years of Western culture, as if there were a clearly identifiable "Enlightenment paradigm" which held virtually unquestioned sway over Europe and North American culture until sometime in the mid-twentieth century. The reality seems to be considerably more complex. And yet, on the model proposed here, although we are still very much within the culture of modernity clearly there are distinct phases and paradigms within this broader culture. And what is today often termed "postmodernity" marks a particularly powerful current phase which is in identifiable ways quite distinct from other phases and paradigms.

The culture of modernity—which is increasingly global and thus cannot be identified simply with "Western culture"—carries with it certain assumptions, values and patterns of living. Regardless of whether one lives in Los Angeles, Tokyo, Mexico City, Nairobi or New Delhi, variations on these common characteristics are identifiable, and it is their presence which makes religious pluralism such a pressing concern today.

Although substantive treatment of the issues is impossible here, we should briefly note some ways in which modernity affects religious belief and practice. For example, it has become commonplace to associate secularization with the process of modernization. But the impact of secularization can be understood in at least two distinct ways.[6] First, there are those who see the impact of secularization primarily in the decline and displacement of religion in mod-

ern life. Secularization leads to secularism.[7] But secularization takes various forms and need not result in the elimination of religious belief and practice. Rather, as is the case in
the United States, secularization can coexist with religion,
but it does so by dramatically altering the ways in which
people are religious.

Related to secularization is the trend toward the privatization of religious belief or the growing dichotomy between the private and public spheres of life. Objective truth
is said to belong to the public realm of "facts." And since
religious statements are allegedly not empirically testable
as are other "public truths," religious beliefs are relegated
to the private sphere and are reduced to matters of personal
preference and private opinion.

Modernity is also linked to a pervasive sense of relativism, due in part to the pluralization of ideologies and
worldviews. Modernization results in the rapid multiplica-
tion of options available to a person—options not only in
fairly trivial matters such as what brand of toothpaste, cars
and clothing to purchase but, far more significantly, options in basic values, beliefs, ideologies, and worldviews.
Observation of diversity ("people believe different things")
often leads to forms of relativism ("there are no universal
truths or values"). Significantly, the intellectual legacy of
the past 200 years has resulted in widespread skepticism
and relativism regarding religion as well. Certainly there
have been times when Western culture has suffered from
an excessive confidence in the powers of reason to solve all
problems—one thinks here of the eighteenth-century Enlightenment and the Logical Positivism of the twentieth
century. But, although such influences are far from dead
today, it seems that the contemporary scene is characterized more by a profound loss of confidence in the ability
of reason to settle fundamental questions in any realm, including religion.

Modernity also fosters a highly pragmatic "consumer
mentality" regarding religion, a tendency exemplified in

301

the eclecticism of the New Age movement, with its shameless borrowing and mixing of attractive teachings and practices from many different religions. Questions of objective truth are minimized or ignored entirely. Various religions are evaluated pragmatically on the basis of how well they meet the needs and desires of their adherents.

Now it is crucial to see that this way of approaching religious issues, influenced as it is by modernity, is not strictly a Western phenomenon. As modernity continues to spread its influence worldwide, it will impact religion in non-Western cultures as well. To be sure, modernization does not occur in a cultural vacuum—modernity breeds upon indigenous cultural patterns which are already in place. The case of Japan is particularly instructive here and has significant implications for missions. In contemporary Japan we find a fascinating blend of a highly advanced stage of modernization with spiritual and cultural values which have their roots in centuries of tradition. There are remarkable similarities between some of the themes of modernity noted earlier and contemporary Japanese culture—e.g., a strong tendency toward religious relativism, lack of emphasis upon belief and doctrine in favor of personal experience, suspicion of exclusivistic claims made on behalf of any tradition, a highly pragmatic "this worldly" approach to religion and so on.[8]

For example, the highly pragmatic, "this worldly" orientation of Japanese religion is well known, and is reflected in the dramatic transformation of Buddhism as it encountered Japanese soil in the sixth century. In contrast to the more pessimistic Buddhism of India, with its emphasis upon *samsara*, the wearisome cycle of birth, death, rebirth regulated by karma and the religious goal of nirvana or escape from this cycle of rebirth, we find in Japanese Buddhism a much more positive affirmation of life and of the "Buddha nature" said to be inherent in all things. The religious goal comes to be identified with "enlightenment" now, in this life, and with the promise of a positive paradise after death—rebirth in the Pure Land.

The pragmatic thrust of Japanese religion is fully evident today and is reflected in the popular saying *kurushii toki no kamidanomi* (turn to the gods in times of distress). In other words, religion is a crutch—it is something to turn to in times of special need, but so long as one is able to cope in life on one's own there is no need to look to religion. The enormous popularity of special charms, oracle-lots, divination, specialty shrines and temples for everything from helping students to pass university entrance examinations to guaranteeing safety from traffic accidents to shrines dedicated to the success of particular businesses such as Toyota or Mitsubishi—all of this illustrates the very tangible, "this worldly" focus of much religiosity in Japan today. Jan Swyngedouw observes:

> Whether in the case of individual persons or in that of groups such as present-day Japanese business enterprises, religions are evaluated primarily in a pragmatic or utilitarian way. The salvation they promise is mainly interpreted in this-worldly terms, as benefits of a material and/or psychological nature with specific self-chosen time limits.[9]

We find in Japanese religiosity, both traditional and contemporary, a highly relativistic, pluralistic and syncretistic approach which is quite tolerant of diversity of belief so long as essential commonalities within the social context are maintained.

Traditionally, the Japanese have had to balance the relationship between three great traditions—the indigenous traditions of Japan, known after the introduction of Buddhism as Shinto; Buddhism; and Confucianism. Although tensions between Shinto, Buddhism and Confucianism were never far below the surface, a kind of accommodation among the traditions developed, so that an "essential unity" of the three religions was popularly affirmed. Depending upon one's own primary commitments, either the Buddhas and bodhisattvas were identified as Buddhist manifestations of Shinto kami, or the kami were seen to be manifestations of the Buddhas. A leading Japanese scholar of Buddhism, Nakamura Hajime states: "The Japanese never considered it necessary to repudiate their religious faith in the native gods in order to become devoted followers of Buddhism."[10]

This syncretistic and relativistic approach is characteristic of Japanese religiosity today as well. The notion of one correct religion, one Savior and one way to salvation, and that one should devote exclusive commitment to one tradition is alien to many Japanese. Government statistics routinely show that the number of total adherents to the many different religious groups in Japan far outnumber the total number of Japanese—a paradox which is accounted for by the fact that many Japanese see no problem in identifying with two or more traditions simultaneously. One can be dedicated as a child in a Shinto ceremony, married in a Christian church and buried in a Buddhist ceremony—and along the way dabble in a number of the "new religions" as well. A traditional saying, when applied to religion, affirms pluralism: "although the paths to the summit may differ, from the top one sees the same moon."

The presence of these characteristics cannot be entirely attributed to the effects of modernization since they have been present in Japanese religiosity for centuries. Nevertheless, the cumulative effect of the influences of modernity combined with the legacy of centuries of earlier Japanese tradition reinforces a social and intellectual environment in which the claims of orthodox Christianity appear highly implausible. I suggest that one of the great obstacles to Christian mission in Asia in the years ahead will come from this peculiar form of "syncretism"—the combination of influences from centuries of indigenous religious tradition with the more recent impact of modernity.

The Challenges of Modernity

In very broad terms we might think of a threefold challenge to Christian faith presented by modernity.

1. The idea that one can know religious truth—that fundamental questions about God's existence, nature and relation to humankind can be answered with any degree of intellectual satisfaction—is widely dismissed as untenable.

This is the challenge with which the Christian church in the West has been struggling for the past 250 years. Accordingly, the agenda for apologetics in the West has been defined largely by the paradigms of post-Enlightenment secularism and philosophical naturalism. The challenges posed by agnosticism and atheism remain and must be taken seriously. Since, however, most discussions of apologetics in the West are concerned with these issues I will not pursue them here. The legacy of the Enlightenment presents just one among many challenges to Christian faith today. For in our pluralistic world the question is not simply that of the choice between theism and atheism or Christian faith and secular humanism. Increasingly, whether in Chicago, Bangkok or Paris, the issue is: Given the many alternative worldviews available today, both secular and religious, why should one become (or remain) a Christian? Pluralism and relativism thus present distinctive challenges to Christian faith.

2. The notion that one particular religious figure and one religious perspective can be universally valid, normative, and binding upon all peoples in all cultures—an assumption central to the biblical understanding of Christ and salvation—is widely rejected today as arrogant and intellectually untenable in our pluralistic world.

Even within the broadly Christian community it is increasingly accepted that there cannot be just one savior and one religion for all of the world's diverse peoples.[11] The widespread shift among recent Roman Catholic and conciliar Protestant theologians toward inclusivist and pluralist paradigms for understanding other religions is indicative of the strength of this challenge.[12] On a popular level among people who have never even heard the term "religious pluralism" there is growing acceptance of the idea that all religions are fundamentally "in touch" with the same divine reality and thus that all religions are more or less equally effective in providing for "salvation" (however that is understood). This, of course, has long been a problem for the Christian church in Asia.

No one in the West has done more to champion the cause of pluralism than John Hick. Hick's model provides a sophisticated epistemological and metaphysical framework for a view which has enormous popular appeal beyond the academic world. Hick's thesis is that the great world faiths embody different perceptions and conceptions of, and correspondingly different responses to, the Real [Hick's term for the religious ultimate] from within the major variant ways of being human; and that within each of them the transformation of human existence from self-centeredness to Reality centeredness is taking place. These traditions are accordingly to be regarded as alternative soteriological "spaces" within which, or "ways" along which, men and women find salvation/liberation/fulfillment.[13]

According to Hick, then, the various religions are the product of a complex interplay between divine and human initiatives—the Real revealing itself to humankind and humankind in turn responding in historically and culturally conditioned ways to the Real. Hick contends that since salvation/liberation/enlightenment is more or less equally available in all religions no single tradition can legitimately claim to be the one true religion.

Christian theology and missiology will need to respond appropriately to increasingly sophisticated forms of pluralism. Hick's pluralistic model of religions cannot be dismissed merely by observing that it is inconsistent with Scripture (which it clearly is), for it purports to be presenting a comprehensive second-order (or higher level) understanding of all religious traditions, including orthodox Christianity. As such, however, its adequacy as a comprehensive model is dependent upon at least two factors: (1) The accuracy with which his model reflects, and the ease with which it can accommodate, the phenomena from the various religious traditions; and (2) the internal consistency and epistemological soundness of the model itself. In spite of its considerable intuitive appeal, Hick's model (as are all pluralist theories) is highly vulnerable on both counts.[14]

For example, in an effort to hold that the concepts, beliefs and symbols of each religion are all just "penultimate" reflections of what is truly "ultimate" Hick is forced to reinterpret key beliefs and concepts within the various religions. Thus "Allah," "God the Holy Trinity," "Dharmakaya," "Nirguna Brahman" and "the Dao" all become historically and culturally conditioned conceptions of "the Real." Not only does this reductionism fail to treat the phenomena from within the various religious adequately on their own terms but it results in severe internal tensions within Hick's theory itself. On Hick's model the ontological implications of the various symbols—including personal concepts of the ultimate such as found in "Allah," "Yahweh" or "God the Holy Trinity" as well as non-personal concepts such as "Nirguna Brahman," "Sunyata" or "the Dao"—are all ultimately mutually consistent. But this is highly implausible if the various concepts are understood as defined within the respective religious traditions. The ontology of Sunyata (Emptiness) rules out the existence of what Christians mean by the Trinitarian God. Significantly, in a later work Hick recognizes that his model results in religious agnosticism:

What can we say about the Real *an sich*? Only that it is the ultimate reality that we postulate as the ground of the different forms of religious experience and thought in so far as they are more than human projection. . . . But we cannot apply to the noumenal Real any of the distinctions with which we structure our phenomena, including our religious experience. We cannot say that it is personal or impersonal, one or many, active or passive, substance or process, good or evil, just or unjust, purposive or purposeless. No such categories can be applied, either positively or negatively, to the noumena.[15]

This, however, merely highlights two further difficulties with Hick's model. Not only is it apparent that we literally know nothing about the Real, but Hick's location of the Real beyond any personal categories—including the moral categories of good and evil—raises the question of internal consistency in his model. For Hick insists that we can apply a moral criterion to various religious traditions in an effort to discern which are in fact authentic manifestations of Real and which are not.[16] Thus, on moral grounds we can conclude that Jesus and Gandhi do reflect the Real but Jim Jones and David Koresh do not. But if the Real itself is neither good nor evil—if these categories simply do not apply to the Real—it is difficult to see how any moral criterion can legitimately be used to make such evaluations.

But our intercultural and interreligious world presents yet a different form of challenge to Christian theology and missiology today. Many in the East reject the kind of eclectic pluralism represented by Hick, regarding it as nothing more than the latest example of the imposition of Western intellectual models upon non-Western cultural and religious traditions. With the resurgence of traditional religions such as Hinduism, Buddhism and Islam there has come a vigorous polemic against Western thinking in general and Christian theology in particular.

3. Even if in principle it is granted that one religious tradition might be superior to the rest, and that one religious figure might be universally normative, why should we assume that Christianity and Jesus Christ are in this

308

privileged position? After all, why Jesus and not the Buddha?

Hindu thinkers such as Sarvepalli Radhakrishnan[17] or Buddhists such as Gunapala Dharmasiri[18] and Masao Abe[19] have studied carefully Western thought and Christian theology and have rejected both in favor of traditional Eastern worldviews. They represent a growing movement, not only among Asians but also among Western intellectuals that is looking to Eastern religious and philosophical traditions for answers not found in Western paradigms. Particularly influential in recent years has been the movement inspired by the Japanese Buddhist philosopher Nishida Kitaro (1875-1945), commonly referred to as the Kyoto School of Buddhism, that seeks a kind of synthesis between traditional Western philosophical concerns (especially as expressed by Continental philosophers) and Zen Buddhism. Significantly, the ontology and epistemology of Nishida and the Kyoto School retain strong Buddhist influences.[20]

The challenge posed to orthodox Christianity by a reinvigorated Buddhism strikes at the very foundation of the Christian worldview. For Buddhism presents an epistemology and ontology diametrically opposed to that traditionally associated with Christianity. Which has ontological ultimacy—Being (God) or Sunyata (Emptiness)? Which has epistemological priority—the intelligible revelation of the *logos* (concepts, words, beliefs) or the silence of *satori* (intuitive enlightenment)? Can reason aid us in ascertaining what is true and false in religion, or is reason itself the problem from which we are to extricate ourselves? How should we even try to settle such questions?

Why should one be a Christian instead of a Buddhist or a Muslim or a Hindu or a New Ager? Clearly there is an important sense in which we might answer this question from within the Christian worldview. Orthodox Christians hold that God has revealed Himself definitively in the Incarnation and the written Scriptures. And if indeed the Bible is the very Word of God, true and fully authoritative, then clearly anything that is incompatible with the teachings of Scripture must be rejected. Thus there is a significant sense in which the Christian, as a Christian, is entitled—indeed is obligated—to reject as false any teachings which are incompatible with the claims of Scripture.

But this response, legitimate as far as it goes, hardly settles the matter. For although from within the Christian perspective one can evaluate competing alternatives on the basis of principles and values internal to the Christian faith, there is a logically more basic question which must be addressed: On what epistemological basis should one accept the Christian worldview as the true one? How is one to determine which among competing religious perspectives is true?

We must not forget that each of the major religions claims to be true (or to be the closest to the truth) and to provide acceptable criteria by which to evaluate other perspectives. The Christian appeals to the Bible as the supreme authority for religious questions; the Muslim rejects the Bible in favor of the *Qur'an*, Allah's definitive self-revelation dictated through the angel Gabriel; the Zen Buddhist claims to have direct access to the ultimate nature of reality through satori; the Advaita Vedanta Hindu appeals to the authority of the Upanishads and the experience of samadhi to validate his claims to truth; and Shirley MacLaine has her own direct channel to religious truth. Obviously, merely appealing to divine authority in and of itself settles nothing, for each tradition has its own authoritative structure. The question is: Which "authority" is in fact ultimately authoritative?

If we are to answer this question satisfactorily we must have access to some principles or criteria that can legitimately be applied to the evaluation of alternative worldviews. One of the more significant new fields within the philosophy of religion is "crosscultural philosophy of religion" which is concerned with exploring precisely these philosophical issues from within a multicultural and multireligious context. According to Ninian Smart, one of the leaders in this movement, a major task of philosophy of religion in the years ahead "is to clarify the criteria for determining the truth as between worldviews."[21]

But in raising this issue we confront a kind of orthodoxy within certain academic circles which rejects out of hand any suggestion that there might be "universal" or "neutral" or "context-independent" criteria for assessing worldviews. A crucial question then becomes: Are we able to transcend the cumulative effects of our socio-linguistic contexts and to apprehend (to some extent) truths which, while expressed in particular linguistic and cultural categories, nevertheless are themselves ontologically independent of all such contexts?[22]

Are there any non-arbitrary epistemological starting points? Or does every perspective (worldview) rest upon one or more assumptions which are all equally arbitrary and must simply be either accepted or rejected? If the second alternative is accepted, I see no way of avoiding some form of cognitive relativism. But relativism comes at enormous cost. Not only does the relativist forfeit the epistemological right to make any claim to universal truth, but he no longer can legitimately reject any other perspective as false. On the other hand, any attempt to avoid cognitive relativism will result in recognizing some criteria which are in some significant sense "context-independent" and thus normative.[23]

Conclusion

Where does this leave us? Am I suggesting that all effective missionaries in the future must become philosophers and expert apologists? Not at all. But I am arguing that in the coming years our world will likely become even more dominated by the values and assumptions of pluralism and thus that the global church must be prepared not only to proclaim the uniqueness of the gospel of Jesus Christ with boldness (Romans 1:16) but also to demonstrate to a cynical and relativistic world why it should accept Jesus as the one Lord and Savior for all humankind. Already we are seeing that as the church grows and matures in Asia there is an urgent need for sophisticated and nuanced engagement with traditional Asian cultural and religious perspectives that is biblically sound, epistemologically tenable and culturally sensitive. The effectiveness of evangelism and discipleship in contexts impacted by religious pluralism will be directly related to the church's ability to challenge and transform some of the values and assumptions which make it so difficult for many to accept the gospel as truth.

Finally, while recognizing the importance of this intellectual dimension, surely the most powerful and persuasive apologetic is a community of believers who have been radically transformed by the grace and love of Jesus Christ and who consistently manifest in their lives the qualities exemplified in Christ's life. Jesus stated the basic principle to his disciples 2,000 years ago: "By this all men will know that you are my disciples, if you love one another" (John 13:35). The failure of the church to live consistently as a community of Christ's disciples undermines all other efforts to demonstrate the truth of the gospel to a skeptical world. May God raise up for His Church gifted men and women who understand the times (1 Chronicles 12:32) and who can demonstrate persuasively—through their lives as well as their words—that in Jesus alone can one find the Way, the Truth and the Life (John 14:6).

Endnotes

[1]Apologetics has a long, if not always distinguished, history in Christian missions. The early church produced some gifted apologists who addressed Hellenistic culture. See Robert M. Grant, *Greek Apologists of the Second Century* (Philadelphia: Westminster, 1988). During the twelfth through fifteenth centuries there was considerable interac-

tion between Christian thinkers and Muslims, with men such as Peter the Venerable, Ramon Lull, Ricoldus de Monte Crucis and others engaging in apologetics against Islam. See Tibor Horvath, S.J., "Apologetics as Dialogue in the Western Church from the Classical Period of Scholasticism to the Beginning of the Reformation," *Asia Journal of Theology* 4 (April 1990): 136-161. The best historical survey of apologetics within the Christian tradition remains Avery Dulles, *A History of Apologetics* (Philadelphia: Westminster, 1971). For a fascinating account of the earliest known debate between a Christian and a Buddhist, see Richard Fox Young, "*Deus Unus or Dei Plures Sunt?* The Function of Inclusivism in the Buddhist Defense of Mongol Folk Religion Against William of Rubruck (1254)," *Journal of Ecumenical Studies* 26:1 (Winter 1989), 100-137. Vigorous use of apologetics against opposing religious traditions was not limited to Christians. Examples of Buddhist apologetic writings against Christianity in seventeenth-century Japan can be found in George Elison, *Deus Destroyed: The Image of Christianity in Early Modern Japan* (Cambridge: Harvard University Press, 1973). For Hindu responses to Christianity see Richard F. Young, *Resistant Hinduism: Sanskrit Sources on Anti-Christian Apologetics in Early Nineteenth Century India*, Publications of the De Nobili Research Library #8 (Vienna: De Nobili Research Library, 1981). A very helpful collection of polemic writings against Christianity by modern Muslim, Jewish, Hindu and Buddhist thinkers can be found in Paul Griffiths, ed., *Christianity Through Non-Christian Eyes* (Maryknoll, NY: Orbis, 1990).

[2]The notion of plausibility structures, understood broadly as the set of factors which helps to reinforce the plausibility of a particular belief for a particular group of people, comes from Peter Berger. See Peter Berger, *The Sacred Canopy: Elements of a Sociological Theory of Religion* (New York: Doubleday, 1967), ch. 6.

[3]Gerald Anderson, "Theology of Religions and Missiology: A Time of Testing," *The Good News of the Kingdom:*

Mission Theology for the Third Millennium, Charles Van Engen, Dean S. Gilliland and Paul Pierson, eds. (Maryknoll, NY: Orbis, 1993), 200-201.

[4]Barry Smart observes, "Indeed one of the remarkable features of contributions to debates on this issue is the extent to which key terms and ideas have evaded clarification, and this applies not only in respect of the family of terms associated with 'modern' but in addition, if not to an even greater extent, in relation to 'postmodern' and its conceptual constellation. In turn it extends . . . to the distinction drawn between the two sets of terms." Barry Smart, "Modernity, Postmodernity, and the Present," in *Theories of Modernity and Postmodernity*, ed. Bryan Turner (London: Sage Publications, 1990), 16.

[5]In turn, we might think of *modernization* as a process consisting of "the growth and diffusion of a set of institutions rooted in the transformation of the economy by means of technology." Peter Berger, Brigitte Berger, and Hansfried Kellner, *The Homeless Mind: Modernization and Consciousness* (New York: Vintage Books, 1973), 9. See also James Davison Hunter, "What Is Modernity? Historical Roots and Contemporary Features," *Faith and Modernity*, Philip Sampson, Vinay Samuel and Chris Sugden, eds. (Oxford: Regnum Books, 1994), 12-28. As such, modernization emerged first in the West around the seventeenth century, with the transformations introduced by the Industrial Revolution, the rise of free-market capitalism, the shift from an agrarian economy to a technological production based economy and the accompanying trend toward urbanization.

[6]See David Lyon, "Secularization: The Fate of Faith in the Modern World?," *Themelios* (September 1984): 16-22; and idem, "Rethinking Secularization: Retrospect and Prospect," *Review of Religious Research* 26 (1985): 228-243. Also helpful is *Religion and Modernization: Sociologists and Historians Debate the Secularization Thesis*, ed. Steve Bruce (Oxford: Clarendon Press, 1992).

[7]And certainly there is ample evidence to support the view that some modern societies are much less religious today than they were a century ago. Os Guinness, for example, points out that since 1900 the percentage of the world's atheistic and non-religious peoples (agnostics, atheists, secularists) has grown from 0.2 percent to 21.3 percent of the world's population—from less than one-fifth of one percent to over one fifth of the world's population. Guinness calls this the most dramatic change on the entire religious map of the twentieth century. See Os Guinness, "Mission Modernity: Seven Checkpoints on Mission in the Modern World," *Faith and Modernity*, 340.

[8]For more on these themes see *Religion and Society in Modern Japan: Selected Readings*, Mark R. Mullins, Shimazono Susumu and Paul L. Swanson, eds. (Berkeley, CA: Asian Humanities Press, 1993) and Jan Swyngedouw, "Japanese Religiosity in an Age of Internationalization," *Japanese Journal of Religious Studies* 5:2-3 (June-September 1978), 87-105. A helpful introduction to Japanese religion is Ian Reader's *Religion in Contemporary Japan* (London: Macmillan, 1991).

[9]Jan Swyngedouw, "Religion in Contemporary Japanese Society," in *Religion and Society in Modern Japan*, 61.

[10]Hajime Nakamura, *Ways of Thinking of Eastern Peoples*, trans. P. Weiner (Honolulu, HI: University of Hawaii Press, 1964), 391.

[11]There is an enormous amount of literature on the subject of religious pluralism. Helpful surveys of the issues and positions can be found in Paul Knitter, *No Other Name? A Critical Survey of Christian Attitudes Toward the World Religions* (Maryknoll, NY: Orbis, 1985); Gavin D'Costa, *Theology and Religious Pluralism* (New York: Basil Blackwell, 1986); and Harold Netland, *Dissonant Voices: Religious Pluralism and the Question of Truth* (Grand Rapids, MI: Eerdmans, 1991).

[12]Speaking of the impact of modernity upon religious belief Peter Berger states, "We do have a problem of belief,

and it not only raises the question of why we should believe in God but why we should believe in *this* God. There are others, after all, and today they are made available in an unprecedented way through the religious supermarket of modern pluralism." Peter Berger, *A Far Glory: The Quest for Faith in an Age of Credulity* (New York: Anchor Books, 1992), 146-147.

[13]John Hick, *An Interpretation of Religion* (New Haven, CT: Yale University Press, 1989), 240.

[14]For a critique of Hick's pluralist model see my *Dissonant Voices*, 208-233.

[15]John Hick, *Disputed Questions in Theology and Philosophy of Religion* (New Haven, CT: Yale University Press, 1993), 177. Emphasis added.

[16]See *An Interpretation*, 316-340.

[17]See especially Sarvepalli Radhakrishnan, *Eastern Religions and Western Thought* (London: Oxford University Press, 1969).

[18]See Gunapala Dharmasiri, *A Buddhist Critique of the Christian Concept of God*, 2nd ed. (Antioch, CA: Golden Leaves Publishing Co., 1988).

[19]See Masao Abe, *Zen and Western Thought* (Honolulu, HI: University of Hawaii Press, 1985).

[20]Nishida's most significant work is *An Inquiry into the Good*, trans. Masao Abe and Christopher Ives (New Haven, CT: Yale University Press, 1987 [1927]). On the Kyoto School and its significance see Robert E. Carter, *The Nothingness Beyond God: An Introduction to the Philosophy of Nishida Kitaro* (New York: Paragon House, 1989); *The Buddha Eye: An Anthology of the Kyoto School*, ed. Frederick Franck (New York: Crossroad, 1982); James Fredericks, "The Kyoto School: Modern Buddhist Philosophy and the Search for a Transcultural Theology," *Horizons*, 15,2, (1988), 299-315; and Thomas Kasulis, "The Kyoto School and the West," *The Eastern Buddhist* 15 (1982): 125-144.

[21]Ninian Smart, "The Philosophy of Worldviews," in *Religious Pluralism and Truth: Essays on Cross-Cultural Phi-*

losophy of Religion, ed. Thomas Dean (Albany, NY: State University of New York Press, 1995), 24.

[22]Two related issues must be carefully distinguished. First is the ontological question whether there are such criteria for evaluation which transcend particular contexts. Related to this, but yet distinct from it, is the epistemological question of the degree of clarity or certainty we can have concerning any particular formulation of such a criterion.

[23]Helpful works which argue for our access to at least some criteria for assessing alternative religious worldviews include Ninian Smart, "Truth, Criteria, and Dialogue Between Religions," in *Religious Pluralism and Truth*, 67-71; and William J. Wainwright, "Doctrinal Schemes, Metaphysics, and Propositional Truth," in *Religious Pluralism and Truth*, 73-86. Also helpful is Paul J. Griffiths, *An Apology for Apologetics: A Study in the Logic of Interreligious Dialogue* (Maryknoll, NY: Orbis, 1991). See also my *Dissonant Voices*, chapter five.

Apologetic Responses To Post-Modernism: A Symposium

*Papers from a Panel Discussion Sponsored by
the Evangelical Philosophical Society
at the Annual Meeting of the Evangelical
Theological Society in Philadelphia
November 1995*

Donald T. Williams, Toccoa Falls College, Moderator;
Millard J. Erickson, S.W. Baptist Theological Seminary;
Kurt Anders Richardson,
Gordon Conwell Theological Seminary;
David K. Clark, Bethel Theological Seminary

Introduction

Donald T. Williams

The analysis of one's own times is always perilous. We know them intimately but also, of necessity, partially, with our noses too close to the data, which seem to be moving in a rapid blur. It is almost impossible to get a critical distance; hindsight is not available; and nobody can tell which contemporary pronouncements will appear ludicrous a century hence. Nevertheless, it is sometimes incumbent upon us to try. Our time seems to be such a time: The one thing we can say for certain about the intellectual and cultural climate in which we are called to serve is that it is changing swiftly. Those of us engaged in the defense of the faith find ourselves shooting at targets that seem to shift with blinding speed.

We have spent the years since the Enlightenment perfecting an apologetic that could deal with a set of challenges that have come to be known as modernism. While it mutated from Enlightenment rationalism to skeptical empiricism to atheistic existentialism to hedonistic relativism, they could all be fairly easily diagnosed as different strains of the same disease. The earlier forms held that objective truth was knowable and known to be incompatible with Christian theism. The latter ones may have held that objective truth is unknowable, but they at least could understand that it would be a nice thing if it *were* knowable. So apologetics could focus on the task of showing that Christianity was *true*, with the possibility of having to demonstrate first that such knowledge could in fact be available. And we finally got to the place where we could do a pretty good job of it, only to discover that nobody cared any more.

All of our carefully developed vaccines suddenly seemed impotent against a new outbreak of spiritual Ebola, a virulent denial not only of the knowability but even the *desirability* of any kind of all-encompassing objective truth. Thomas Oden is probably right in diagnosing it as a new and deadly strain of the earlier plague that ought rightly be called the ultramodern; but it seems so different that popular usage has prevailed in giving it the appropriately self-contradictory label of postmodernism.

Trying to find an altar to an unknown god in *this* anti-Athens presents us with a new and troubling dilemma. Our biggest liability with this new audience is not lack of sufficient evidence so much as our quaint notion that evidence matters. Selling truth to postmodernists is like trying to sell air conditioners to Eskimos. A whole new set of stumbling blocks seems to have arisen; in addition to the scandal of the cross and the scandal of particularity, we now have the scandal of objectivity.

How, we must now ask, can we make the Christian message appealing and compelling to a generation that can no longer understand that truth in the old sense is desirable? And how, even more importantly, can we do it without compromising the essence of the answer we offer: that Jesus and Jesus alone is the Way, the *Truth* and the Life? To people who do not like the idea of truth, is it even possible to make the gospel attractive without changing it into something else? Must we simply write off either this generation, the gospel itself or the relevance of apologetics to its presentation? These are questions which must now be seriously faced. The older cliché maintained that you could lead a horse to water (the apologist's job?) but you couldn't make him drink (though you could try to salt the trough and appeal to the conviction of the Holy Spirit). But the more we consider the challenges of postmodernism, the more we must wonder whether deconstructed horses can even be led to water.

In the following essays, three cutting-edge evangelical thinkers point toward some constructive answers to these problems. First, Millard Erickson picks up on the horse-and-water analogy to give a helpful analysis of the options and some sound "horse sense" concerning their evaluation. Then Kurt Richardson shows how Christianity provides an alternative to the tribalism and barbarianism that postmodern fragmentation produces. Finally, David Clark insightfully suggests the practical relevance of all this analysis for evangelism and ministry.

Postmodern Apologetics: Can Deconstructed Horses Even Be Led to Water?

Millard J. Erickson

The question before us actually involves several elements: the horse; the means of leading (the halter and rope); and the water. Several answers might be given to this question. I want to outline these answers and then give a brief indication of my personal reaction to the question and the options.

I see basically four answers that are being given to this question. These are variously proposed and practiced by different evangelical and non-evangelical writers.

1. *Yes, but it must be deconstructed water*. This basically says that the only kind of water that a deconstructed horse will drink or to which he will let himself be led, is deconstructed water. If the horse is genuinely deconstructed, then the water presented to him must be suited to the horse. This, of course, involves conceding the truth of the deconstruction of the horse. It grants that the horse is deconstructed and that deconstruction is here to stay and must be accepted. In terms of a set of categories that I have borrowed from my doctoral mentor, William Hordern, and used several times over the years, these persons are not merely translators, but transformers. They are prepared to alter the understanding and even the content of the Christian faith, if necessary, in order to make it acceptable to the postmodern deconstructionist.

A number of the contentions of the deconstructionists conflict with tenets of evangelicalism as generally understood. These must therefore be abandoned. Among these are the following: the objectivity of truth; a referential understanding of language; a correspondence theory of truth; the existence of "meta-narratives"; and the presence of some universal qualities of human nature. One theologian who represents and advocates this approach is a person who would not claim to be an evangelical, Mark C. Taylor.

2. *Yes, but we must use deconstructed rope.* This view may or may not hold that the water needs deconstruction in order to be appealing to deconstructed horses (i.e., that the message needs to be altered). It does maintain, however, that it is necessary to alter the form of leading, that is, the method and means. It is more the form or the style of presentation rather than the content that needs to be changed. This would mean, for example, that instead of a propositional presentation, what would be done is to make a narrative approach. Generally speaking, this approach would hold to the objectivity of truth but the relativity of knowledge and would acknowledge that all knowers are to some extent historically and socially conditioned.

3. *Yes, but the horse is not really deconstructed.* This affirms that the horse, although it may think it is deconstructed, really is not. Consequently, no adjustment, either of the water or the technique of leading, is needed. The same methods of leading horses can be used with deconstructed or postmodern horses that have been used before. The world has not really changed all that radically, according to this third response. There is a belief that the deconstructionist is engaged in sort of unintentional self-deception. There are two varieties of this type of response, which we may term respectively, the kerygmatic and the apologetic.

The kerygmatic variety believes in the self-authenticating character of the biblical message. Usually this view is combined with a strong belief in the convicting, illuminating power of the Holy Spirit. Thus, all that needs to be done is to present the truth, and it will bear fruit. To take seriously the idea that humans can cut themselves off so fully from the grace of God that they cannot be reached with a plain presentation of the truth is to concede the point which the deconstructive postmodernist is making, and thus in effect denying the message which is being presented.

The apologetic variety of this response suggests that we

can engage in some of the traditional types of arguments. These may have to be carefully selected, but are still useful. Persons are still rational, despite changes that may have taken place in the world. Consequently, rational arguments can still be utilized.

4. *Yes, but we must first de-deconstruct the horse.* This approach says that the horse is deconstructed, but it is not possible to live on such a basis. There is a more pessimistic and a more optimistic version of this view. The more pessimistic holds that deconstructed horses simply have to be written off, but that our aim is to be to prevent other non-deconstructed horses from being deconstructed. Apologetics, on this view, is primarily a defensive endeavor. The more optimistic approach says deconstructed horses can be reached, but they must first be de-deconstructed, and this requires that they be more thoroughly deconstructed. This is done by pushing such horses to be consistently and thoroughly deconstructed, whereupon they will discover that it is not possible to live on this basis. The problem with deconstructed horses is not that they do not believe enough, but that they believe too much—more than they really are entitled to believe, on their premises.

On one occasion, Jacques Derrida, the prophet and patron saint of deconstruction, was involved in a debate with John Searle, the Stanford philosopher, and objected vigorously that Searle was misunderstanding and misrepresenting his ideas. But this objection is a highly non-postmodern, non-deconstructed idea. A similar incident occurred in a debate between James McClendon and Mark Taylor. We must help finish deconstructing the horse, before the horse can be de-deconstructed, or reconstructed.

Part of this process involves asking what kind of language we are using when we talk about language. When a deconstructionist discusses deconstruction, is he or she really using deconstructed language? If such were the case, the deconstructionist would probably remain silent, or at least would not expect anyone else to understand and agree with him or her. One other way of doing this is to show what consequences flow from deconstructing meaning and language. What happens is often a new kind of authoritarianism, such as is found in political correctness, where only one answer is permitted. Thus, deconstruction may lead to a new form of oppression. Such horses must be de-deconstructed.

A Beginning of a Response

For myself, I believe that a combination of forms of response #2 and response #4 holds the most promise. We are talking here not about going all the way with #2 but taking some aspects of it on a provisional basis. It may be that at least in initiating conversation with a deconstructionist we must modify the way in which we do the leading or present the message. This may mean that a more narrative presentation, not in the hermeneutical or heuristic but in the communicational sense of "narrative," will have to be the beginning of the conversation, to enable us to cross the bridge to where the horse is, rather than standing on our side of the bridge and trying to coax the horse to come to us. Eventually, of course, we must bring the horse across the bridge, but that may not be possible initially. It means that we will have to listen to the deconstructionist, rather than simply talking, which tends to be an occupational disease of theologians, and sometimes of other Christians as well. There is a point in the deconstructionist's contention of relativity, and that is that we all see reality from our own perspective or our own presuppositions. The truth is objective, but our understanding may be in part affected by the angle from which we look at it. We will need to look through our deconstructionist's eyes long enough to understand why for him or her the view makes good sense. Then we will better understand how to relate the message to the person in a way that can be understood.

One of the most valuable courses I took in college, although I did not see it that way at the time, was a course in debate. The value of it was that one week my partner and I would have to argue one side of the issue and the next week we would have to take the opposite side. Something of that approach is what I think might help us here. Because we have the truth, the absolute truth as revealed by God, we may be tempted to feel that we ought simply tell people that, and there is no point in listening to their errors. But the way to respond to the authoritarianism of some deconstructionists is not to be similarly dogmatic.

The other approach that I believe can be used partially is the fourth. I have thought in just the past few weeks that perhaps we need to take a new look at the apologetic approach of Francis Schaeffer. Schaeffer was dealing with deconstructionists before it was popular to call them that. His approach was to push such a person to the end of his or her view, to live out consistently that position, believing that no one could actually live on the basis of such a view. I believe that we may need to help the deconstructionist to "hit bottom," like an alcoholic, before there will be any significant sense of need to move beyond that approach.

The New Barbarism: Toward an Apologetic of Desire

Kurt Anders Richardson

*I*deologically, modernity has been characterized by various universal civilizing goals: democratic principles, literacy and education, technological amelioration of the human environment, the creation of new wealth in a free market and cultural tolerance through acculturation to the above norms. As Stephen Carter has shown, this naturalistic or secular universalism is not anti-religious in essence but tends to be so in practice. For the modern ideal of religious pluralism to work, even members of a majority religious group must maintain a privatized relationship to public life. Thus we have the present so-called "culture wars." This strife over the privatization of religious life shows that the forces of modernity are hardly dead. Opposition to the public influence of religious ideas comes largely from a view of secular knowledge as society's regulative force, presupposing the Enlightenment ideal that the education of the human race is the one truly universal goal. Because universal agreement on religious tenets is deemed impossible and probably undesirable, only the virtually contentless references to deity in the American Constitution can be suffered—and in numerous cases even these can be challenged. For modernists the secular values described above became essential to their ideals of civilization for American culture.

There are, however, other forces, called "postmodern," arising out of the deep structures of private life within America and the West in general. The postmodern by its very name indicates a dissociation with the universalism of modernity. Rooted deeply in the democratic right of dissent and the American frontier spirit, numerous clusterings of people representing alternative beliefs and lifestyles are emerging. They range from youth rock-band disciples to a myriad of neo-pagan religious associations, from sports fanaticism to lifestyles imitating the "art" of pornography and violent combat. Within America's great public institution, the university, an alternative institution has arisen, as Stanford philosopher John Searle has declared.

The common characteristic of these forces is the principle, not of public knowledge, but of private passions. Richard Kadrey identifies this phenomenon in his *Covert Culture Sourcebook*. Even in Christian motivational literature passion is typically the operative principle in realizing one's goals; insidiously passion and its release often becomes the goal. To the extent that passion begins to guide the personal ambitions, a profound indifference to the claims of truth and knowledge sets in. Once this indifference shapes one's form of life, an essential component of the modernist foundation of secular knowledge (or the

Christian hope of knowing God) becomes seriously undermined if not eliminated.

In modernist culture, therefore, the primary apologetic challenge was confronting the problem of knowledge. Christian apologetic concerned itself primarily with attempts to demonstrate the validity or warrant of its claims to the knowledge of God, the uniqueness of Christ and the supreme explanatory value of the biblical worldview. But with postmodern indifference to the problem of knowledge, this approach will not work. Life conceived as dominated by passion calls for a different apologetic that confronts the problem of desire. To do this successfully, we must draw upon the many signals from sociology that identify a culture dominated by desire as *barbaric*. References to the amazing phenomenon of barbarism arising within the structures of civilization abound. One of the leading texts is Stjepan G. Mistrovic's *The Barbarian Temperament: Towards a Postmodern Critical Theory* (New York: Routledge, 1993).

I would offer nine theses in view of this phenomenon of barbarism and the postmodern apologetic situation. They are a preliminary statement of principles for responding constructively to this situation and its many needs.

1. Barbaric forms of life arise through processes of ritualization. Since unbridled passion is quite dangerous, ritual helps channel passion so one can survive one's own release. Current ritual practices include forty-eight hour dance fests, body mutilation and a host of extreme behaviors at or near the commercial levels of society.[1]
2. Barbaric forms of life often rest upon a remystification of life.[2] Life guided by desire often requires religious speech and symbols to justify and order it. Because mystified, enchanted, often delirious experience is what people are after, life must be re-cloaked in naturalistic or even supernaturalistic senses of mystery.
3. Barbaric forms of life go beyond subcultural groupings

to a new tribalism. Traditional public allegiances of every type—clubs, volunteer societies, churches, etc.—are all in decline. The next generation is simply not joining. Instead, the pursuit of highly specialized ritual behavior has led to a tribal clustering of persons.[3]

4. Barbaric forms of life reduce all rivalries of perspective to the amassing and control of power. Personal liberty becomes all-important. As a result, any unifying structures within society are perceived as oppressive and hostile, no matter how constitutional or benign they might be.[4] The crying need is for evangelicals to enter the fray and encourage a nonpolitical unity based on genuine standards of civility and morality.

5. Barbaric forms of life promote the disappearance of personal identity and an affirmation of the bestial, however intelligent the beast within may be. This development most clearly indicates the retrograde quality of the barbarism that has arisen. Oddly, this is where the modern or hyper-modern has led. In seeking a revolutionary way of life, people revolt against their own human nature. The tragic loss of memory on the point that the human is truly distinct from the animal should be recovered through the application of Christian sensibilities to public life.[5]

6. Apologetic response to barbarism requires the classic demystification of life. From the first chapter of Genesis to the last of Revelation, the Christian understanding of the world and its history is its openness before God. The ancient reference point in Scripture can bring about a healthy renewal of civility and sensibility about public life.[6]

7. Apologetic response requires a demonstration of the channeling of desire through the redemptive structures of Christian community and commitment. Christian alignments with nonbelievers who also care about civil and moral forms of life can also be achieved to much common benefit. Of course, every act of a Christian

should be done with prayer in the name of Christ and with the model of Jesus Himself in mind and heart, and this will surely supersede what other members of these alignments achieve. Nevertheless, deep humility and mutual respect through these cooperative efforts could become the best form of evangelism of all.[7]

8. Apologetic response to barbarism requires a non-political stance. It seems clear that both the left and the right are wrong about the sources of social reform. Political processes do not accomplish the kind of public good that is necessary for a civil society, no matter how refined an ideology the left may present. Nor, on the other hand, is a moral society cultivated simply by the promotion of a free market, as the right sometimes seems to assume. It is extremely important that the Christian apologist/evangelist rise above these political interests. If the Christian influence within public life is truly to help members of that public deliver themselves from their worst behaviors and habits, it will have to be by something greater and far more inspiring than the coercion of civil laws and punishments.

9. Apologetic response to barbarism should lead to a recovery of the classical apologetic of knowledge. At present, the younger generation is so overwhelmed by the bombardment of social practices that place a premium on the gratification of desire at its most extreme that there is hardly any room for the life of the mind. This life can be recovered if and only if these severe ethical and moral crises are brought into a new equilibrium through reform. When this does take place, the classic problems of understanding and the struggle with intellectual skepticism will return.

From these points of contact and response there can be, I believe, a true overcoming of the tragic effects of the barbaric tendencies which beset civilized society. Of course, the project of civilization has always remained unfinished.

There are many beneficiaries of the civilizing ideals of the American experiment, including immigrants and those coming up from formerly disenfranchised minorities. If evangelicals will return to the public places of Western life and contend for the truth and what is ethically and morally right, not only by their voices but by providing a demonstrable alternative in their own community to the tribalism and barbarity that surrounds them, great reform is possible. Indeed, it will come. The question for us is, will we be involved or leave it to others?

Apologetic Responses to Postmodernism

David K. Clark

"**M**y roommate and I believe the same thing. The only difference is that he's a Christian and I'm not. We both know there's no person or thing or being called *God*. But we agree that the concept *God* is real and very important. My roommate chooses to live by this concept. I don't."

One night, after I made a presentation at a prestigious local college, a young philosophy major named Eric shared with me this perspective about God.[8] The unaffected manner in which Eric proposed his antirealist view of God surprised me. That his roommate, a self-described evangelical Christian believer, should interpret *God* in that same antirealist way *really* surprised me. Surely this is symptomatic of our postmodern time. Since seventy-two percent of eighteen to twenty-five-year-olds in a recent survey said they do not believe in absolute truth,[9] Eric's is the sort of position that Christians will no doubt increasingly encounter. So how can apologists make Christianity attractive to people for whom absolute truth is neither possible, conceivable nor *desirable* without compromising the absolute truth claim which is an essential part of the Christian message?

Postmodern Epistemic Ethos

To some, postmodernism entails the end of epistemology. The epistemic ethos of postmodern thought and culture involves several interlocking pieces:

- Human persona, individually or collectively, have no access to a unified ultimate truth.
- All human knowing is relative to any one of many socially-constructed, linguistically-shaped conceptual frameworks.
- Many webs of belief are conceptually coherent, empirically adequate and pragmatically compelling; none is decisively refuted by external criteria.
- The plurality of epistemically felicitous perspectives is treasured as a means of enhancing personal freedom.
- Conversely, claims to know a unified ultimate truth are dangerous because they hide personal prejudice, cultural bias or thirst for political power—all of which are threats to personal freedom.
- Threats to personal freedom should be countered by an undercutting of all grandiose intellectual pretensions which lead to abuse of power.
- The commitment to any particular conceptual framework is not a claim to know the true nature of things, but an affirmation of an antirealist (virtually real?) *mythos* by which a group of people have chosen to live out their freedom.[10]

And with this we are back to Eric's antirealist view that a religion (like all intellectual pursuits or philosophies of life) amounts to socially constructing a set of concepts, not necessarily connected to anything real, by which a person or community could simply choose (sheer *choice* being a highest value) to live. Eric's creative, postmodern, Goodman-like antirealism now stands alongside the dominant modernist perspective—secular naturalism—as the significant viewpoints that oppose Christian theism in the academy.

Apologetic Assumptions Regarding the Postmodern Epistemic Ethos

For believers in God who hold that *logos* existed in the beginning with God, this network of ideas is unacceptable. But we must admit certain things about our context:

1. The Enlightenment is dead for some people. Eric's antirealism seems to such people the better alternative. For these people, if evangelical theology adopts the *ethos* of modernism, it adopts intellectual baggage that significantly limits its attractiveness.

2. But the Enlightenment is alive for other people. Among scholars, those in the know about the death of modernism are concentrated in certain academic disciplines (e.g., literature or sociology). Among lay people, this may be influenced by profession (e.g., the world of business is largely modernist—progress is expressed in the growth mentality, reason is applied through technology, etc.).

3. The death of the Enlightenment model of knowledge does open the door to perspectives that were marginalized in the past—including orthodox Christianity. As Diogenes Allen argues, the "massive intellectual revolution" now occurring in which the modern world is disappearing before us means that "not only are the barriers to Christian belief erected by the modern mentality collapsing, but . . . philosophy and science, once used to undermine belief in God, are now seen in some respects as actually pointing toward God."[11]

4. The birth of the postmodern *ethos* pulls the rug out from under anyone—including the orthodox Christian—who thinks that one perspective is more adequate while contrary views are less so. Christian apologists have before them the slippery task of affirming Christian truth claims without buying into modernist modes of thought and expression.

In a word, the current dilemma is that some non-Christians think that one perspective can be known as most adequate—but it is clearly not Christian theism—while others think that no perspective can be known as most adequate—and Christian theism cannot be known in this way either.

Apologetic Pedagogy and Practice

This situation calls for response at many levels. As Christian apologists who are also academics, we should of course do our work in our fields as best we can to God's glory. This means becoming "very serious about Christian scholarship." We should monitor postmodern trends without capitulating to subtle pressures to mimic its fads. This means doing our scholarship in distinctively Christian ways.[12] As philosophers, we who follow the divine *logos* ought not to join those who mock meaning and cast shadows in their futile attempts to attack the existence of light.

I will focus, however, not on our work as scholars, but on pedagogy and practice. I commend the following strategies to those who teach and live as Christian apologists:

1. We must learn both to distinguish and to connect knowledge and truth. If *truth* describes sets of propositions that depict the real world,[13] *knowledge* denotes some person's grasp of or apprehension of those propositions. *Absolute* truth, I take it, is coextensive with God's omniscient understanding. Truth is absolute in the sense that God's grasp of the way things are is adequate extensively and intensively. He comprehensively knows all facts and knows them in a conceptual framework that is as complex as reality.

Any human apprehension of truth is always conditioned historically. In speaking of absolute truth, Christians too quickly infer the absoluteness of their own knowledge from their conviction about the absoluteness of truth. Conversely, critics infer the relativity of truth from their awareness of the historical conditioning of human knowledge.

Critics hear incredible arrogance (with potential for destructive power-grabbing) in Christian claims to absolute truth. Student apologists need to have their consciousness raised about this postmodern reality: any claim to absoluteness seems in the contemporary context like vicious intolerance.

Human apprehensions of truth can be objective, however, in the sense that the objective world can, if we so allow, decisively shape or refute our constructs. (An ideology, of course, is a mentality that does not allow external reality to shape the mental constructs.) Our apprehensions cannot be objective if we insist that this means that we rise above the historical situation we find ourselves in. We do rightly use a variety of strategies and tests to make rational choices about when our perspectives are doing a better job of capturing reality. But we do not escape the problem of the veil.[14]

Apologetics teachers should nurture in their students a certain comfort level with the dual nature of human knowing as both limited and yet objective. Too many young evangelical students react to contemporary relativism by asserting strongly the absoluteness of Christian truth. But we need not abandon the concept of absolute truth even though we must recognize the relative-yet-objective character of human knowledge.

2. We should recognize we live in a pluralist culture, not a monolithically postmodern culture. Postmodernism is one response to the pluralism—it delights in that pluralism. But other responses to plurality, including modernist and premodernist ones, are possible. If we counted noses, I guess we would encounter more modernists in our society than postmodernists. This calls for apologetic practice that is situationally sensitive. It calls for apologetic practice that is dialogical, responding to individuals in their context, recognizing the uniqueness created by each dialogue partner's experiences and perspectives.[15] It calls for a mentality that can, with equal facility, deconstruct both the flippant

cynicism of the social constructivist and the arrogant empiricism of the positivist.

Yet we should not assume that the social constructivist and positivist are always different people. Several years ago, I talked to a lawyer from Minneapolis who specializes in suing companies for making defective products. He is at once thoroughly modern—skeptical and combative (his paycheck depends on his being skeptical of all sorts of evidence)—and relativistic and tolerant—"Your view makes good sense to you, of course, but I just don't choose to adopt it." Apologetic practice in a pluralistic, postmodern era faces both the perspectivism that erases truth and the political correctness that arbitrarily reinstates it.

3. We can use vivid analogies to express the unliveability of postmodernism in its deconstructive mode. Here concrete language—stories, imagery, illustrations—are invaluable (as narrative theologians have rightly argued). There are those who have trouble believing that our language (understood in a critical realist sense) describes a real world. (I talked with a woman this week who disbelieves in dinosaurs: "Aren't those skeletons really just plaster?") To show that critical realism matters (e.g., my conversation with Eric), I use illustrations: "Suppose you have pain in your chest. You consult a doctor. She considers whether the pain is heartburn, an ulcer or stomach cancer. Does her assessment matter? Absolutely. Successful treatment of your potentially life-threatening problem requires a real connection between the diagnosis and the actual state of your stomach."

Though concrete illustrations are critical, we should not abandon a vigorous use of abstract and conceptual modes of discourse in a total acquiescence to narrativism.[16] Stories are extraordinarily powerful, but deceptively ambiguous. Even Jesus' parables often left his audiences scratching their heads. As Dallas Willard says, "The role of the Scriptures and scriptural interpretation is to provide us with a general understanding of God and to inspire and cultivate a corresponding faith. The power of stories alone to generate life-changing faith is much overestimated today."[17] *Alone*, of course, is the key word here.

4. Gene E. Veith points out that some facets of postmodernism seek retrieval of tradition rather than deconstruction of past. Retrieval does not merely reinstate the premodern past. It critically appropriates bits and pieces of the past, inserting them into a new postmodern mosaic. Veith says, "It is not yet apparent which version of postmodernity—the chaos of relativism or the renewal of the past—will win out."[18] But the utter destruction implied in deconstructive or eliminative postmodernism lays out for all to see the ultimate implications of the secular modernist experiment: unliveability of life without God. It is an apologetic boon that the Western social fabric is now entirely threadbare.[19] Books by Diogenes Allen, Roger Lundin, John Warwick Montgomery, Thomas Oden and Herb Schlossberg are resources here.[20]

5. Who we are counts most. The life of covenant relationships in Christian community is a potentially powerful argument to those who understand and experience the negative side of postmodernism's total liberation from tradition. To be traditionless is to be entirely freed of the constraint of the community that embodies that tradition. To be traditionless is also to be spiritually homeless.

I have a friend who was a member of a young adults group I led for four years. Over a two-year period, I spoke to him several times about becoming a Christian. He enjoyed talking, but he always pulled back when we got down to the issue of personal faith in Jesus. Yet he kept coming back to our group. He told me that a major reason he kept coming back was that he saw something in our family, and he wanted to be part of a Christian family. Growing up in an unhealthy home, he experienced emotional blockages to trust and intimacy. The thought of trusting God scared him. I had not seen this man for a couple of years, but last Sunday, I took him to lunch. After hanging around Christians for five years, he had finally became a believer under the ministry of a booming, seeker-oriented church in Minneapolis. Now he was quizzing me about how he could help other people follow Christ.

Summary

Apologetics expresses absolute truth through relative modes of thought (the "treasure in earthen vessels"). Now more than ever, given the postmodern pluralism we live in, apologetics is a *personal* matter, not *merely* an intellectual one. We should defend the faith to particular persons (not to pure, disembodied minds) using concrete analogies and narratives. In an era where postmodern experientialism is prominent, effective apologists can highlight the contrast between postmodernism's downward spiral into deconstructed despair and the genuine joy and love that God nurtures in the context of covenantal relationships within God's Kingdom.

Endnotes

[1]Nick Land, "Making It with Death: Remarks on Thanatos and Desiring Production," *Journal of the British Society of Phenomenology* 24 (1993): 66-76.

[2]Cf. Jacquelyn N. Zita, "The Male Lesbian and the Postmodernist Body," *Hypatia* 7 (1992): 102-127.

[3]Cf. Andreas Kronenberg, "Where are the Barbarians: Ethnocentrism versus the Illusion of Cultural Universalism: The Answer of an Anthropologist to a Philosopher," *Ultimate Real Mean* 7 (1984): 233-36.

[4]Cf. Ed Block, Jr., "Radical Hermeneutics as Radical Homelessness," *Philosophy Today* (1991): 269-76; R.G. Collingwood, *The New Leviathan, Or, Man, Society, Civilization, and Barbarism* (Oxford: Clarendon, 1942); and Leroy S. Rouner, *To Be at Home: Christianity, Civil Religion, and World Community* (Boston: Beacon, 1991).

[5]Cf. Karen L. Carr, *The Banalization of Nihilism* (Albany, NY: SUNY Press, 1992); Jay Newman, "Two Theories of

Civilization," *Philosophy* 54 (1979): 473-83; Louis A. Sass, "Civilized Madness: Schizophrenia, Self-Consciousness, and the Modern Mind," *History of Human Sciences* 7 (1994): 83-120; and Charles Taylor, "Two Theories of Modernity," *Hastings Center Report* 25 (1995): 24-33.

[6]For illustrations of the problem of reading Scripture and classic tradition from an all-too-modern viewpoint, see Jean-Luc Marion, *God Without Being*, tr. Thomas A. Carlson (Chicago: Chicago University Press, 1991); Alicia Suskin Ostriker, *Feminist Revision and the Bible* (Cambridge: Cambridge University Press, 1993); and David Owen, *Maturity and Modernity: Nietzsche, Weber, Foucalt and the Ambivalence of Reason* (New York: Routledge, 1994).

[7]Cf. Stanley Rosen, *The Ancients and the Moderns: Rethinking Modernity* (New Haven, CT: Yale, 1989) and Charles Taylor, *The Ethics of Authenticity* (Cambridge: Harvard, 1992).

[8]For any among us who are critical realists, I changed Eric's name. For any antirealists, I suppose I should say I replaced one concept (which I'll not mention) with another concept, *Eric*.

[9]George Barna, *The Barna Report: What Americans Believe* (Ventura, CA: Regal, 1991), 83-85.

[10]Themes of this sort generally represent a deconstructionist mode of thought, perhaps the most prominent of several forms of postmodernism. David Ray Griffin, for example, lays out four varieties. In addition to deconstructive or eliminative postmodernism are constructive or revisionary (e.g., Griffin's process theism), liberationist (e.g., Harvey Cox's communitarianism) and restorationist or conservative (e.g., George William Rutler's *Postmodern Theology*, ed. David Ray Griffin, William A. Beardslee and Joe Holland (Albany, NY: SUNY Press, 1989), 1-7. These four do have in common a certain revulsion for things modern. The degree to which they are really postmodern is subject to debate. I see deconstructive postmodernism as postmodernism's most representative form. The other three have

significant modern parallels. I admit the deconstructive form, with its "belief in a self-contained universe, and belief in unlimited human freedom," does as well. Diogenes Allen, "Christianity and the Creed of Postmodernism," *Christian Scholar's Review* 23 (1993): 121.

The problem is that any negative definition includes objects merely because they lack a certain attribute. The positive attributes of this class of objects are likely quite varied. For example, the actual physical structures of animals that lack a backbone—invertebrates—vary tremendously.

[11]Diogenes Allen, *Christian Belief in a Postmodern World: The Full Wealth of Conviction* (Louisville, KY: Westminster/John Knox Press, 1989), 2.

[12]Alvin Plantinga, "On Christian Scholarship," *Religious and Theological Studies Bulletin* 5 (1994): 18.

[13]Suppose someone asserts, But God *is* truth (John 14:6). I'd respond that this means that God, and Jesus as His incarnate Son, is genuine, the real McCoy, not a counterfeit. This is a perfectly legitimate use of *truth*. Which is logically prior, God's being truth or God's knowing true propositions? The former. Our *knowledge* of the genuineness of God depends on the truthfulness of the propositions that describe God. The *truth value* of those propositions depends on the nature of the case, on the inherent reality the propositions describe, viz., that God is indeed the most real Reality.

[14]The problem of the veil is that we cannot get outside our point of view in hopes of gaining an understanding of reality that is independent of any viewpoint. For this reason, we cannot step back to judge how our point of view stacks up against reality as perceived without a viewpoint.

[15]This is the point of my *Dialogical Apologetics: A Person-Centered Approach to Christian Defense* (Grand Rapids, MI: Baker, 1993).

[16]See my "Narrative Theology and Apologetics," JETS 36 (1993): 499-515.

[17]Dallas Willard, *In Search of Guidance: Developing a Con-*

versational Relationship with God (San Francisco: Harper-Collins, 1993), 62.

[18]Gene E. Veith, "Postmodern Times: Facing a World of New Challenges and Opportunities," *Modern Reformation*, September/October 1995, 19.

[19]"When grave persons express their fear that England is relapsing into Paganism, I am tempted to reply, 'Would that she were. . . . If such a state of affairs came about, then the Christian apologist would have something to work on. For a Pagan, as history shows, is a man eminently convertible to Christianity. He is essentially the pre-Christian . . . religious man. The post-Christian man of our day differs from him as much as a *divorcée* differs from a virgin." C.S. Lewis, "Is Theism Important?" in *God in the Dock: Essays on Theology and Ethics*, ed. Walter Hooper (Grand Rapids, MI: Eerdmans, 1970), 172.

[20]Diogenes Allen, *Christian Belief in a Postmodern World*; Roger Lundin, *The Culture of Interpretation: Christian Faith the Postmodern World* (Grand Rapids, MI: Eerdmans, 1993); John Warwick Montgomery, *Human Rights and Human Dignity* (Grand Rapids, MI: Zondervan, 1986); Thomas C. Oden, *After Modernity . . . What?: Agenda for Theology* (Grand Rapids, MI: Zondervan; Academie, 1992); Herbert Schlossberg, *Idols for Destruction: Christian Faith and Its Confrontation with American Society* (Washington, DC: Regnery Gateway, 1990).

List of Contributors

Michael Bauman is Professor of Theology and Culture and Director of Christian Studies at Hillsdale College, Hillsdale, Michigan

David K. Clark is Professor of Theology and Director of the Center for Biblical and Theological Foundations at Bethel Theological Seminary, St. Paul, Minnesota

Matthew A. Cook is Pastor of Grace Church, Millersville, Ohio

Millard Erickson is Professor of Theology at Southwestern Baptist Theological Seminary, Fort Worth, Texas

Gary R. Habermas is Professor of History at Liberty University, Lynchburg, Virginia

David W. Hall is Pastor of Covenant Presbyterian Church, Oak Ridge, Tennessee

Michael A. Harbin is Assistant Professor of Theology at Taylor University, Upland, Indiana

Gordon Lewis is Professor of Theology at Denver Seminary, Denver, Colorado

Ronald B. Mayers is Professor of Theology at Cornerstone College, Grand Rapids, Michigan

John Warwick Montgomery is Professor of Law and Humanities at University of Luton, England

J.P. Moreland is Professor of Bible at Biola University, La Mirada, California

Harold Netland is Assistant Professor of Philosophy of Religion and Mission at Trinity Evangelical Divinity School, Deerfield, Illinois

Robert C. Newman is President of the Evangelical Theological Society and Professor of New Testament at Biblical Theological Seminary, Hatfield, Pennsylvania

Thomas C. Oden is Professor of Theology at Drew University Divinity School, Madison, New Jersey

Kurt A. Richardson is Professor of Theology at Gordon-Conwell Theological Seminary, South Hamilton, Massachusetts

Charles B. Thaxton is Director of the Konos Connection and Adjunct Professor of Physics at Charles University of Prague, Czech Republic

Donald T. Williams is Associate Professor of English and Director of the School of General Studies at Toccoa Falls College, Toccoa Falls, Georgia